Medicine is a Practice

The Rules for Healthcare Marketing

Neil Baum, MD

Published by **American Association for Physician Leadership, Inc.**
PO Box 96503 | BMB 97493 | Washington, DC 20090-6503

Website: www.physicianleaders.org

AAPL books are available at special quantity discounts to use as premiums and sales promotions, or for use in corporate training programs. For more information, please write to Special Sales at journal@physicianleaders.org

This publication is designed to provide general information and is sold with the understanding that neither the author nor the publisher is engaged in rendering legal, accounting, ethical, or clinical advice. If legal or other expert advice is required, the services of a competent professional person should be sought.

13   8 7 6 5 4 3 2 1

Copyedited, typeset, indexed, and printed in the United States of America

PUBLISHER
Nancy Collins

PRODUCTION MANAGER
Jennifer Weiss

DESIGN & LAYOUT
Carter Publishing Studio

COPYEDITORS
Karen Doyle
Pat George

ACKNOWLEDGMENTS

These book chapters began as articles for the American Association for Physician Leadership, and they have been curated with the assistance of the staff members, Jennifer Weiss and Nancy Collins. As editors at the AAPL, they have been a true north star guiding me in publishing for business of medicine for 30 years. They have made valuable suggestions and additions to these articles as well as honest recommendations for appropriate deletions. Together we have created a collaborative team that has made the publication of this collection possible. I am truly grateful for their direction in the publication of these chapters, content that I hope will help our colleagues promote their practices and serve their patients.

TABLE OF CONTENTS

ABOUT THE AUTHOR

Neil Baum, MD, is Professor of Clinical Urology at Tulane Medical School in New Orleans, Louisiana.

Baum is the author of *Marketing Your Clinical Practice—Ethically, Effectively, and Economically*, which is in its 4th edition, has sold over 175,000 copies, and has been translated into Spanish. He also wrote *The Complete Business Guide to a Successful Medical Practice*, published in 2015. He has written a book, *What's Going on Down There?*, which has served as a guide for women's health. He has written ten books on practice management and the business of medicine

Baum was the columnist for *American Medical News* for more than 25 years. He wrote the popular column, The Bottom Line, for *Urology Times* for more than 20 years. He has authored or co-authored over 350 articles that have appeared in peer-reviewed medical publications on various urologic topics, as well as articles on practice management.

Baum has recently published a book, *The Business Basics of Building and Managing a Healthcare Practice* (Springer 2020), which emphasizes the importance of being involved in the business of medical practice.

Neil Baum, MD
Professor of Clinical Urology
Tulane Medical School
New Orleans, Louisiana
doctorwhiz@gmail.com

INTRODUCTION

May you always have work for your hands to do. May your pockets hold always a coin or two. — Irish Blessing

Physicians who aren't good at business won't survive, according to career coach Joyce Russell (*The Washington Post*, May 10, 2010).

I have been a practicing physician for 44 years and have enjoyed sharing my experiences and knowledge about the business of healthcare through the more than 200 articles I have written for American Association for Physician Leadership publications. The articles in this book, compiled through the years, offer a comprehensive look at modern healthcare — what has changed and what remains the same.

There have been tremendous changes in the clinical aspect of medical care and tsunami-like changes in the business aspects of practicing medicine. Examples include managed care (perhaps *mis*-managed care), capitation, the passing of the Affordable (are they kidding?) Care Act, the introduction of relative value units to determine compensation, the concept of the employed physician, the implementation of the electronic medical record, and more recently, the use of telemedicine to provide care for patients without the doctor being eyeball-to-eyeball with the patient.

Today, nearly every doctor who graduates from medical school leaves their postgraduate training with excellent skills for diagnosing and treating medical illnesses. However, the majority leave their training programs with no skills or with, at most, a few skills to become successful businesspeople. In fact, most physicians have earned a reputation as being deficient in the business of medicine, of being good at caring for their patients but poor at managing the business aspect of their practices.

Graduating students, residents, and fellows often complain that the medical school curriculum hasn't changed much since 1910 when educator Abraham Flexner proposed standardization of pre-clinical and clinical years in his groundbreaking Flexner Report.[1] Unfortunately, only a few medical schools offer courses or guidance on the business of medicine. That's the bad news. The good news is that there has been a quantitative rise in the opportunity for dual MD\MBA degrees — from six programs in 1993 to approximately 65 in 2019.[2] Although it isn't necessary to have an MBA to be able to grasp the basic concepts of business that will affect a practice, incorporating the principles of business discussed here into their knowledge base will serve physicians and their patients.

In response to those who claim there is no time in most education and training programs to teach about the business of medicine, I ask that we be honest. Do medical school students need to know how many ATPs are created within the Krebs Cycle to be good clinicians? There are a lot of things they memorize in medical school that are not as relevant to the practice of medicine as basic accounting, creating a business plan, practice management, and leadership. These are the skills that physicians can use on a regular basis and far more often than the names of the cranial nerves and what they innervate.... unless they are neurologists or neurosurgeons!

Learning the basics of business with its application to healthcare is also important in creating a doctor who will have a profitable and ultimately enjoyable career. If they don't understand the business component of their practice, they may not be able to survive in today's marketplace, where profit margins are razor thin. American healthcare is different than every other profession or business. Healthcare is the largest and most regulated industry in the U.S. economy, and because of excessive regulation, it doesn't follow the basic laws of supply and demand.

Another area that is covered in these articles is the importance of marketing and practice promotion. Of course, physicians can place an announcement in their local newspaper, list their name in the Yellow Pages, or have a high school student transfer a trifold brochure into a website template and hope to attract patients to their practice. However, many of the articles herein discuss ethical, effective, and economic methods of promoting the practice that actually generate new patients.

This collection of articles is intended to be a roadmap or GPS for doctors to follow to be good clinical physicians *and* good businesspeople who make a difference in the lives of their patients and make good financial decisions.

What's the bottom line? A physician who doesn't understand the business of medicine won't be able to survive in today's market. That would be a terrible waste of 12 to 15 years of education.

I hope readers benefit from these articles and will let me know how useful they are in their own practice.

NEIL BAUM, MD
Professor of Clinical Urology
Tulane Medical School
New Orleans, Louisiana
doctorwhiz@gmail.com

REFERENCES

1. Duffy TP. The Flexner Report—100 Years Later. *The Yale Journal of Biology and Medicine.* 2011; 84(3):269.

2. D'Souza N. The Rise of the MD/MBA Dual Degree: Revitalizing Healthcare through Physician Leadership. Honors Thesis, University of South Florida at St. Petersburg. December 13, 2019.

CHAPTER 1

Identifying and Then Managing the Zero Moment of Truth in Your Medical Practice

Neil Baum, MD

The traditional method of marketing and promoting a practice consisted of "hanging a shingle" on the door; placing a small, paid, announcement in the paper that indicated your name, address, and phone number; and, finally, depending on word of mouth from satisfied patients to the rest of the community about your areas of interest and expertise and the excellent care you provided your patients. This process was used for several hundreds of years and was considered the ethical approach to practice development. Only rarely did medical practices avail themselves of newspapers, magazines, billboards, radio, and television, because this was considered verboten, and the word "advertising" was considered unethical.

Next came the 1990s and the incorporation of the Internet into medical practice. The doctor took his or her tri-fold, tri-colored brochure, electronically transferred the document to the Internet, and declared that the practice had a website. This kind of marketing was unidirectional, or "push marketing"—the information was created and there was no means for the viewer of the website to interact with the practice except by telephone. At this time there was little opportunity for patient feedback outside of snail-mailed letters or word-of-mouth comments to friends and family.

In the 2000s, medical marketing became permissible, and two-way communication between the prospective patient and the doctor and the medical practice became possible. Doctors contributed content on a regular basis to their websites and even encouraged patients to communicate with the practice through blogs, emails, and videos. After the website was created, there was little to be done by the practice but to sit back and wait for patients to make a connection with the office. The next step, the "moment of truth," occurred when the patient called the office, the point where he or she started to have an experience with the practice. These crucial interactions—the telephone call, the reception area, the exam room, and the encounter with the doctor—were the ways that patients decided whether they had a favorable or negative experience. The next moment of truth was the decision to remain a patient in the practice. Considerations in making this decision included whether access to the practice was easy to obtain, whether there were value added services, and whether the doctor and staff were compassionate and caring.

Since 2010, the landscape has changed significantly. Today 88% of U.S. consumers will conduct Internet research before buying a product or using a service such as healthcare. Contemporary consumers rely on 10 or more sources in making a purchase decision. By 2015, this number climbed to 22 sources in healthcare and other hospitality industries. Most patients will solidify their decision-making before actually calling a medical office to make an appointment or entering the reception room of the medical practice. New technologies have become readily available to facilitate discovery and engagement of these sources that our patients are using to make a healthcare decision.

The adoption of mobile devices and social media networks and unbiased third-party review sites really launched the new era of medical marketing. In 2011 that Google coined the term "zero moments of truth" (ZMOT) and released an e-book called *Winning the Zero Moment of Truth*.[1] The premise of the book is that decisions to select a healthcare provider break down into a series of multiple moments of truth, each of which requires special understanding to help nudge patients along their search journey. For example, when a patient is considering making an appointment, whether driven by a stimulus or need, patients are essentially going to "Google it." Anyone involved in the art and science of search wins in this moment by ensuring that their web pages are optimized to outperform competitive pages as people search. One suggestion for identifying those keywords that patients are going to use is to go to ads.Google.com and use their "discover new keywords" to identify the keywords, ranked from highest to lowest, that patients are using to find your practice. When you start creating content for your website and social media programs, use these keywords in the titles of your articles and blogs, and use the most commonly used keywords in the content of your articles. This is just one of the many ways that search engine optimization will use to place your practice on the first page of the Google search.

Stimulus* ⟶ **ZMOT** ⟶ First Moment Of Truth** ⟶ Second Moment Of Truth

* Often word of mouth
** The office telephone

FIGURE 1. The zero moment of truth (ZMOT) is the interval between first hearing about a doctor or medical practice (the stimulus) and the first moment of truth, which usually takes the form of a phone call to the office.

ZMOT is the interval between first hearing about a doctor or medical practice (i.e., the stimulus) and the first moment of truth, which usually is a phone call to the office (Figure 1). It is during this interval that potential patients use the nearly unlimited resources at their fingertips for research, fact checking, testimonials, and insurance checking for authorization and pricing. Most of the resources patients use to inform their decision fall outside the direct control of the practice. The ZMOT represents the first time in a conservative business milieu that patients have owned a piece of the decision path. And never forget that patients revel in their new role.

WHAT DOES ZMOT LOOK LIKE?

Let's look at a simple scenario of someone encountering the ZMOT during a decision to select a healthcare provider:

1. Lisa, a marketing director at a software company, has just moved to a new location in the community and is looking for a pediatrician for her children. She types in "pediatrician" plus her new zip code into the Google search window. She sees a list of 8 to 10 pediatric practices within her area. This list functions as the stimulus in this example, because it piques her interest enough for her to want to learn more about these practices.

2. Lisa decides to do some research on several of the pediatric practices. This is the ZMOT, where she looks at online reviews and testimonials to help her decide which practice to choose for her children.

3. Next comes the first moment of truth, where Lisa decides to call one of the practices and request an interview with the doctor(s).

4. Lastly, there is the second moment of truth, or the ultimate moment of truth, which is the experience that Lisa has after taking her children to the practice and having either a positive or negative experience. Lisa will share those experiences with others by word of mouth or go to one of the online physician rating services and weigh in on her experience with the pediatric practice. Lisa's experience becomes the next potential patient's ZMOT.

The most important lesson from Google's eBook about the zero moment of truth is that practices need to be aware of the ZMOT, be prepared for it, and, finally, to ensure that the ZMOT has been managed and not missed or ignored.

If you're available at the zero moment of truth, your customers will find you at the very moment they're thinking about becoming a patient.

PASSING THE ZMOT TEST

Make sure information about your practice is readily available and easy to find. Patients will be looking for the following types of content to help them make a decision: patient testimonials; answers to FAQs for the medical conditions where you have an area of interest and expertise; and case studies where you have treated patients with medical problems you are interested in attracting to your practice. They want reviews from your existing patients and also from their family and friends who have had a positive experience with your practice. Honestly, they are not interested in hearing directly from you and having you toot your own horn.

Focus on optimizing both the desktop and mobile versions of your site. Most product research starts with an online search on a computer or smartphone, so it's important that your site is properly optimized for search engine optimization. Try doing some of the following searches on Google: your practice area and medical conditions you treat. An example from my practice might be "vasectomy + New Orleans." You will see that I'm on the first page of the Google search (Figure 2). You want to be sure that your online reviews of your practice are as close as possible to four stars. Best of all are testimonials and opinions from others in your area

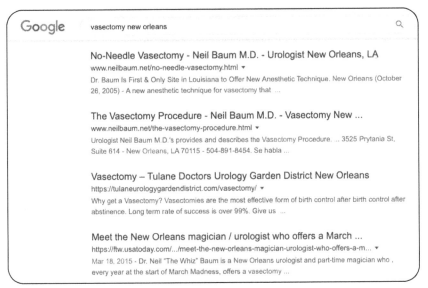

FIGURE 2. Use search engine optimization to place your practice on the first page of the Google search.

and your industry. This search will show you exactly what a patient sees (or does not see) when researching your practice or your name.

Think video/YouTube. It's not a coincidence that YouTube is the second most popular search bar on the internet. Consumers are looking for visuals and audio to help them decide. For healthcare, this means incorporating patient testimonials and discussions about disease conditions on blog sites. (I use WordPress.com, which easy to use—and it's free.)

Don't get lulled into thinking that because you have a presence on Facebook, Google, Twitter, YouTube, and Pinterest, you are doing all that you need to do attract and maintain patients in your practice. That's just the beginning. Once the patient enters the practice, this is where the rubber meets the road. The experience the patient has now will determine that patient's satisfaction and his or her willingness to share that experience with others.

Bottom Line: Putting a strategy in place to prepare for the ZMOT should not drastically change your current marketing strategy. After all, the fact that patients research before becoming a patient isn't earth-shattering news. But it is important to be aware of what information potential patients need during this process, and how easy it is for them to access it.

REFERENCE

1. Lecinski J. Winning the Zero Moment of Truth. Google; 2011. www.thinkwithgoogle.com/marketing-resources/micro-moments/2011-winning-zmot-ebook/.

CHAPTER 2

The Vital Two Minutes of the Patient Encounter

TOM HARBIN, MD, MBA, AND NEIL BAUM, MD

Imagine two scenarios:

The doctor enters the room without introducing himself or herself, sits down and looks at the computer screen, interrupts the patient after 15 seconds, never looks at the patient, and then writes a prescription and leaves.

The doctor enters the room, looks the patient in the eye while shaking hands and does the same for all the family members present, including children. The doctor then asks about the latest vacation, prompted by a note in the chart. After taking a history, the doctor examines the patient, even though the lab values have given the diagnosis and make an exam moot. Then the doctor sits down, faces the patient directly, and interacts with both the patient and family when discussing the diagnosis and treatment plan, allowing time for questions. The staff provides a written treatment plan before the patient leaves.

THE FIRST SIXTY SECONDS

As the cliché goes, you never get a second chance to make a good first impression. This truism makes it very important for the doctor to favorably impress the patient from the beginning, especially when seeing a patient for the first time.

First, consider your appearance. Patients expect you to look like a doctor. Traditionally, this means wearing a white coat, a powerful symbol of being a physician. Conservative dress for women, and white coat and tie, clean shaven for men will create the best impression. The exceptions to the white coat include pediatricians and psychiatrists.

Second, think about your initial behavior. We suggest that you smile and make eye contact. A smile indicates that you are receptive to listening and will be helpful to the patient. Communication theory has shown that words are only a small part of a face-to-face encounter. Words impart only 7% of the message that you convey. Voice inflection imparts another 28% of a message, and the remaining 65% is conveyed nonverbally by body language, facial expression, and eye contact.[1]

Next comes the first touch of the patient, usually a handshake. (And don't forget the rest of the people in the room.) Use hand sanitizer in front of the patient, tactfully indicating good hygiene. Then sit down so you're at the same level as the patient, with no barrier such as exam table or computer between you and the patient. This implies that you're not in a hurry and that the patient has your undivided attention. Sit erect, lean forward, and look the patient in the eye, not at the chart or the computer screen. By so doing, you are using that nonverbal 65% of a message to its best advantage.

You should start the dialog with nonmedical questions and discussion (e.g., books read, trips taken, interests in common). Once the patient has started talking about his or her symptoms or medical history, don't interrupt. Let the words flow. In a study of physician/patient interviews, Beckman and Frankel noted that patients were allowed to complete their opening statement without interruption only 23% of the time.[2] Doctors interrupted in 18 seconds, on average. Allowing the patient to speak without interruption makes the first few seconds count.

Ask new patients the name of their referral source; and when possible, make a nice comment about the doctor or referral source. Make a note in the chart so you can send a letter to the referrer. If the patient found you via the Internet or your Web site, ask what words or names he or she used in the search. Keep these as key words, and be sure they're included in the titles or body of your articles, blogs, and other social media.[3] Some doctors give patients a card on which they can write out the questions they will want answered by the time they leave.

With all these steps followed, you will have made a good first impression, and you can go on to the physical examination, office testing, and whatever else is involved in the full evaluation of the patient.

THE LAST SIXTY SECONDS

It's now time to discuss your findings and treatment plan. We suggest allowing the patient to be dressed and sitting in a chair while you adopt the same posture and body language as suggested above. Avoid standing over a patient lying on the exam table and covered only with a gown or drape, as this lessens the likelihood of the patient recalling what you said.

After you have presented your findings and plan, conclude by asking if all questions and concerns have been covered. Make sure the family's questions are answered as well.

Finally, reassure the patient and offer hope regardless of the severity of the diagnosis. Make every assurance that you will help the patient, make him or her comfortable, and avoid pain and discomfort to the best of your ability. Giving hope is a learned skill that many physicians have not mastered. Jerome Groopman, MD, in his book *The Anatomy of Hope,* points out that a physician cannot impart hope unless he or she believes in it personally. He further says, "I see hope as the very heart of healing. For those who have hope, it may help some to live longer and it will help all to live better."[4] Medicine has seen dramatic improvements in all specialties, and the promise of stem cells, genetic advances, and other treatments makes it very legitimate to offer hope to almost every patient.

CONCLUSION

The best opportunities to impress a patient favorably are in the first and last minutes of the encounter. If these time periods are wasted, we lose our ability to be effective. Ultimately, we risk losing patients and/or receiving poor reviews.

REFERENCES

1. Dibble J, Langford B. *Communication Skills and Strategies: Guidelines for Managers at Work.* Atlanta, GA: Southwestern Educational Publishing, 1994.
2. Beckman HB, Frankel RM. The effect of physician behavior on the collection of data. *Ann Intern Med.* 1984;101: 692-696.
3. Baum NH, Maley C, Schneider A. *Social Media for the Health Care Profession.* Phoenix, Maryland: Greenbranch Publishing, 2011.
4. Groopman J. *The Anatomy of Hope.* New York, NY: Random House, 2003.

CHAPTER 3

The Role of Positive Psychology in the Modern Medical Practice

SCOTT E. FRIEDMAN AND NEIL BAUM, MD

In daily conversations with colleagues, and in regular conversations with physician clients and friends, we hear a constant refrain of pessimism about today's healthcare profession. Many of these doctors unabashedly share with us that if they had to do it again, they wouldn't become doctors—nor would they recommend to their children that they enter the healthcare profession. This pessimism trickles down and infects professional colleagues, administrative staff, and, ultimately, our patients and the care we provide to them.

What has happened to this once-prized career path? And how is the climate of today's typical medical practice not only deleterious to our practice of medicine but also to our health and well-being? And most importantly, what can we do to improve the quality of healthcare, our practices, and our lives? This article offers answers to this question based on new research from the fields of social neuroscience and positive psychology. To appreciate these insights, however, it is first helpful to step back and revisit the pathophysiology of stress.

THE PATHOPHYSIOLOGY OF STRESS

To understand how stress impacts our practices, our health, and our interpersonal relationships, including those with our staff and our patients, we need to appreciate a little bit of evolutionary psychology and biology. Thousands of years ago, our ancestors faced true threats to their continued existence, encountering predatory animals (e.g., saber-tooth tigers) on a regular basis. To enhance their prospects of surviving, primitive humans developed a virtually instantaneous response that prepared them to fight or run from the danger. The "fight-or-flight" response became so finely developed that our ancestors, and now we, often are able to anticipate danger even before it exists. This prompts most of us, for example, to avoid dark alleys at night—although often we wind up anticipating (and worrying about) dangers that don't exist. Winston Churchill is credited with recognizing this byproduct of our evolutionary heritage when he observed that "I am an old man and have known a great many troubles, but most of them never happened."[1] (Think "overprotective parent" or hypochondriacal patient.)

Although most physicians practicing in the United States today no longer need to fear encounters with predatory animals, our brains remain "hard-wired" to react in fight-or-flight mode to modern day threats—threats that are more accurately and fairly characterized as petty nuisances and annoyances, such as, for example, when supplies are unavailable, having to wait a few extra minutes for an operating room to become available, or needing to complete extra paperwork for (declining) reimbursement. Beyond mere petty annoyances, we are prone to experience stress in any number of critical care circumstances, such as when a patient's condition is inexplicably deteriorating or when dealing with a patient (or that patient's family members) who feel that they are not receiving sufficient attention. Finally, of course, come all the other stresses we might face in our personal lives, including those that relate to our spouses and children.

Whenever our primitive fight-or-flight response kicks in—and for whatever reason—the physiological events that we experience today are the same as those our ancestors experienced when facing true physical threats. Nerve cells release chemicals such as adrenaline, noradrenalin, and cortisol into the bloodstream. These chemicals, in turn, trigger enhanced blood flow into the muscles of our limbs (and away from the digestive tract and the pelvis), making it easier to run away from the danger. Simultaneously, there is also an increase in the heart rate and the respiratory rate to increase the oxygen evolutionarily necessary to help make legs run faster when trying to flee a charging tiger. Other physiological changes include dilation of the pupils, improved (sharpened) eyesight, and increased awareness, all of which enhance a human's ability to focus on getting out of harm's way.

These automatic stress responses are our body's way of protecting us from danger. When they work appropriately, they help us stay focused, energetic, and alert. In an emergency, these stress responses are lifesaving, giving us extra strength to protect our loved ones and ourselves. It is this very reaction that allows a soccer mom to pick up a car off of a trapped child—something she wouldn't normally be able to accomplish under nonstressed conditions.

Unfortunately, our bodies and our neuroendocrine responses cannot differentiate between the threat posed by a saber-toothed tiger at the cave entrance and that posed by an irate patient complaining about not being seen on time. As a result, the reactions that occur in our bodies for nonexistential threats—including such things as an increase in cortisol and adrenaline into the bloodstream, and increased heart and respiratory rate—often are overreactions.

Worse, particularly in today's medical milieu, the nonstop action and responsibilities healthcare workers face every day can result in a lifestyle where one's fight-or-flight alarm system is constantly "on." Medical science has discovered that repeated negative events, multiple times each day, lead to a build-up of stress hormones that, in turn, can have unhealthy consequences on a number of areas, including mood (e.g., increased anxiety, depression, irritability), behavior (e.g., drug or alcohol abuse, smoking), and, of course, on one's health (e.g., high blood pressure, heart disease, obesity).

Fortunately, a variety of strategies are available to help manage these fight-or-flight reactions and, in so doing, enhance one's personal and professional quality of life and job performance. In this article we share some of these strategies that have been scientifically validated by researchers in the burgeoning fields of positive psychology and social neuroscience for physicians and other healthcare workers to draw upon.

POSITIVE PSYCHOLOGY IN THE MODERN MEDICAL PRACTICE

Positive psychology is the scientific study of happiness and human potential. The Positive Psychology Center at the University of Pennsylvania describes the field as "the scientific study of the strengths that enable individuals and communities to thrive...[Positive psychology] is founded on the belief that people want to lead meaningful and fulfilling lives, to cultivate what is best within them, and to enhance their experiences of love, work, and play."[2] The field is focused on understanding, and helping to apply, new tools for optimal living—for individuals, families, and organizations. Unlike pop psychology's often unsubstantiated conclusions and recommendations, positive psychology is a science, and, therefore, the insights, conclusions, and recommendations it offers are based on empirical data generated from research conducted pursuant to the scientific method. This research has demonstrated that small shifts in how we communicate and behave not only make us happier and healthier, but also can enhance an organization's bottom line, including "31 percent higher productivity, 25 percent greater performance ratings, 37 percent higher sales, and 23 percent lower levels of stress."[3] Of particular relevance is research that shows that physicians who are in a good mood—feeling positive and optimistic—come up with the correct diagnosis 19% faster than doctors who report feeling "neutral."[4]

We offer the following 10 key recommendations that we believe will be of interest to physicians.

1. Use Words that Prime Positivity

Physicians depend on team work, including with partners, other healthcare professionals, administrative staff, and others. Researchers at Stanford University have found that simply including the word "together" helps motivate people to work longer hours and produce better quality work.[5] Consider beginning a conversation or meeting with positive news or observations that emphasize the importance of teamwork and collaboration. In her book *The Morning Meeting Book,* Roxanne Kriete asserts that related research demonstrates that emotions, whether positive or negative, are highly contagious, and, so, beginning positively—"positive priming"— enhances cooperation, empathy, and a sense of shared responsibility."[3] Of special note, consider beginning an e-mail with a positive comment to help reduce the risk of being misunderstood, as so often happens with this form of communication because of the absence of nonverbal cues such as body language, facial expressions, and tone of voice.

2. Adjust Your Positivity Ratio

Barbara Frederickson, the Kenan Distinguished Professor of Psychology at the University of North Carolina, is well known for her work on the importance of positivity ratios—the ratio of positive comments to negative comments. Decades of work by Frederickson and others has amassed considerable empirical data on the correlation of a higher positivity ratio with happiness and success.[6,7]

Informal observation over the years suggests that too many physicians and healthcare workers suffer from low positivity ratios. Catch people doing things right! There are so many instances when staff members do something above and beyond the job description and their efforts go unnoticed. One of us (NHB) remembers a time when a staff member took sample medication to a patient's home when the prescription she received caused her to have side effects that precluded her using the expensive medication. When this kind of "extra mile" behavior is observed, compliment or reward the staff member for going above and beyond what was "required." Strive to be as positive as possible, but, at least, to have four or five positive comments for every negative one. Having a higher positive-to-negative ratio is likely to lead to a more productive team or practice.

3. Avoid Negative People

Scientists are identifying biologic evidence that validates the existence of positive and negative people.[8] Being around negative people can bring us down. Doctors going to hospital lounges and cafeterias often find themselves surrounded by swirling pessimism. Avoid those encounters and seek out others who don't participate in "pity parties." Avoid "negative" staff meetings by starting with something positive, perhaps even asking each staff member to tell something positive that happened to them in the practice since the previous meeting. This simple idea gets everyone thinking positively and, as a result, the staff meeting becomes more meaningful and more productive.

4. Dealing with Bad News

Physicians often find themselves in the position of having to deliver bad news, such as to a patient who has just been diagnosed with a terminal illness. Michelle Gielan[3] describes how physicians at the Children's Hospital of Philadelphia seek to shift their conversations with patients and their families to "something positive," such as "Given what your family is up against, what are you hoping for?" Describing Dr. Chris Feudtner's approach, Gielan writes:

Dr. Feudtner says that families usually have a list of seven or eight wishes, including to make happy memories before the end of the child's life, to manage the child's pain well, and to let the child spend the remainder of his or her days at home rather than in the hospital. [His approach moves the conversation from no cure] to modest success in achieving some of those wishes.

Related research suggests how physicians would benefit by using "plain English" rather than medical jargon when delivering news, particularly bad news, expressing compassion through words, tone of voice, or even a hug.

5. Express Compassion

Compassion, a major tenet of the world's major religions, has been increasingly studied by researchers, revealing amazing results that physicians would be wise to pay attention to. (Unlike empathy, where one experiences another person's emotions, compassion is generally defined as experiencing another person's suffering and involves an authentic desire to help.) Research conducted at the Lexington Veterans Affairs Medical Center in Kentucky found that a hospital's policy of permitting doctors to say "I'm sorry" in the event of suspected medical malpractice resulted in a 627% lower payment per claim than hospitals that didn't have such a policy.[3] Learn to say "I'm sorry!"

6. Offer Constructive Feedback

Notwithstanding its emphasis on "positivity," positive psychology does not ignore the reality that we encounter disappointments and adversity in our lives. Researchers help us understand that the most constructive way to manage such situations caused by others is to be encouraging and provide constructive feedback, similar to what a great coach might offer.[9] Constructive feedback will help others bounce back faster and help create energy for renewed efforts. Next time one of your colleagues makes a mistake, try taking a moment to create a learning opportunity rather than yelling, griping, or expressing some negative emotion.

A pat on the back is better than a kick in the pants. It is so much nicer to compliment someone, patient or staff member, when they do something well as opposed to giving them a kick in the pants when they don't do what is expected. For example, if a patient is overweight and the obesity is contributing to his or her poor health, even a modest weight loss should be celebrated. This motivates the patient to continue with the process and not "let the doctor down" by not being a compliant patient.

7. Offer a Helping Hand

We depend on others to help us do our jobs and accomplish our goals in countless ways. Research reveals that when we help others, even if we do no more than lend a listening ear, we boost our own happiness and that of others. So-called "work altruists" have been found to be 10 times more engaged at work than those who do not offer help to their colleagues and are 40% more likely to be promoted.[6] Find the time to help a colleague. Volunteer to take an extra day of call to give an obviously overworked colleague a much-needed break. Scrub-in to assist with a difficult surgery. Or help a colleague with an administrative matter that he or she is uncertain about how to best handle.

8. Find Time to Socialize

We suspect that most physicians' days are filled with too much to do and too little time to do it—seeing patients, talking to family, paperwork, etc. The hectic and harried pace often leaves little time for colleagues to socialize. A by-product of this harried pace and modern forms of technology is that communication today too often takes place through impersonal e-mails and text messages, rather than in face-to-face conversations. With little or no socializing, relationships become more distant and, in turn, more stressed. Research suggests that finding some time to socialize—such as over a cup of coffee at the start of the day, a quick bite to eat during the day, or a cocktail or dinner at the end of the day—improves social bonds and the quality of interpersonal relationships.

9. Express Appreciation and Gratitude

Write a thank you note every day. One of us (NHB) met Lou Holtz when he was the head football coach of Notre Dame, and learned that he was famous for writing at least one thank you note every day. He also encouraged his staff *and* his football players to do the same. After seeing how successful Coach Holtz was, I adopted the same letter writing approach and make

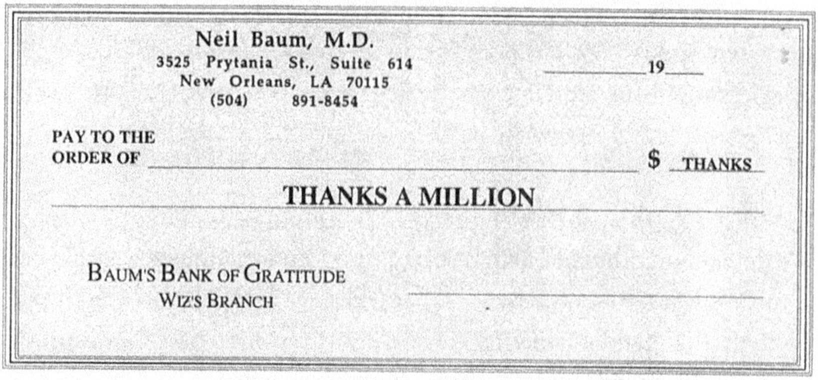
Neil Baum, M.D.
3525 Prytania St., Suite 614
New Orleans, LA 70115
(504) 891-8454

19___

PAY TO THE ORDER OF ________ $ THANKS

THANKS A MILLION

BAUM'S BANK OF GRATITUDE
WIZ'S BRANCH

FIGURE 1. Thank you note from Dr. Baum.

every effort to say thank you to someone every day. I also encourage my staff to write notes of appreciation (Figure 1).

10. Smile!

Finally, researchers are finding out some interesting facts about smiling that we urge physicians to consider. Aside from making us feel better, researchers who tracked the lives of women who had the best smiles in yearbook photos found that they reported living happier lives, having happier marriages, and having fewer setbacks than their classmates whose smiles weren't as big.[10] In another study, researchers found baseball players who had big smiles on their baseball card photos lived, on average, seven years longer than those whose smiles weren't as big.[11]

Beyond these personal benefits, saying "hello" and smiling has been proven to have "bottom line benefits" to healthcare systems. Consider Ochsner Health System, a large Louisiana healthcare provider, that has garnered widespread attention for implementing what it calls the "10/5 way." Ochsner employees are encouraged to make eye contact if they're within 10 feet of someone, and say hello if they're within 5 feet. Ochsner reports improvements in patient satisfaction scores and patient referrals—and its bottom line![12]

SUMMARY

Is it any wonder that modern day forms of stress lead to problems with our staff, our patients, and even our health? In today's society, it is neither socially acceptable nor generally helpful to come to blows with someone who is annoying us, nor can we always run away from (avoid) the stressful situation. Instead, we need to learn how to avoid the stress whenever possible ("self management"), or when that isn't possible, to control the stress ("stress management") and dissipate all those chemicals, cortisol, and adrenaline, as quickly as possible so that they don't create unhealthy and counterproductive reactions that can wreak havoc on our practices and our personal lives as well.

Without the right tools to handle these events, we are prone to overreacting or reacting inappropriately, reactions that often backfire and can exacerbate the situation—often, for the physician, negatively impacting the quality of our relationships with our colleagues, our staff, our patients, and even our families and friends. The consequences of too much negativity in our lives include impaired bodily functions, reduced productivity, and negative effects on the quality of relationships with others and, ultimately, our quality of life. Fortunately, ongoing scientific research suggests a number of easy-to-adapt strategies that can help all of us live more productive, satisfying and healthy lives. We hope you explore some of this exciting research and test some of the suggestions described above!

REFERENCES

1. Langworth R. *Churchill by Himself: The Definitive Collection of Quotations.* New York: PublicAffairs; 2008:531.

2. Positive Psychology Center. Our mission. http://ppc.sas.upenn.edu/our-mission. Accessed August 1, 2015.

3. Gielan M. *Broadcasting Happiness: The Science of Igniting and Sustaining Positive Change.* Dallas, TX: BenBella Books; 2015.

4. Estrada CA, Isen AM, Young MJ. Positive affect facilitates integration of information and decreases anchoring in reasoning among physicians. *Organ Behav Hum Decis Process.* 1997;72:117-135.

5. Carr PB, Walton GM. Cues of working together fuel intrinsic motivation. *J Exp Soc Psychol.* 2014;53:169-184.

6. Fredrickson B, Losada M. Positive affect and the complex dynamics of human flourishing. *Am Psychol.* 2005; 60: 678-686.

7. Fredrickson BL. Updated thinking on positivity ratios. *Am Psychol.* 2013;68:814-822.

8. Michigan State University. Biological evidence of positive and negative people in the world. *ScienceDaily.* April 2, 2014; www.sciencedaily.com/releases/2014/04/140402100052.htm. Accessed August 1, 2015.

9. Black SJ, Weiss MR. The relationship among perceived coaching behaviors, perceptions of ability, and motivation in competitive age-group swimmers. *J Sport Exerc Psychol.* 1992;14:309-325.

10. Harker LA, Keltner D. Expressions of positive emotions in women's college yearbook pictures and their relationships to personality and life outcomes across adulthood. *Journal of Personality and Social Psychology*. 2001;80(1):112-124.

11. Abel EL, Kruger ML. Smile intensity in photographs predicts longevity. *Psychological Science*. 2010;21:542-544.

12. Porath C. No time to be nice at work. *The New York Times*. June 19, 2015; www.nytimes.com/2015/06/21/opinion/sunday/is-your-boss-mean.html?_r=0. Accessed June 21, 2015.

CHAPTER 4

Marketing Funnel: Visualizing the Patient's Journey

Neil Baum, MD

MARKETING FUNNEL

The marketing funnel (Figure 1) can be used to understand the process of attracting patients to your practice. There are several distinct phases of the patient journey where this funnel is applicable to your medical practices. The funnel is wide at the top and narrow at the bottom because every stage represents the amount of potential patients entering the funnel. Because you are likely to lose some potential patients along the way, the funnel gets narrower toward the bottom. This article reviews each state of the marketing funnel.

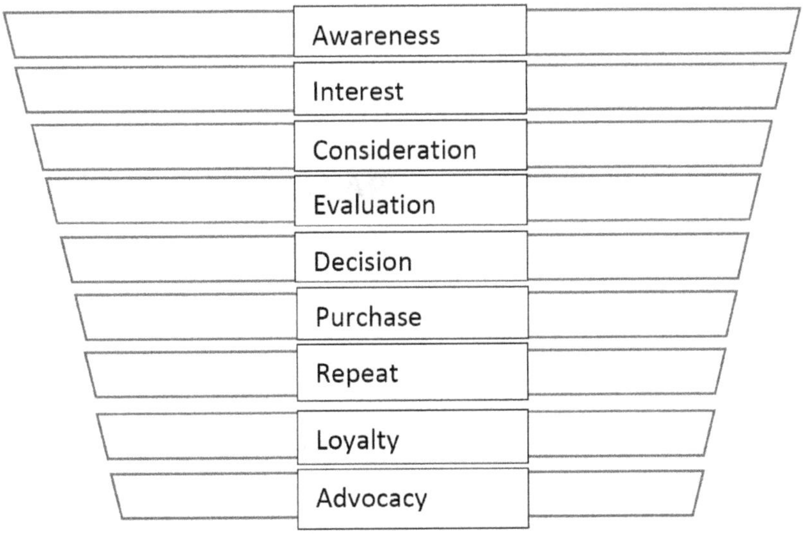

FIGURE 1. Marketing funnel.

AWARENESS

The marketing funnel starts off with the awareness stage, often called the *attention-seeking stage*. The goal of this stage is to gain presence and to introduce your practice to potential patients—they need to know that you exist. You can either actively reach potential patients through newsletters, marketing campaigns, or word of mouth, or help them discover you more easily with their own (online) search. In order for patients to more easily find you online, search engine optimization (SEO), both organic and nonorganic (i.e., pay per click) is the best method.

INTEREST

Now that you have the patients' attention, you want to create some interest. The goal of this stage is to show who you are and what your areas of interest or expertise are. You are trying to build a relationship with your potential patients and gain trust. Give patients and potential patients valuable information, but don't focus on selling your practice. Throughout this second stage, potential patients begin to develop attitudes, opinions, and, hopefully, interest in your practice. Providing new, excellent content is required for this stage. Think about using blogs, webinars, free e-books, and newsletters. Keep in mind that patients can also develop negative feelings toward your practice, so be careful with what kind of messages you convey to potential patients.

CONSIDERATION

Once patients' interest in your practice has grown, they might be willing to consider availing themselves to your services and making an appointment in your practice. In order to establish that relationship, you have to help them understand that your practice fulfills a medical *need* or *desire* that they might have. Furthermore, you have to explain that your practice is the best option for solving that medical need. This stage is therefore all about positioning and showing off your unique aspects that differentiate you and your practice and what extra value you have to offer to patients compared to other practices in the area or region. Studies have shown that people usually consider only two to three different practices before calling one of the practices for an appointment, so you want to make sure your practice is the one selected.

EVALUATION

Now that your brand has made it to the consideration stage, patients are likely to evaluate their options based on their own personal criteria. Even though selection criteria may vary from patient to patient, you might be able to detect some general patterns by looking at the criteria that patients most often use to select a medical practice. Continuous patient feedback, which can be obtained through surveys and focus groups, will help you figure out what patients in general find most important about a certain disease or condition. Once you are aware of these attributes, you can guide your marketing efforts in such a way that you highlight these features when showcasing your practice. Attributes that patients commonly use to evaluate a practice are price, quality, appearance, durability, and what happens after the doctor–patient encounter is over.

DECISION

The next stage is when the patient will decide either to accept you as a physician or to seek another physician. It is important to note here that the person making the decision to call for an appointment is not always the same person as the one *calling for* the appointment or becoming part of the practice. For example, a child who needs pediatric care might not be the one calling for the appointment. Another example is a caregiver who may be contacting the practice to make an appointment for a family member or a friend. It is crucial to keep in mind when targeting your marketing efforts to certain groups of people that you use material that focuses on those who can make the decision to be patients in your practice.

PURCHASE

The actual "purchase" phase has been kept separate from the decision-making phase for two reasons:

- There can be a difference between the buyer and the decision-maker.
- Potential patients might ultimately decide to not purchase your product even though they have decided that your product is their first choice. This could happen because:
  - The potential patient is searching online for your practice and has trouble locating the contact information; or

— The decision-maker may have issues with the insurance plans that cover your services.

Once your potential patients have decided that they want your service, it is the job of your marketing efforts to make it as easy as possible for them to become a patient. For example, if a patient wants to make an appointment online, you want to make the procedure seamless and easy, with only one or two clicks on the mouse needed to secure an appointment. Making it easy for patients will help you to boost the conversion rate from viewer to paying patient.

REPEAT

Many marketing funnels stop after the patient has made an appointment. However, in today's hypercompetitive and dynamic healthcare environment, it is key to keep patients in your practice for as long as possible. Retention of patients is just as important as getting the patient to make his or her initial office visit. Good patient relationship management increases the chance that patients will become repeat customers. One of the best ways of impressing a new patient is to have someone in the practice—ideally the doctor—call the patient after an initial visit to be sure all the questions have answered during their visit to the office.

LOYALTY

In the loyalty stage, customers start to develop a preference for your practice and will tell others about their outstanding care and service. If their experience has been outstanding, patients will share their experience by word of mouth with family and friends. Patient loyalty is far more important than return visits. Loyalty means patients are hanging in there even when there may be some problems or negative rumors about your practice. In order to create loyalty, your patients need to believe the relationship between you and them is more than just a transactional relationship, which means connecting with your patients on a personal level is crucial.

ADVOCACY

The final and optimal stage to reach with customers is the advocacy stage. Advocacy happens when your patients become something more than just paying patients: they become fans. Fans usually are so excited about something that they tell their friends and family all about it; they share positive reviews on social media, and they might even try to convince others to become fans as well. In other words, they are now helping you creating awareness just like at the beginning of this marketing funnel. When customers decide to become your own practice's ambassadors, you know you are doing something right!

Bottom Line: The marketing funnel is a great tool that helps you visualize the patient journey or the path that patients take as they become more familiar with your practice and your services and move from awareness to conversion to (hopefully) the advocacy stage. It allows marketers to use a more structured approach to map out the marketing campaigns that need to be considered. Keep in mind that this is a general version of the marketing funnel and that you might need to adapt it somewhat to fit your practice. Let the marketing begin!

CHAPTER 5

Finding the Sweet Spot in Your Medical Practice

Kendra Reed, PhD, Sean Presti, and Neil Baum, MD

"If you don't know where you are going, any road will get you there."
Lewis Carroll in Alice in Wonderland

Finding the sweet spot begins with identifying your strategy.[1] Practices that lack a simple and clear strategy are likely to fall into the categories of those who: (1) failed to execute their strategy; or (2) worse, never even had one. In an astonishing number of practices, doctors and practice administrators face overwhelming obstacles because no clear strategy exists to guide decision and behaviors of those people who "make or break" the practice. Complaints and questions abound in such practices, such as the following:

- We are so busy with patient care that we don't have the time to develop a strategy.
- Should we expand our operation and take on a new associate or create a satellite office in the suburbs?
- Should we offer early morning hours, which will certainly increase the cost of our overhead/personnel?

A successful practice can increase power and focus with a strategic statement that all team members can internalize and use as a compass to point the direction for every decision and action.

Think of a large medical practice as consisting of 100 discrete iron filings, each one representing an individual and valued employee. By scooping up the filings and dropping them onto one piece of paper, you will create an artistic mess, with each filing pointing in a random direction. In other words, if you take 100 smart hard-working people and plop them into a practice, each individual will make what they think are right decisions

27

for the practice—but the result will be a lot of good decisions leading in a variety of directions and resulting in confusion and frustration.

Rather than trying to scoop up all 100 metal filings, if you pass a magnet under the piece of paper those filings and consider your Physics 101 knowledge, the filings will line up in one unified direction. Similar to the magnet pulling the filings, a well-articulated and internalized statement of strategy aligns individuals' decisions and behavior within a practice. A clear, concise, meaningful strategy enables everyone in one practice to make decisions that reinforce one another and move the practice in one strategic direction. With everyone in the practice moving in the same direction, the practice will more likely benefit from improved patient outcomes, decreased costs, and reduced overhead—the "triple win."[2]

Unfortunately, physicians and office managers commonly lack awareness of the fundamental elements of a strategy statement, making development of a strategy nearly impossible. With the knowledge of the elements, articulation of the strategy, and clear consistent communication of the strategic direction, the leadership team can create a roadmap for everyone on the team to follow and instill a competitive advantage that becomes a part of the practice's DNA.

THREE ELEMENTS OF A STRATEGY STATEMENT

The three components of a good strategy statement are (1) objective, (2) scope, and(3) advantage. "These elements are a simple yet sufficient list for any strategy that addresses competitive interaction over unbounded terrain."[1]

The Objectives

A strategy statement must begin with a clear articulation of the ends the strategy will achieve. "To begin with the end in mind means to start with a clear understanding of your destination."[3] If a practice has an unclear sense of what that practice aims to achieve, then the odds are stacked against the practice reaching the goal or objective. The objectives should be specific, measurable, attainable, results-oriented, and time bound. In other words, the strategic objectives include not only a clear endpoint but also a realistic date for reaching it. For example, an objective of attracting the highest percentage of new patient retention would be made more powerful by adding specifics, such as increasing the number of new patients by 3% in nine months. Objectives should be on the leadership level of a successful practice, should be limited to two to four objectives, and should provide the basis for creating the entire practice as well as individual performance objectives.

Strategic objectives act as the catalyst, and, therefore, should not be confused with the mission, vision and values of a practice. Mission statements explain why a particular practice exists or the value proposition in a particular competitive space, with a vision depicting what or how the practice wants to be seen by customers, competitors, and the community.

Medical practices often confuse a strategic objective with cliché or mission statements. A strategic objective is not, for example, the platitude of "maximizing patient satisfaction." A strategic objective reflects the mission of the practice. For example, a practice whose goal is to offer superior customer engagement might consider a strategic objective including "responding to patients' inquiries within 24 hours for non-urgent calls or e-mails." Of course, urgent or emergency calls will be returned sooner.

Because most medical practices compete without a clear vision, they rarely act in alignment with a clear mission and reach specified objectives. For example, if your vision aims to focus on being highly responsive to patients' phone calls and e-mails, then a strategic objective would be needed for accomplishing this behavior that differentiates your practice from others in the community.

Defining the Scope

Defining the scope sets the strategic boundaries of the practice. More specifically, the scope clarifies what is included and excluded from a practice in term of three dimensions: (1) patients; (2) staff; and (3) services. Clearly defined boundaries clarify activities the practice should emphasize and, more importantly, activities the practice should avoid. For most practices in most situations, clearly defining the desired patient takes precedence. A practice may set one boundary as treating only women, and then the scope can be further to focus on services to treat women with infertility issues or to focus on nutrition and weight loss. With clear boundaries, the staff's talents and activities can be better aligned, and can become more efficient and more productive in achieving strategic objectives that drive the mission and fuel the vision.

Defining the Advantage

"Clarity about what makes the [practice] distinctive is what most helps everyone in the practice understand how they can contribute to the successful execution of its strategy."[1] An advantage that positively differentiates your practice from others in the community increases the probability of success in a competitive environment, in which medical teams strive to increase the number of patients with a staff that provides distinct, reproducible, and value-added services. You must ask, "What will our practice do differently, better, faster compared with other practices in the region?" For example, if you declare that your unique advantage to your patients is that they will wait less than 15 minutes to see a physician or mid-level provider, then you must deliver on that advantage to provide a competitive strategy. If a patient waits 60 minutes to see the doctor, the practice will disappoint patients and possibly find patients leaving the practice to find a practice that keeps their promises.

The strategic advantage statement includes two parts: (1) the value proposition; and (2) supporting activities. The value proposition explains why targeted patients should avail themselves of the services that the practice offers. For example, does your practice provide ready access to the practice and guarantee that patients can have same-day appointments, evening appointments, or appointments on weekends? Next, supporting activities address the unique aspects, services, or complex combination of activities allowing the practice to deliver the enhanced value that was promised to the patient. If you have a concierge practice, your promise offers house calls that few other physicians in your community offer or provide. With increased interest in telemedicine, your sweet spot may be offering scheduled virtual visits on the same day the patient requests a virtual visit; thus, your strategic advantage would create value within your area of expertise and propel the success of your strategic objectives.

INCREASED STRATEGIC POWER WITH BRANDING

Branding allows practices to find that sweet spot and turn tap water into Evian. Let us explain. Most of the population drinks water from the tap that is free and safe. Yet millions of people will buy bottled water (e.g., Evian, Fiji, SmartWater) at $1.50 or more for 16 ounces. That cost is 20% more than an equivalent amount of Budweiser beer and 40% more than the same volume of nutritious milk! That is an example of the power of branding.

FIGURE 1. Location of the "sweet spot."

Everyone *believes* their practice is special, unique, and offers the very best healthcare. When you hit the sweet spot, you clearly demonstrate your uniqueness and your superiority to other practices in the community. When you consistently hit the sweet spot, you can "sculpt" your practice and create an ideal medical practice where the patient is the focus, the staff enjoys caring for the patient, and the doctor does what he or she does best—that is, take care of patients in a uniquely distinct and valued matter and not be just a data collector for the electronic medical record.

It was just a few decades ago that doctors attracted patients by having an in-column ad in the Yellow Pages or placing an announcement of the intention to open an office in the newspaper. Doctors often had to wait several years for word of mouth to create a busy practice. Today, most doctors will not want to wait for years in order to have a busy practice. Now it is possible, even in the current healthcare crisis, to find the sweet spot in your practice and become very busy and successful very quickly.

An excellent approach to strategic planning for medical practices is to create a strategic worksheet (Figure 2). This worksheet would first list what has to be done within 24 to 48 hours, then start another column for what to do in the next 5 to 7 days, and finally add column for strategic action steps to be taken in the next 30 to 60 days. This is an excellent way to create and prioritize working strategy.

Time	24-48 hrs	5-7 days	30-60 days
Current situation			
Action to take			
Priority			
Preparation			

FIGURE 2. Sample sweet spot worksheet.

STRATEGIC IMPLEMENTATION: PREPARATION AND FOCUS

Any tennis player worth his salt will tell you that hitting the sweet spot requires preparation and focus. Preparation means getting ready even before walking on to the court, including stretching, applying a new grip on the handle of the racquet, adding new strings to the racquet, and even making sure the player's tennis shoes are tied securely. Preparation to hit the sweet spot is equally critical for a successful practice. For example, the staff needs to be prepared to see patients before starting the clinical day in the office, including ensuring that all the reports and lab tests are in the electronic medical record, the exam rooms are fully stocked with the supplies and equipment needed for patient care, and even that the restrooms are clean and there are ample supplies of paper towels and toilet paper. Preparation helps to get each employee to narrow in on the sweet spot, get their heads in the game, and, in other words, focus on implementing a successful strategy. One way to prepare your team by communicating your strategy and strengthening your team's focus on the win is a "morning huddle."

In today's turbulent, chaotic, and rapidly changing environment, the success of the modern practice depends on the promise to see that every patient has a positive experience. In most practices, the patients will spend more time with your staff than with the doctor. Therefore, it is essential to see that the staff is highly motivated to ensure that the patient's interaction with everyone in the practice remains at a high level from the moment the patient walks into the reception area and checks in at the desk right up until they make their next appointment and check out of the office. One technique that one of us (NB) has found useful, practical, and effective is to have a morning huddle. This is a 1- to 2-minute meeting with the doctor and the entire staff to be sure that everyone is on the same page and all working together to create that positive experience for every patient. The doctor and the office manager have an immeasurable impact on staff motivation.

The morning huddle is a pause or time out at the beginning of the day, to ensure that the game plan for the whole day is executed properly, safely, and efficiently. The doctor arrives before the first patient is seen and reviews the daily schedule with the staff. Each appointment is reviewed for potential "gotchas" or sources of delay. For example, if a patient is returning to discuss a biopsy report, be absolutely certain that the pathology report is on the chart and has been reviewed by the doctor before he or she enters the room. Nothing is more discouraging to a patient than having to wait for the report to come from the pathologist or the hospital. Patients who have had a biopsy are anxious about the findings, and a delay of even a few minutes can add to their anxiety. Just as patients have been preparing for several days for the visit, it is reasonable to expect the practice to take the same care in preparing to review a report or even a simple blood test.

Another example is anticipating the special needs of a patient with limited mobility. Having a wheelchair ready before the patient arrives sends a powerful and caring message. You also can make certain that a room that accommodates a wheelchair is available for the patient and they aren't kept waiting in the reception area until a room is available.

If a patient is going to have an office procedure, the morning huddle is a time to be sure that all of the instruments, medications, and a plan for achieving a comfortable room temperature are in place for the procedure. The doctor doesn't want to be in the room doing the procedure and have to send someone out to obtain more medications or supplies. The morning huddle also may be used to alert the staff about any VIPs that will be coming to the practice and to be extra vigilant for their needs and wants.

This time also can be used to inform the staff about any visitors that are expected that day and to be sure that everyone knows about the visit and is ready to make sure that they are welcomed and escorted into the office or lounge area.

Let the staff be aware of any last-minute developments that could affect the daily schedule: for example, the need for a doctor to leave at lunchtime for a meeting, a lecture, or a short case in the operating room. If the staff knows about the time that the doctor has to leave, they will work hard to have patients in the room and ready to be seen in a timely fashion in order for the doctor to depart on time.

The morning huddle motivates the doctor to start on time and stay on time. If the doctor is consistently late, then the day starts out already behind schedule before the first patient is seen. This leads to stress on the part of the staff, and they cannot perform at the highest level when there is stress in the office setting. For the morning huddle to be effective, the doctor has to be part of the process and *must* be on time. We know that there are urgencies and emergencies that sometimes make it difficult or impossible for the doctor to be on time. But this should be the exception and not the rule for most practices. We can do a far better job to be on time for our patients.

The morning huddle gets the entire staff on the same page and creates a sense of camaraderie and team spirit. The huddle can identify potential problems before they have a chance to wreak havoc with the schedule or create a negative experience for the patient.

The morning huddle takes only a few minutes. It just might be the best two minutes you spend with your staff each day to ensure that every patient has a positive experience with the practice.

The take-home message on the morning huddle: the morning huddle may help you consistently hit the sweet spot in your practice.

Bottom Line: Behind every successful practice lies a powerful strategy that includes the sweet spot. Any strategy statement that cannot explain why patients should avail themselves of your expertise is doomed to failure. Take the time to identify the sweet spot of your practice and make every effort to strike the ball at the sweet spot and you will have a very sweet practice.

REFERENCES

1. Rukstad DJ, Collis D. Can you say what your strategy is? *Harvard Business Review.* 2008;86:82-90.

2. Logan D, Loh LC, Huang V. The "triple win" practice: the importance of organizational support for volunteer endeavors undertaken by health care professionals and staff. *J Glob Health*. 2018;8(1):010305. DOI: 10.7189/jogh.08.010305.

3. Covey S. *The 7 Habits of Highly Effective People: Powerful Lessons in Personal Change*. New York: Simon and Schuster; 2013.

CHAPTER 6

Kaizen and the Contemporary Medical Practice

RON HARMAN KING, MS, DAVID P. SPICIARICH, BS, AND NEIL BAUM, MD

The secret of getting ahead is getting started. The secret of getting started is breaking complex overwhelming tasks into small manageable tasks, and then starting on the first one.

—*Mark Twain*

BRIEF HISTORY OF SUGGESTION PROGRAMS

The first modern employee suggestion program was reported in a British Navy journal in 1770. Before this date, a junior naval officer who offered a suggestion or contradicted a captain or admiral's order could be punished by hanging! The first suggestion box appeared in 1880 in a Scottish shipyard. The concept was to query all employees and then reward them financially for any ideas that were implemented.

The first U.S. company to implement a company-wide employment suggestion program was the National Cash Register Company. The idea did not catch on and was soon abandoned, because those at the top of the hierarchy expected the managers to do the thinking and the workers to do what they were told.

The suggestion box became more popular during and after World War II. Now it was possible for customers to offer their ideas for improvement in the product or service. This is not Kaizen, though, because suggestions submitted in a suggestion box are initiated by patients or outsiders and are intended for others to make the changes rather than front-line employees offering ideas that can be implemented by the staff.

The first evidence of the use of suggestions seeking improvement in healthcare was published in 1915 by Frank Gilbreth, who filmed surgical procedures with the goal of eliminating waste and improving efficiency in the operating room.[1] He observed that surgeons spent more time searching for instruments than actually performing the operation.

Gilbreth's revolutionary idea was to have a surgical "caddy" to hand instruments to the surgeon, thus allowing the surgeon to focus on the patient and the operation. To show you that medicine has been and still is bogged down in the status quo and does not accept change easily, it took another 16 years for the American Medical Association to accept the caddy system as a best practice.

Next came Dr. W. Edwards Deming, considered the father of the continuous improvement method. Deming took his ideas of continuous quality improvement to Japan, where they were adopted by the Toyota manufacturing company and became famous as the Toyota Production System, or Kaizen. This, in Deming's words, is "the process of making incremental improvement, no matter how small, and achieving the goal of eliminating all waste that adds cost without adding value."[2]

GETTING STARTED WITH KAIZEN IN HEALTHCARE

Kaizen is arguably the best tool for easily implementing changes in the modern healthcare practice. The goal of Kaizen in healthcare, including managing responses from a suggestion box, is to make small changes that will improve the patient experience.

The first step is to look for opportunities to do things in a different or fresh way. In their book *Seeing David in the Stone*,[3] authors James B. Swartz and Joseph E. Swartz studied 70 of the world's greatest innovators, from Galileo to Edison to the founder of Federal Express. The book emphasizes that these pioneers found opportunities first and then identified the problems that needed to be overcome to take advantage of the opportunities. The-take home message is that the more clearly the problem or the opportunity is defined, the easier it will be to solve with the available resources.

For healthcare providers, the process often starts with a suggestion. Ideas often will appear as complaints or improvement ideas. Even when idea comes in as a solution, it's best to look first at the problem to be solved. A well-defined problem statement focuses the efforts of the team and helps set the scope of the project. Problem statements must be specific and should not include solutions. For instance, a patient once noted on a comment card that he didn't like putting his clothes on the floor in the changing room. The problem is easily stated: patients have no place to put their clothes as they change into gowns for examinations or procedures.

KAIZEN IN ACTION

Here is an example from our practice (NB). On most Fridays, we commonly performed three to five vasectomy procedures. Sterilized trays of instruments, medications, and suture material were available for each procedure. There were approximately 20 to 25 instruments on each sterile tray. However, one of the nurses noted that only four instruments—the scalpel, the ringed hemostat to grasp the vas, the Hemoclip applier, and the specialized vasectomy hemostat—were routinely used.

She suggested that we reduce the number of instruments on each tray from 20 to the four instruments that are most frequently used. The inefficiency was that too many instruments are prepared for every vasectomy when only four are generally used. However, even though in nearly all of our cases we used only four instruments, sometimes we'd have a special case that required one or more of the additional instruments. We couldn't just eliminate those tools altogether—they needed to be available just in case they were needed. We reviewed the medical records from the last 200 vasectomies, and we found that we only needed additional instruments in four instances.

Once we have identified a problem statement, we form a small team of participants with responsibility for or knowledge of the problem. The team looks at the current situation and asks the question, "What is true today?" Then we look at the data that reflect or illuminate the problem statement.

The next step is to define the desired target state: what do we want to be true? In the case of the vasectomy trays, we wanted to have make the most frequently required instruments immediately at hand, while still having the larger selection available.

After defining the target state, it's time to identify the gap: what keeps you from achieving the target state? Solving the problem of the instruments on the vasectomy trays was easy. We had always made all 20 instruments available. "This is the way we've always done it" is one of the greatest obstacles to improvement and comes up often! It's common for the team to jump straight to solutions, but it's important to spend time here to be sure you have developed a good list of obstacles.

Now it's time to develop solutions. Have the team brainstorm ideas that will eliminate the issue. Once there is a good list of potential solutions, have the team choose which they want to work on. Other considerations will affect your ideas.

Develop a plan to try out each proposed solution, and then conduct a limited-scope experiment. For our vasectomy trays, we had the four most commonly used instruments open for each procedure; the remaining 16 tools were in the room, but remained in the sterile packaging. Those packages could be opened if they were needed.

Did your experiments work? Be open to the possibility of an unforeseen occurrence. With our surgery tray, we pretended we needed one of the 16 tools. When we opened the pack, we found that the paper wrapping the tray of instruments was punctured, and the pack wasn't sterile. A compromised pack is a rare occurrence, but we decided we needed two additional packs in the room, just in case.

Setting up the procedure room, we used preference cards to detail which tools and instruments should be present. We updated the preference cards to show three packs of instruments, one with 4 instruments and the other two with 20 instruments, that would be available for each procedure. We suggest creating whatever work-aids or instructions are needed to let everyone know about the new process.

Lastly, share the results. Your team has done some great work, and they deserve to be recognized. The Kaizen Report is a great tool to let the entire practice know what the team did. Be sure the person who made the original suggestion is aware that you took action, and that his or her input was instrumental in making these improvements.

ADVANTAGES OF KAIZEN

Kaizen levels the playing field between management and staff. When entry-level employees see opportunity for positive change, Kaizen empowers them to become agents of change—and providing leadership encourages them to recognize needed improvement and to suggest solutions.

Many practices and hospitals have an unfortunate mindset that instructs the staff only to show up on time, keep their heads down, refrain from complaining, and do the job as it is outlined in the employee manual. If leaders don't engage the staff in improvement of their work, they waste an opportunity to improve efficiency, productivity, and patient care. A successful practice is not just about clinical skills, but also about the participation of everyone in ongoing quality and process improvement.

Bottom Line: Many practices request comments and suggestions from patients but fail to follow up. The lack of follow-up includes failure to even acknowledge and thank the patient for taking the time to submit a suggestion. This approach sends a terrible message to patients: give us your suggestions, and we will ignore them. This is one of the many examples that healthcare is in dire need of improvement. Kaizen is perhaps the best tool for closing the loop between receiving suggestions and implementing solutions. Improvement can occur at any level within practices and hospitals. Often it is the patients, employees, doctors, and staff who see the problems and have the best ideas for solving those problems. Remember, no problems are too small or big for Kaizen to solve. All it takes is to identify a problem, develop a solution, experiment, make the change permanent, and share the experience.

REFERENCES

1. Towill DR. Frank Gilbreth and health care delivery method study driven learning. *Int J Health Care Qual Assur.* 2009;22(4):417-40.

2. Gabor A. *The Man Who Discovered Quality: How W. Edwards Deming Brought the Quality Revolution to America.* New York: Penguin; 1992.

3. Swartz JB, Swartz JE. *Seeing David in the Stone: Find and Seize Great Opportunities.* Carmel, IN: Leading Books Press; 2006.

CHAPTER 7

Creating the Almost Perfect Medical Practice: Part I

NEIL BAUM, MD

It is important first to identify the criteria of an ideal practice and then to prioritize those areas that you deem most important for your practice. This will enable every doctor to identify the areas that will make his or her practice nearly perfect.

1. In an ideal practice, the doctors serve the patients they enjoy providing care for.

You can have a full practice, but if your patients are not the type for whom you enjoy providing care, you will not be a happy, fulfilled doctor. Therefore, it is important to think about the medical conditions that you enjoy treating, the kind of patients that you would like to have, and the lifestyle you would like to live. This process takes careful planning and decision-making. If you are a sports medicine orthopedist, for instance, you will look for patients with elbow, hip, knee, and ankle problems. If you are a pediatrician and enjoy taking care of teenagers and the unique problems of adolescents, then you can seek out those patients and refer younger children to your partners or other pediatricians. This approach can be used by primary care doctors, internists, and specialists. Although it is nice if 100% of your patients are the ones that you would most like to treat, it is unlikely that you can ever achieve that goal. However, if 90% of your patients fall into the category of those that you like to treat, and only 10% are not in the favored category, then you are likely to be satisfied and enjoy your work.

2. In an ideal practice, patients have ready access to the practice and the doctors.

You have to determine how many patients you are comfortable seeing in an hour, a day, a week, or a month. It is important to leave time slots for emergencies or urgencies so when a patient needs to be seen immediately, he or she can be added to the schedule seamlessly, rather than being squeezed into an already full schedule. That prevents unanticipated appointments from wreaking havoc with the schedule and keeping those patients who had scheduled appointments from being seen on time. It also makes sense to leave a few time slots during the week open for new patients. If a patient calls for an appointment and is told that the first new appointment is more than a few weeks away, it is likely that he or she will call another physician where there is more reasonable access to the practice. There should be room for an ample number of new patients to replace patients who are leaving the practice for one reason or another. I don't believe an ideal practice can ever be totally closed.

3. Ideal practices have loyal employees and no expensive turnover.

Employee commitment is one of the most important requirements for creating an almost perfect practice. Employee commitment is delicate: it must be earned and can easily be destroyed if the physicians and the administration do not pay attention and listen to the employees' concerns and issues. Employees with a high level of commitment will be loyal to you and your practice. They will not look elsewhere and leave the practice, resulting in costly turnover.[1]

4. Ideal practices control their accounts receivable.

Any monies left in your accounts receivable (AR) are dollars that belong to you and are being used by someone else, usually an insurance company or the patient. The goal is to keep most of your AR in the 30- to 60-day bucket. Money that has been in AR for more than 120 days is historically difficult, if not impossible, to collect. An ideal practice looks at the AR on a monthly basis and monitors AR and tries to maintain the majority (i.e., 60%–65%) in the 30- to 60-day category, with less than 10% over 120 days.

5. Ideal practices submit clean claims and have few or no denials or rejected claims.

A claim to an insurance company should be made within 24 to 48 hours after the service is provided. This includes surgical procedures. A clean claim usually is paid in 10 to 14 days. Most claims that are denied are a result of improper data input by the billing clerk. For example, if a patient has a hyphenated last name, and the hyphen is not used in the submission, the claim is often denied. Therefore, attention to minute detail is necessary for anyone charged with submitting claims to insurance providers. Denied claims are an unnecessary cost and take time to resolve, but they can be processed in a timely fashion if the claims are scrubbed clean. It is estimated that the cost of dealing with a denied or rejected claim can be about five times the cost of submitting a clean claim. The perfect practice has no denied claims. If your denial rate is higher than 3% to 5%, using a claim scrubber is a worthwhile investment.

6. Ideal practices answer the phone in no more than three rings and do not use a phone tree.

Patients want to speak to a human, not listen to an endless menu of choices from a phone tree before reaching someone in the office who can help with their problem. The take-home message is that trees are for fruit and acorns and not for patients. Also, an ideal practice doesn't turn the phones over to an answering service during lunch. Lunch hours can be staggered so that the phone is always answered during office hours.[2]

7. Ideal practices do not make excuses.

Ideal practices do not make excuses when a problem or error occurs. They apologize and fix the problem. It is not a sin to say "I'm sorry" to a patient when a mistake has been made. If a lab result or the result of an imaging study was promised to a patient and the patient was not contacted, then it is important to make amends with the patient. I suggest that the doctor him- or herself call the patient and apologize, even if the error was the result of a mistake made by a staff member.[3]

Remember: the buck stops with the doctor, and patients really appreciate hearing from the doctor when mistakes have been made. It is even a nice gesture to send a written apology note to the patient who feels a mistake or an error has been made and also make a note in the patient's record or in the electronic medical record that acknowledges that the error occurred and that action has been taken and the patient has been notified.

An ideal practice anticipates problems and tells patients in advance what may happen during or after treatment. There is a natural tendency for doctors and staff to become defensive or to offer reasons why something didn't go as planned. Making an excuse or offering up explanations in self-defense is the worst customer service mistake, whether you are the receptionist, the nurse, or the doctor. Ideal practices avoid surprises. If there is a problem, the best solution is bringing up the issue before the patient does. I am a firm believer in making use of the two magic words, "I'm sorry," and apologizing profusely. You gain the patient's confidence and rapport by acknowledging the patient's feelings. Whenever possible, give the patient a reason for the problem. Remember the saying that holds true: patients don't care how much you know until they know how much you care. You can show you care by listening to the patient. Avoid being defensive, acknowledge the patient's concern with empathy, and find a solution that is acceptable to the patient.

Ideal practices avoid surprises that can upset a patient. The best and most compliant patient is the one who is educated and has all the information that is needed to feel comfortable proceeding with the treatment plan. I find it useful to provide patients with FAQs of anticipated risks and complications associated with the procedure or surgery. FAQs that cover many of the possible risks and complications can inform them before they undergo a procedure or surgery. I also provide FAQs for the medications most commonly used by our practice; this also reduces the phone calls from the patients to the staff or doctor.

8. Ideal practices survey their patients and place an emphasis on patient satisfaction.

Most physicians assume that most of their patients are satisfied and appreciate the care they receive from doctors, nurses, and allied health professionals. Patient satisfaction is an elusive concept, one that often is difficult to measure. However, systems and metrics do exist that provide objective evidence of patient satisfaction that go beyond mere patient satisfaction surveys. For example, our practice surveys patients on every visit by giving them a survey card. Action is taken for all positive or negative comments (Figure 1). Also note that on the front of this card is an opportunity for patients to write down what questions they would like answered during the visit to make their doctor-patient encounter complete (Figure 2).

The need to improve quality in healthcare delivery is increasing. The CMS, hospitals, and insurance providers alike are striving to better define and

Thank you for helping us serve you better

Was it easy for you get an appointment in this office?

___Yes   ___No

Is your general impression of this office favorable?

___Yes   ___No

Was the office staff friendly and understanding?

___Yes   ___No

Did the doctor answer all of your questions?

___Yes   ___No

Do you have any additional comments or suggestions?

FIGURE 1. Patient survey card, back.

Dr. Neil Baum, M.D.
Urology

What three questions would you like to ask the doctor today during your visit to our office?

1. _____

   _____

2. _____

   _____

3. _____

   _____

Please complete the back of this card

FIGURE 2. Patient survey card, front.

measure quality of healthcare. Doctors and staff must understand that a major component of quality of healthcare is patient satisfaction. Furthermore, patient satisfaction is critical to how well patients do; research has identified a clear link between patient outcomes and patient satisfaction scores.[4]

9. Ideal practices monitor the practice's online reputation.

Whenever a negative review is given, the practice sees this as an opportunity to improve its services to the patients. Even an ideal or almost perfect practice cannot make everyone happy and satisfied, although that is the goal or objective. It is possible for an unhappy or disgruntled patient to make damaging, disparaging remarks with a simple click of a mouse. Just a few negative comments online can significantly affect your online reputation and take you from five stars to two in no time. Therefore, it is imperative that you "dilute" those negative responses with an abundance of positive comments and compliments. That is why I try to capture every positive response—of which I receive several every day—with a testimonial that is posted on my website, or by having the patient complete a brief survey he or she is still in the office that goes to healthgrades.com, Yelp.com, and a few other online reputation management sites.

10. In an ideal practice, the doctor is not interrupted when he or she is engaged in a patient encounter in the exam room.

Doctors should not be interrupted when they are with a patient. The only exceptions are calls from the emergency department, operating room, or intensive care unit. If another physician calls and wishes to speak to the patient, the receptionist might respond, "The doctor is with a patient (doing a procedure) and will be available in [state number of minutes] and will call you back shortly. However, if it is an emergency, I can interrupt him/her at this time." Now the physician or other caller has been given an explanation and has the option of interrupting the physician if he or she deems it is urgent to speak to the physician.

11. In an ideal practice, the doctors have great communication skills and are able to motivate patients to make positive lifestyle changes.

Doctors in ideal practices are able to motivate patients to make positive lifestyle changes (e.g., improved nutrition, regular exercise, smoking cessation). Having great communication skills means being in the present and looking at the patient, not keeping your back to the patient and focusing on the computer and the electronic medical record.

Bottom Line: I hope you can honestly state that you are accomplishing or performing many of these suggestions, all of which can contribute to creating an almost perfect medical practice. In the next article in this series, I will offer eight more ideas that will make you perfect in the eyes of your patients.

REFERENCES

1. Hills L. Increasing medical practice team commitment: 25 strategies. *J Med Pract Manage.* 2016;31(4):223-228.
2. Peller S. *Own the Phone: Proven Ways of Handling Calls, Securing Appointments, and Growing Your Healthcare Practice.* Phoenix, MD: Greenbranch Publishing; 2014.
3. Groopman J. *How Doctors Think.* New York: Houghton Mifflin; 2007.
4. Manary MP, Boulding W, Staelin R, Glickman SW. The patient experience and health outcomes. *N Engl J Med.* 2013;368:201-203.

Creating the Almost Perfect Medical Practice: Part II

1. Ideal practices offer positive reinforcement.

Ideal practices have office managers and physicians who appreciate the staff, offer praise for good performance, and say "thank you" for a job well done. It is true that you can accomplish more with a pat on the back than a kick in the pants.

2. Ideal practices are HIPAA compliant.

In order to avoid any violations that will generate fines and penalties, the ideal practice has to be crystal clear about the guidelines for HIPAA compliance and must adhere to those standards. The best practices have a HIPAA compliance officer who has the authority and the clout to identify and correct deviations and then stick to the rules to keep the practice in line and avoid any risk of penalties or fines.

3. Ideal practices have a front desk that collects 100% of the copays and remaining patient balances.

Copays, cancellation fees, and deductibles are all part of the everyday vernacular of medical practices. Our staff is taught to request copays and explain that we can no longer bill the patient for the copay. Contemporary patients understand that they cannot fill their cars with gasoline or buy an airline ticket without paying in advance for the product or service. Healthcare is no different, and payment is expected at the time of service. There are few exceptions where patients are exempted from paying their copays and deductibles before seeing the physician.

4. Ideal practices are not involved in costly, emotionally draining lawsuits.

For the most part, preventing litigation comes down to good documentation in the medical record. Ideal practices provide educational material to their patients on the procedures and surgery that they plan to perform. There are no shortcuts for this process.

5. Ideal practices have a cross-trained staff.

Cross-training creates the opportunity for staff to perform each other's duties for the purpose of maintaining productivity when any person is absent or unavailable. For example, when there are more phone calls than can be handled by the receptionist, any cross-trained staff member can help answer the phone calls. Instead of asking patients to leave a message, thereby possibly losing the patient and his or her business, a staff member trained to be a receptionist for short periods of time can be a huge benefit to the practice.

6. Ideal practices empower employees to make decisions that are in the best interest of the patient.

I have a monetary ceiling of $200; up to that amount, a staff member can make a decision at the time of the encounter with the patient without having to get approval from the office manager or the physicians. For example, if a patient is delayed in the office because of a problem with the practice (e.g., the physician was running late or the computer system was uncooperative), and the patient is concerned about parking costs, the staff is empowered to pay the patient's parking and to apologize for the delay.

The combination of cross-training and empowerment becomes a powerful set of tools for achieving an ideal medical practice. Cross-training and empowerment can achieve dramatic improvements in productivity without increasing staff size and also can enhance patient satisfaction.

7. Ideal medical practices embrace technology.

The ideal practice makes good use of technology in the clinical setting and indicates to patients that the doctor and the practice are up-to-date with all the current diagnostic and treatment options.

Technology costs for medical practices have increased in recent years. All of us who have implemented electronic medical records, however, have seen substantial decreases in both the cost and complexity of our hardware and software, as well as the cost of support or maintenance. You can plan to spend 18% of the cost of your software for annual maintenance and the new upgrades. Moving to cloud-based EMR and outsourcing the billing can significantly reduce your technology costs.

8. Perfect practices embrace continuous growth and improvement.

The need to improve quality in healthcare delivery is increasing. The CMS, hospitals, and insurance providers are all striving to better define and measure the quality of healthcare. Doctors and staff must understand that a major component of the quality of healthcare is patient satisfaction. Furthermore, patient satisfaction is critical to how well patients do; research has identified a clear link between patient outcomes and patient satisfaction scores.

Bottom Line: Physicians aren't powerless to craft and sculpt their practices. I believe that the methods described in this article are easily implemented and can be easily accomplished in a cost-effective manner.

CHAPTER 8

Steve Jobs Provides Lessons for Any Medical Practice

HAL ORNSTEIN, DPM, AND NEIL BAUM, MD

We both just read the biography *Steve Jobs* by Walter Isaacson (Simon & Schuster, 2011). Steve Jobs was probably the greatest innovator since Thomas Edison, doing more than anyone to change technology by providing products and computers that have simplified our ability to communicate with others. Although the book paints Jobs as a ruthless and self-centered leader, he had the admiration of most of his employees, and his employees were enthralled by his knowledge, energy, enthusiasm, and ability to identify products that would transform the lives of all of the world's citizens.

Below are 10 ideas you can borrow from Jobs to enhance your medical practice:

1. Create an organization in your office of only A-players. Get rid of the average B and C players and the riff raff. It's a cold reality, but they are doing damage, especially those who have the most contact with your patients. Jobs surrounded himself with only the best. He challenged them to go beyond their potential and to create products that have changed the world. Doctors and office managers have the potential to do the same in their offices. They can challenge their colleagues and their staff to provide not just a diagnosis and treatment of medical conditions, but also to provide stellar care to patients. A-players display empathy, understand the specific needs of patients, and have the ability to help your patients understand their benefits. The A-players can give patients a wow experience, and the patients will leave happy and tell others about the outstanding care you offer. Other doctors in your practice and employees who are not able to exceed patients' expectations need to be given two options: step up to the plate or find a new job. It is that simple.

2. Challenge your people to take your practice to the next level. Patients get very angry when they hear, "No," "We can't," "Our policy says . . . ," or "I'll try." Empower your team to make on-the-spot decisions; let them know that at times it is OK to make mistakes, as it is a sign of growth. At office meetings, role-play so they understand what empowerment really means and the trust you have in their judgment and knowledge. Work on achieving what you may feel is impossible. Jobs told his engineers, "I want to get 1000 songs in my pocket." The engineers said impossible, and he encouraged them that they could do it, and they did it. Today, millions of consumers have iPods. The same can be accomplished in your practice by setting reachable goals and giving the staff the tools, time, and training to reach those goals. If you have an issue with patient wait times, challenge your staff members to come up with a solution, and then listen to their suggestions even though they may feel like it is a hopeless case. If you want to expand the practice 20% when numbers have been slowly declining, do not accept that it is just not possible; put your heads together, and make a plan with small, achievable goals along the way. Many ideas are abandoned because the project looks large and intimidating, but when broken into small pieces, it becomes clear that you can achieve your goals.

3. Be a master of the details. Jobs wanted the inside of the computer, which no one would see, to look just as pristine and aesthetically pleasing as the slick black, silver, or white of the outside case. Your patients may not see the employee lounge, but if the lounge contains dirty dishes, a filthy microwave, or food left on the tables, that tells your staff that cleanliness is not an important issue. As Herb Kelleher, the previous CEO of Southwest Airlines, once said, "If there is old food on the drop-down trays from the previous passengers, you may question how the airlines mechanics take care of the plane's engines." Make every effort to pay attention to the small details, and you will find that the big details will be much easier to follow. We often say in our offices "It is the 5% that makes 95% of the difference." Most practices do the 95%, so the opportunity for you to shine in the eyes of you patients is found by doing the 5%.

We recommend you hand out a sheet to all your staff members and ask them what they feel are some small things you can do for your patients to make a significant difference. And for each idea, they get a $1 scratch-off lottery ticket. Some ideas include:

- Ending each visit with, "What other questions do you have?" and then "Thank you for coming in today and never hesitate to call with any questions";
- Calling every new patient the night of his or her visit to see if the patient has any additional questions;
- Having a comment box visible to all patients but not where front desk team can see it so patients are not afraid of dropping in a comment;
- Getting new patients' e-mail addresses and e-mailing all forms and directions to them;
- Giving all postop patients a box of nice candy;
- Giving movie tickets to patients whose wait times are excessive;
- Providing gift cards to employees as a thank you for dedication; and
- Leaving random notes for employees at their desk or work area recognizing something outstanding they did.

4. Create a brand that easily identifies your product. Jobs' Apple stores reinvented the role of the retail store in defining a brand, a service, and outstanding products. Have a strong logo for your practice that is used as often as possible, including color coordinated scrubs for all your employees. The uniform should always have a name tag or embroidered name. Create a tag line that is used on all printed materials and other items. Consider getting reusable bags with your logo, tag line, office address, and contact information to give to patients when dispensing any items.

5. Step outside of the box. Be a contrarian. Do what others say can't be done. The iPhone turned mobile phones into music, photography, video, e-mail, and Web devices all contained in a device that could fit in palm of the hand. You don't need a market study to decide if a product or service is going to work. Jobs was once asked if he did a market study on the Macintosh. His response was, "Did Alexander Graham Bell do a market study before he developed the telephone?"

6. Look at the trend and create a game changer. Newspapers and magazines are losing readership to the Internet. The iPad launched

tablet computing and offered a platform for digital newspapers, magazines, books, and videos. Do you want to be like the newspaper or like the Internet? You have a choice. The status quo is going to leave you behind and playing catch up. Catching the next wave or trend will catapult your practice to a success level that you will enjoy and find challenging and exciting.

7. Simplify. Less is more. Trying to use the computer, the cell phone, the MP3 music player, and the video recorder can be daunting especially when trying to organize your data or trying to retrieve your files. The iCloud changed the role of the computer from its central role in managing your files to letting all of your devices sync seamlessly. How can you incorporate this into your medical practice? Can patients come to your office and receive all of their care at one location, or do they have to go to multiple locations and practices in order to receive their care? If you can organize patient care to one place and one visit, you will become a darling of healthcare, and patients will even pay a premium to have all of their care provided during a single visit.

8. Do it perfectly. When he had a ship date for the Macintosh but the handle on the computer was not attached like Jobs wanted, he sent the design team back to the table and delayed the launch for several weeks until the handle was perfectly molded onto the console of the computer. So if you renovate your office and it is not perfect, accept the temporary loss of revenue and don't see patients until the work is complete.

9. Focus on the product and not the profit. Jobs led a company where his people were motivated to make great products. Everything else, including earnings, was secondary. Healthcare should follow his example: Do what is in the best interest of the patients; everything else is secondary. Today's practices are led by number crunchers looking at overhead, accounts receivables, collections, and numbers of patients seen each hour. Perhaps if we looked at quality of care, patient satisfaction, and outcomes, we would have very successful practices. The formula for value is outcomes divided by cost. Think about finding metrics to determine outcomes and measure your cost of care, which can be translated into a value number. Those

who are capable of measuring value will be attractive to insurance companies and bean counters.

10. Become a fortune teller. Jobs could hold his metaphorical moistened finger up in the air and magically foretell the direction of the wind, speed of the wind, when the rain would come, how much rain would come down, and when you should leave the community to get out harm's way. He was that prescient with a magical sense of what was going to happen and how he could ride the wave of the future building products that would make the lives of everyone better. Knowing the changing future of medicine, it is best to be proactive rather than reactive. We strongly recommend that all practices spend a few hours with all the doctors and employees and perform a SWOT analysis, listing your strengths, weaknesses, opportunities, and threats. (An Internet search will show you how to complete this type of analysis and apply it to your practice.) Then lay out a plan to be revisited on a regular basis to help ensure a bright future for your practice.

Bottom Line: We all can't be, or perhaps choose not to be, like Jobs. However, no one can deny his success and the impact he had on technology and communication on a global level. There are aspects of his leadership style that are worth emulating in your practices, and we hope that we have given you an app (i.e., appetite) for that!

CHAPTER 9

Patient Satisfaction: What We Can Learn from Other Industries

LYNN HOMISAK, PRT, AND NEIL BAUM, MD

I (NHB) was able to make a reservation online through OpenTable for a local restaurant and was seated promptly at the designated time. The meal and service were excellent, and the next day, an e-mail (Figure 1) was received asking for feedback on the dining experience at the restaurant.

Dear Neil,

Thank you for booking your recent reservation through OpenTable. We would appreciate your feedback about your experience at Amici Ristorante & Bar on 8/25/2013.

Please take a moment to fill out our Dining Feedback Form:

http://www.opentable.com/feedback/dff.aspx?re=%252bQPxCJHhJVA%253d&cmpid=em_trigger_dff_anon
Thank you, and we look forward to seeing you again at OpenTable.com.

Bon appétit!
Your OpenTable Team

FIGURE 1. Customer service feedback request from Open Table.

On another occasion, I ordered coffee pods for an espresso machine from Amazon.com. An e-mail was received two days after delivery of the product asking for feedback (Figure 2).

We can go on and on citing instances not only from OpenTable and Amazon.com but from many other businesses that deliberately make the effort to contact their customers for feedback. Why are they intent on getting this feedback (good *or* bad); and, more importantly, why isn't the medical profession as a whole just as determined to follow their lead?

Most companies would agree that customer experience and loyalty go together, and that both are vital to the success of any business and worth pursuing. Both authors travel extensively and have found that the travel industry—airlines, hotels, rental cars—is very keen on capturing repeat

Hi Dr. Neil H Baum,
Will you please take a minute to share your experience?
You Purchased: 50 Nespresso Capsules Decaffeinato Coffee NEW (New)
From df89 (Fulfilled by Amazon) - Estimated Delivery Date: August 24, 2013
How did the seller do?

Item arrived by August 24, 2013?	Yes No
Item as described by the seller?	Yes No
Prompt and courteous service?	Yes No Did not contact
How would you rate the seller?	5 (Excellent)
	4 (Good)
	3 (Neutral)
	2 (Poor)
	1 (Awful)

Tell others about this seller:
(e.g. delivery experience, item as described, quality of customer service)
Unfavorable Experience? (Rating 1-3 Stars)
If you haven't yet, please contact Amazon Customer Service and allow them to
resolve any issues before submitting feedback.

FIGURE 2. Customer service feedback request from Amazon.

business. United Airlines, for example, asks for feedback after every flight. I (LH) make sure to respond, because if they care enough to take the time to ask, it's important for me to take the time to share my thoughts. What they are saying when they ask for my opinion is, "Your voice is important" and "We are listening." In addition, they make a point of delivering this consistent message: "You have a choice in airline carriers. Thank you for choosing United." There are many times I am able to fly a different airline for a lesser fare; however, my allegiance is rooted in United's desire to keep me as a customer and make me feel important and satisfied at the same time. And it works. Wouldn't it be great if patients had the same level of loyalty toward the doctor and the practice that many frequent flyers have toward their airline carriers? Of course we would like that kind of loyalty, and it can be attained if we, too, focus on improving patient satisfaction.

You can be sure that other entities, such as insurance companies and employers, are going to ask patients about the care they received not only from the face-to-face time with the doctor but also from the staff. In fact, it appears that the trend in healthcare is moving toward using patient satisfaction as a viable metric according to which doctors will be judged and even compensated.

According to an article published by *The Wall Street Journal*,[1] one pay-for-performance measure that we can expect to see with the Patient Protection and Affordable Care Act is tying hospital payments to consumer satisfaction by surveying patients about the service they received while hospitalized (using a scale of 0 to 10). According to the article, one of the survey questions is: "How often did doctors treat you with courtesy and respect?" *The Wall Street Journal* states that "high-performing hospitals will be rewarded with a Medicare 'bonus' while low-performing hospitals have to live with the reimbursement rate cut."

This is certain to shed new light on the expectation and delivery not only of exceptional clinical care, but also the combination of clinical plus customer care. Hospitals are already starting to pay attention by emphasizing the importance of this to their doctors and staff through in-house, customer service-focused training programs. I (LH) can attest to this personally, as I have been called in to deliver such programs, and I am seeing more and more cutting-edge physician offices on a similar path.

Customer service training is nothing new; it's what medicine has been practicing for years, but perhaps it was more identifiable back in the days of TV Drs. Welby, Kildare, and Casey than it is now. The portrayal of doctors back in the 1960s and 1970s was different than it is today. Connecting with the patient was never anything less than a mixture of professionalism, the Golden Rule, acts of kindness, and even house calls. Aside from those now almost nonexistent house calls, has the way we communicate as a healthcare nation changed so drastically that we no longer take or make the time to get to know the patient and build the doctor–patient relationship, even though we know that it almost always leads to improved patient satisfaction and better overall compliance? And if we know, then why don't we pursue it more assertively? Is it because medical professionals have become too overburdened with all the new HIPAA security compliance regulations, dramatic coding revisions, electronic medical records, Meaningful Use requirements, charting and documentation obligations, soaring overhead, claim submission penalties, and on and on? It is no wonder doctors are unwilling to take the extra initiative given that their days lately are filled with more stress and less reimbursement.

Those of us on the inside know the negative impact that these everyday headaches can have on a doctor's diminishing time and revenue; however, patients are blind to them. Their expectations are greater than ever, despite all the changes. Competition, an Internet-savvy population with information at their fingertips, and choices (just as the airline suggested) demand we provide quality care *and* quality customer service. Despite the changes we face, it's the customer service piece that remains a constant in whether practices thrive or just survive. Practices that thrive don't just have a mission statement of delivering quality patient care and satisfaction written on the wall of the employee lounge or on the first page of the employment manual; instead, they believe it, they practice it, and they live it. Likewise, those who just go through the motions fall short of reaping the rewards.

The fact that newer, tighter regulations have taken a toll on today's medical practices is no excuse for not asking our patients the simple question (to paraphrase Mayor Koch), "How are the doctors and staff doing?" So why is it that too many doctors are unwilling to ask? Perhaps they think that customer service no longer drives patient loyalty; rather, insurance plans do. Maybe some of that is true. However, it doesn't cost a thing to tap into the minds (and hearts) of our patients and find out what we are doing right, what we are doing wrong, and how to make things better in an effort to reestablish trust and allegiance between doctors and patients.

Patient engagement should not be underestimated. It is vitally important, today more than ever. And it's critical to keep your finger on the pulse of your practice. Pretending things are fine, longing for yesterday, or hoping things will get better is not productive. What is helpful is utilizing a tool similar to those that restaurants, retail Internet sites, or airlines use to help gauge why customers keep coming back and, more importantly, why they leave. That tool is the customer (or patient) satisfaction survey.

It may be that some practices refuse to conduct surveys because they are not prepared to handle criticism, when in reality, they should be viewing these unexpected critiques as gifts. Customer Service Manager[2] points out statistics from Lee Resource, Inc., that indicate that for every customer who makes an effort to complain, 26 other customers remain silent. The silent "wronged customer" will tell between 8 and 16 people about it, and over 20% will tell more than 20. What's more, 91% of unhappy customers or patients will not willingly do business with you again.

Equally important is knowing whether the "exceptional service" you think you provide is actually seen as exceptional in your patients' or customers' eyes. Interestingly, 80% of companies surveyed said that they offer superior customer service, but only 8% of their customers agreed with them.[3] Never look a gift horse or a negative survey report in the mouth! This is your opportunity to fix the wrongs, make things better, and win over an unsatisfied patient.

One of the biggest obstacles to starting a survey is to start. The mind may be willing but the unknown ("What questions do I ask?" or "How do I distribute a survey . . . how often . . . and for how long a period of time?" or "How do I collect them?") can be enough to stop you from taking those initial necessary steps. One of the goals of this article is to help you get started by sharing with you some "hows and whats" and "dos and don'ts." The other, more important, objective is to help you understand why this simple and crucial tool will offer better management of your practice and also create an edge for your more successful future.

First, keep it focused. Don't get carried away. Focus on the most critical five or six core topics. Asking what kinds of magazines your patients prefer to have in the waiting room is not as valuable as knowing how convenient it was to get an appointment or how they may have been treated (or mistreated!) on the phone.

Second, keep it brief and effective. How much is too much or not enough? If you hand your patients a 3×5 index card with one or two questions, it may appear you are not really serious about what they think and are just going through the motions. Don't be surprised if their responses are equally trivial. On the other hand, overwhelming them with a lengthy survey that requires flipping one or more pages is disrespectful of their time. A one-sided, one-page survey is (in the words of Goldilocks) "just right" to hit the important issues and yield an adequate assessment. Your survey should not take more than five minutes to complete.

Third, keep it effortless. Make your questions easy to respond to by creating a four-option numeric or "excellent, good, average, poor" rating system. Patients will be more inclined to participate in a survey that allows them to simply circle, check, or mark their responses with an X as opposed to writing time-consuming sentences.

Finally, for those patients who feel the need to speak out, give them space to do so via a "comment" section. Directing them to the reverse side of the survey does not limit their thoughts to just one or two allotted lines, and some people appreciate the extra space.

Now, what questions do you ask? Simple! . . . the ones you want answered. Suggested survey content might revolve around such topics as the appointment process, facility, staff, and doctor(s) (Figure 3). Be prepared for criticism. Understand that the comments you don't want to hear are likely the ones you *need* to hear so that you can take action and resolve them (e.g., "The wait is too long!"). So thicken your skin and be prepared to handle the truth.

To gather enough data to effectively evaluate your practice, a survey should extend for one full month. This permits an adequate amount of time to reach a good number of patients. The results should be tabulated immediately (using an Excel spreadsheet), analyzed, and dealt with.

Because staff have a greater opportunity to engage the patient, it is preferable to have them roll out the survey. Those fully committed to this team project will try to involve every patient, which should be the objective. If their presentation is patient interest–based (as opposed to self-interest-based), and patients feel the outcome will benefit them, they may be more inclined to participate. An approach might be, "Mrs. Jones, we'd like to make some changes that will help to improve the service you receive here. We value your opinion. Will you help us by taking a few minutes to complete this short survey?"

If this is done at check-in, patients have the ability to complete the survey either in the reception area or the treatment room. They are instructed to drop completed surveys them into a designated mailbox (available for $10 to $15 at local hardware stores) located at the front desk on their way out. Of course, we encourage them to be as honest as possible, and this is usually accomplished by making it "name optional."

Conducting onsite written surveys is one sure way to get patients to participate. To reduce paper shuffling, however, you might also consider setting up one (or several) digital workstations. At each station, arrange an immobile practice iPad and a sign welcoming patients to conduct their survey digitally, hit "send," and be done. Also, don't forget to upload a survey onto your Web site. While you likely will not get as much activity, it makes patient feedback available as a year-round option, if they choose to use it. You can also hire a company that will e-mail your patients immediately following their visit for feedback, much like Amazon.com does.

We Aim to Please You!

	Excellent	Good	Fair	Poor
RATE YOUR APPOINTMENT				
1. Length of time to get an appointment				
2. Convenience of available appointment				
3. Wait time in reception room				
4. Time waiting for Dr. in treatment room				
Other comments:				
RATE OUR FACILITY				
1. Office hours and location				
2. Cleanliness and comfort				
3. Parking				
4. Reading materials				
5. Ease and accessibility of website				
Other comments:				
RATE OUR STAFF				
1. Courtesy and helpfulness				
2. Professional				
3. Friendly				
4. Knowledgeable				
Other comments:				
RATE YOUR DOCTOR				
1. Completely explained my condition & treatment				
2. Knowledgeable				
3. Thoroughness of examination				
4. Attentiveness to my problem				
5. Spent enough time with me				
Other comments:				
Overall experience at our office.				
How can we improve our services? (please use reverse side for additional comments)				
				Thank you!

FIGURE 3. Suggested office visit survey.

For the most part, your patients will be very cooperative and appreciate having the opportunity to voice their opinion and make it count. Remember: do *not* initiate a patient satisfaction survey if the plan is just to go through the motions and pretend to care. Patients will be paying attention and will notice whether or not changes were made based on their responses. Conversely, if your intent is to sincerely try to make improvements, consider doing so with their help. They're only too happy to offer input and be included.

Bottom Line: Denial is not just a river in Egypt, and customer service is not just a department. *Entrepreneur*[4] defines customer service as "the degree of assistance and courtesy granted those who patronize a business." It is, in fact, what drives patient satisfaction in our practices. Patient satisfaction is essential, and it is not static. Many other professions and industries are conducting customer surveys. It is time for the medical profession to take similar action and start asking the Kochian question, "Hey, how am I doin'?" If we do, we have the golden opportunity to find out what's on the minds of our patients and how we can improve the customer service that will move us forward.

REFERENCES

1. Adamy J. U.S. ties hospital payments to making patients happy. *Wall Street Journal*. October 14, 2012. http://online.wsj.com/news/articles/SB10000872396390443890304578010264156073132.

2. Customer Service Facts. Customer Service Manager. www.customerservicemanager.com/customer-service-facts.htm.

3. Lawrence A. Five customer retention tips for entrepreneurs. *Forbes*. November 1, 2012. www.forbes.com/sites/alexlawrence/2012/11/01/five-customer-retention-tips-for-entrepreneurs/.

4. Customer Service. *Entrepreneur*. www.entrepreneur.com/encyclopedia/customer-service#.

CHAPTER 10

The Elephant and the Chains: Breaking Old Habits and Improving Practice Efficiency and Productivity

Neil Baum, MD

Tell the truth—didn't you ever want to run away and join the circus? Perhaps we all had that fantasy at one time. If you had joined the circus, you would have observed that large, two- to three-ton elephants are tethered to a small stake with a small chain around the ankle of one of their hind legs. This tiny wooden stake driven into the ground could be pulled up in a nanosecond, and the elephant could be free and run away. But the elephant never pulls on the stake; it just rocks back and forth, peacefully eating hay and drinking water.

Have you ever wondered why the elephant is so passive with the chain around its ankle, which is attached to such a small stake driven into the ground? When a baby elephant is first being trained, it is staked to a large log or a big tree and cannot possibly extricate itself from the chain around its ankle. The baby elephant will pull on the chain, and the large log or tree will not move. Eventually, the baby elephant gives up and knows that the chain around its ankle means that it cannot break free. Once it has been conditioned by the chain around its back foot, the elephant, even the largest weighing two to three tons, will not try to break loose because it believes it is tied to a big stake or large tree.

Like these elephants, how many doctors are conditioned by habits that they learned years ago? Many of us don't take risks or challenge the boundaries of something new. Instead, we become creatures of habit and perform our craft with the skills and behaviors that were learned many years earlier.

This article will provide some examples of chains and stakes that are preventing us from reaching new heights and offer suggestions on what we can do to leave our comfort zones, break loose of old habits, and embrace new ways of doing things that will make us better doctors.

Read on for some examples of metaphorical chains and stakes that might be holding you back.

ELECTRONIC MEDICAL RECORDS

Moving from paper charts to electronic medical records (EMRs) is a challenge to every practice. You can demonstrate an ostrich mentality and continue with paper charts, or you can make the quantum leap to EMRs. Not only do you have an opportunity to earn $44,000 per physician if you meet the meaningful use requirements, but you can also realize the following benefits:

- Capture data to demonstrate quality of care;
- Automatically check for drug- drug interactions and be alerted if you write a prescription for a drug to which the patient is allergic; and
- Calculate the E/M, taking all the guesswork out of the coding process.

Implementation of an EMR system can be a daunting experience for everyone in the practice, but it doesn't have to be that way. The expectations of implementing EMRs in a practice are to enhance the quality of patient care, improve physician and staff efficiency, and increase office profitability. All of this is doable and easily accomplished with a clearly executed implementation process.

E-PRESCRIBING

The "prescription" is culturally embedded in the practice of medicine today, and often is a tangible record of the encounter between physician and patient. Manually writing a prescription is widely acknowledged to be an error-prone activity involving paper, multiple parties, and opportunities for miscommunication. The traditional process is inefficient; by one estimate, three person-hours/physician/day are spent dealing exclusively with prescription drug management. Now there are financial motivations for doctors to begin e-prescribing.

E-prescribing has the advantage of alerting for drug-drug interactions and also will notify the doctor if he or she writes a prescription when the patient has an allergy to the medication. As a result, the e-prescribing process enhances patient safety. Prescriptions of the most frequently used drugs can be added to a favorite list, and these medications can be sent to the pharmacy from the EMR with a single click. Finally, you will never have a call from the pharmacist who can't read your writing, which is always a waste of doctors' time.

DELEGATION

Until recently, only doctors performed procedures or touched patients. Now there are physician assistants and nurse practitioners who are able to do many procedures and conduct care on behalf of the doctor that result in improved efficiency and ultimately in improved productivity of the practice. Assistants can remove sutures or change a dressing. These are just a few examples of tasks that could be delegated to others. Physicians need to break the chain of doing everything and embrace the notion that doctors should do only what doctors can do and should allow others with training to perform other aspects of care.

USING A SCRIBE

Use a scribe to take a history of the present illness (HOPI), review of systems, and medical history. There is no reason for a doctor with 12 to 15 years of training to be asking patients about their smoking habits, allergies, and current medications. This can be done by a scribe, perhaps even more efficiently than by the physician.

The scribe interacts with a new patient after the doctor introduces himself or herself to the patient. The scribe then takes the HOPI, records the medical history, and conducts the review of systems. The scribe then presents the HOPI to the physician and accompanies the physician into the room. At this point, the doctor may ask a few additional questions or probe any aspects of the HOPI that are not clear or that require more in-depth questioning. The doctor conducts the physical examination, and the scribe records the positive findings in the chart or EMR. At this juncture, the doctor can have a discussion with the patient regarding the diagnosis and the plan of management, and the scribe records the doctor's plan of action. The doctor can then answer any questions the patient may have, and the scribe can give the chart or the computer to the nurse who will make the necessary arrangements for any lab tests, studies, or surgeries; provide the patient with sample medications and written instructions for the use of the medications; provide pertinent educational materials; and make follow-up appointments. While the nurse is taking care of one patient, the scribe can move to the next patient, staying one patient ahead of the physician. But more importantly, while the scribe is spending 15 to 20 minutes with the patient, the doctor can be doing a procedure, seeing two or three other patients, or returning calls. As a result, the practice becomes much more efficient and productive.

CHANGING BUSINESS PRACTICES

There is nothing in the Hippocratic Oath that states that a medical practice has to open at 9:00 AM and stop seeing patients at 5:00 PM. You can break the chain of traditional office hours by starting earlier in the morning or ending later in the day. This will make your practice very attractive to those wishing to see doctors before they go to work or at the end of their work day.

Traditionally, doctors' offices give a patient a bill at the end of the doctor-patient encounter. Instead of billing patients for your services *after* you have provided the service, you can collect the copay and balances *before* the patient is seen. This can be accomplished by using touchscreen technology in the reception area.

Currently used by millions of patients in all 50 states, there are wireless, touchscreen devices such as the PhreesiaPad (www.phreesia.com). This technology collects and updates critical patient information, verifies patient insurance, and automatically collects payments during the check-in process before the patient is taken from the reception area to the exam room. This new technology is HIPAA-compliant and captures electronic signatures on all required consent forms, and it integrates with existing practice management and EMR systems. This new technology automates and simplifies the entire check-in process, allowing office staff and clinicians to focus on customer service and patients' health concerns, rather than on administrative burdens.

BOTTOM LINE

Doctors have numerous chains that hold us back and prevent us from being more efficient, more productive, and more profitable. Let's not forget we are businessmen and businesswomen; and the reality is, we need to understand business practices to survive in today's market.

CHAPTER 11

Zap Your Gaps: Closing the Gaps in Your Practice

Kendra Reed, PhD, and Neil Baum, MD

A gap analysis can be used by a medical practice to determine what steps need to be taken to move from its current state to the desired, future state. Gap analysis consists of the following steps:

1. Listing characteristic factors (e.g., attributes, competencies, performance levels) of the present situation (i.e., "what is");
2. Listing factors needed to achieve future objectives (i.e., "what should be"); and
3. Highlighting the gaps that exist and need to be filled.

Gap analysis forces a practice to reflect on the current situation and what can be done in the future to bridge the identified gap.

Medical practices are different from other services or products. Doctors and hospitals are in charge of far more serious aspects of our patients' needs and wants than any other profession or occupation, with the possible exception of an airline pilot! Often there are gaps between what patients request and what we deliver in the services we provide.

BENEFITS OF CONDUCTING A GAP ANALYSIS

A gap analysis can help you understand and prioritize problems and deficiencies by identifying gaps that need to be overcome. Once you uncover the gaps, it becomes easier to quantify them and identify the work effort that will be required to address them. Certainly, you are likely to identify several gaps that need to be bridged, but once discovered, you can prioritize them so that the largest gaps or the ones that are affecting patients the most can be addressed first.

Gaps usually appear in one of three categories: people, processes, and technology:

- **People gaps,** for example, might be that the staff or an employee lacks the right skill set, or that their job descriptions aren't clearly defined.
- **Processes gaps** might include redundancies or unclear handoffs between steps in a process. One example is asking patients to fill out insurance forms and health questionnaires each time they have an appointment. This irritates patients and results in inefficiency in patient flow.
- **Technology gaps** would include situations such as incompatibility between the computer system at the practice and the one used by the hospital.

Each type of gap requires a similar approach: identify the gap; find the cause; and then provide the solution. A thorough gap analysis can help identify the gaps, their root cause, and the solutions that can overcome them.

A gap analysis can either give decision-makers a comprehensive overview of the entire practice or focus on a particular function, such as billing, accuracy of coding to prevent denials, information technology, or operations. This allows doctors and office managers to determine whether the practice has the resources needed to meet their goals and objectives. The gap analysis helps the practice focus its efforts and make informed decisions. After the gaps are identified, the gaps are categorized as high, medium, and low priority.

The larger gaps between expectations and experiences or between "what is" and "what should be" generally lead to patient dissatisfaction. Therefore, measuring these gaps is the first step to patient satisfaction. Having the realistic ability to reach identified strategic goals and targets puts your practice at a distinct advantage. This inevitably leads to better patient care, enhanced reputations both on- and off-line, more new patients, and greater productivity.

If you conduct patient surveys of your practice, you will also find unmet needs in your practice. Certainly, all the unmet needs or gaps can't be solved, but the ones that appear over and over again should be given a high priority.

Gap analysis also applies to your internal customers—that is, your staff. Gaps between their expectations and their work experiences can lead to low morale and poor productivity as well as increased and costly turnover of your employees.

IDENTIFYING THE GAPS

A gap often reveals itself when a patient or staff member expresses a need that is not being met. Such gaps often are identified by listening to our patients and our staff. Think about your patients and which of their needs are not being met. For example, if patients are having to wait weeks or months to obtain an appointment, this is a gap that should be bridged or repaired. Yes, it may fuel the doctors' egos to feel that they are in demand by having a long wait-time, but this is not meeting patients' expectations or their needs. Another example is seen when patients call the office or e-mail the doctors with a question and do not have the call returned or e-mail answered in a timely fashion . . . currently a reasonable response time is 24 hours.

Gaps also can be identified by conducting a survey of your patients. This survey can be a formal one, such as those that can be created at no cost on SurveyMonkey.com, or informal, as when you look at online reviews of your practice. Another type of informal survey that will identify gaps is merely to ask patients about their experience with your practice. The key here is to speak to the patients and your staff and identify what are their pain points or what are their needs.

Other gaps in your practice might include revenue and productivity, profit, market share, patient complaints, or staff issues such as absenteeism or frequent turnover.

For example, if surveys show that patients are complaining about waiting four to six weeks to have access to the practice and then waiting nearly 60 minutes after their appointed time to be seen by the physician, you have identified a significant gap that needs fixing.

Also, look at your online reviews. Anything less than a score of 3.5 out of 4.0 should be cause for concern, because that indicates that there is a gap between patients' expectations and the experience they received.

Don't forget to ask your employees for gaps in what they are experiencing in the workplace. If you notice increased employee turnover and see that employees are leaving after a short period of employment and not even giving two weeks' notice that they are leaving, you have identified a gap that needs fixing. An efficiently conducted gap analysis is designed to improve the entire practice, including deficiencies in the staff. If your employees are better motivated and enjoying more satisfaction at work, there will be less turnover, enhanced productivity, and, ultimately, happier patients and happier doctors.

KEY ELEMENTS OF EFFECTIVE GAP ANALYSIS

In gap analysis, you typically list elements in the practice's current state, then list its desired state, and formulate a comprehensive plan to fill in the gap between these two states, i.e., the current situation or the "is" and the future or improved state or "should be" (Figure 1). The first step in gap analysis is identifying your current state and your future desired state.

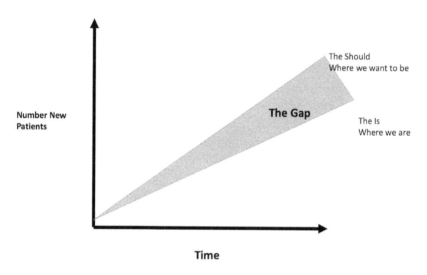

FIGURE 1. A gap analysis designed to reach the goal of attracting new patients.

Every gap analysis starts with taking an honest look at existing situation or your current state. Then you list the areas you'd like to see improved. Your focus can be as wide (e.g., the whole practice) or narrow (e.g., staff morale in the collections department). The analysis can be quantitative (e.g., currently see 25 patients per day); qualitative (e.g., patients are not taking their medications properly); or both. The key thing is to be specific and factual with an emphasis on identifying weaknesses or shortcomings.

Other examples of gaps to be filled might include the practice's revenue—for example, increasing revenue of your practice from $1.25 million to $1.75 million in 18 months, or increasing annual profit from $.5 million to $.75 million over the same time period. An orthopedic surgeon might consider a gap to fill as increasing your market share for hip replacement surgery in the three zip codes around your office from 5% to 8.5%. Finally, if you have patients waiting to obtain an appointment, then consider goals of decreasing wait times for a new appointment from four to six weeks to no more than two weeks and decrease the time waiting to be seen by the doctor once they arrive in your office from the "is" of 60 minutes to less than 15 minutes.

Next, consider the future state or the ideal condition you'd want your practice to be in or the "should be." This state can be highly specific (e.g., increase by three new patients a day, decrease no-shows from three to five to one, or better yet, zero), or generic (e.g., enhance morale in the workplace). Your gap analysis template should record all the changes you would like to make as they correspond to the current state (Figure 2).

Gap Analysis

Category	The "Is"	The "Should"	Corrective Action	Priority	Owner	Due Date
Quality\Content						
Users						
Data Processes						
Tools						
Team Training						

FIGURE 2. Template for gap analysis.

Look for Causes *Before* Providing Solutions

Start looking for causes or gaps. This is where the rubber hits the road and you identify the factors responsible for the difference between your current and future desired state. Only after identifying the causes of any problems can you then use this template to come up with a remedies and action plans to zap the gaps.[1]

The next part of your gap analysis template should list all the factors responsible for the gap identified in the previous column. This list should be specific, objective, and relevant. For example, poor prescreening of employees can be responsible for increased workplace absenteeism, or patients having to wait four to six weeks for an appointment can result in an increase in no-shows.

The last step in the gap analysis is to list out all the possible solutions or remedies for bridging the gap between the current and ideal state. These remedies should directly address the factors or causes that you have identified as producing the gap. For example, having patients complete their demographic information and health questionnaire online before coming to the office will reduce their wait time in the reception area. The remedies must be action-oriented and specific, such as arranging automatic prescription refills in order to enhance patient compliance with their medications. You might consider hiring a physician assistant in order to shorten the time a patient needs to wait to gain access to the practice.

Bottom Line: American healthcare is becoming fragmented, and patients are left with a less than optimal experience during their interactions with doctors, hospitals, and payers. Most physicians are experiencing time constraints, making it difficult for them to enhance the doctor–patient relationship. Also, spending more time with patients has the additional detractor that additional time spent with patients typically is not reimbursed. As a result of such barriers, gaps are generated in the doctor–patient relationship. Conducting a gap analysis is the first step to identifying the problem, finding the cause of the problem, and then proceeding to the solution of "zapping the gap."

REFERENCE

1. Blanchard K, Robinson D, Robinson J. *Zap the Gaps—Target Higher Performance and Achieve It!* William Morrow, 2002.

CHAPTER 12

Barriers to Entry or Exit: Which Ones Are You Building?

Michael T. Harris, MD, and Neil H. Baum, MD

Think of your practice as if it were a castle. The goal is to get as many patients as possible into your castle. This also includes getting doctors to refer to your practice and/or insurance companies to include you on their panels. So regardless of your target market, by lowering the drawbridge for easier entry you are likely to attract more business to your medical practice. Continuing this metaphor, we want to raise the drawbridge to prevent people from exiting. If it is easy for patients to enter the castle, and they have a positive experience within the walls, and it is easier to continue to live there than to go elsewhere, then the castle is well-designed.

Therefore, it is important to think of barriers in both directions: barriers preventing access to your practice, which are to be minimized, and barriers to exit the practice, for which you should strive. This article will describe how to make your castle a fortress by removing barriers to entry and constructing barriers to exit the practice.

BARRIERS TO ENTRY

Before the Patient Arrives

Poor Initial Contact

Most doctors don't answer their own phones. So the first impression new patients and referring physicians get from your practice rests on the shoulders of your receptionist. If the phone is answered by a harried, stressed-out person whose first words are, "Doctor's office, please hold," all he or she may hear in return is "click." This is a true barrier to entry that may result in the caller hanging up and calling a competitor. This is easily remedied by scripting the greeting for all incoming calls. "Good morning, you've reached Medical Associates, my name is Elizabeth. How may I help you?"

Can't Get an Appointment for Weeks

What message do you send a potential patient who calls for an appointment and is told "nothing is available for three months?" If a woman with an acute onset of new symptoms (even ones the doctor or staff member thinks are minor) calls for an appointment, you can be sure she will be calling a competitor in a nanosecond if you don't plan to see her within the next 24 hours. You will have lost an opportunity for a new patient because you don't have a provision for seeing new patients with urgencies or emergencies. Leaving open slots for emergencies or utilizing scheduling templates available in most physician computer software will go a long way to help capture that new business.

No Web Site

If you are still depending on your *Yellow Pages* ad to let patients know where you are located and what your telephone number is, you are practicing in the era of leeches, ledger cards, and rotary phones! Patients are going to the Internet in large numbers and are looking there for health-related information. If you are not on the Web, you are missing out on a great opportunity to attract and interact with your existing patients as well as attract new patients.

Hospital with a Poor Reputation

Have you checked the reputation of the hospital where you admit your patients? The quality of the hospital can easily be checked on the Web site of the Centers for Medicare & Medicaid Services at www.hospitalcompare. hhs.gov. Now you can compare your hospital with other hospitals in the community with three clicks of a mouse. And all of your patients will check. If your hospital is deficient in quality measures, this is generating a barrier for entry not only for your hospital but also for your practice. (As an aside, you *must* participate in your hospital's quality improvement programs or you *will* suffer the consequences of diminished patient volume and lower income.)

Poor Online Ratings

Have you seen your scores on Healthgrades.com? Your patients have. You must monitor your own online profile to see what patients see when they Google you. In the very near future, doctors will be compensated based on metrics that judge the quality of the services they provide to their patients. One measure of quality is patient satisfaction. You must start measuring your practice-based metrics so you will be in a position to favorably compare with your competitors—for patients and for dollars.

Getting There

Location of Office in a "Bad" Part of Town

In real estate, the key to sales success is location, location, and location. Location of your office is also important and can serve as a barrier to entry if the office is situated in a less than desirable area.

Bad Signage

How do patients arrive at your practice? Are there are well-marked signs on the building? Is it clear to patients entering the building how to locate your practice once inside the building? Are there directions on your Web site that describe how to find the practice? These are important questions that each doctor and practice has to answer because your patients are asking these questions on a regular basis.

Paying for Parking

Does your practice offer free parking? Are there ample parking facilities in close proximity to your practice? Practices that offer free or validated parking have a distinct advantage over practices that require patients to pay $15 to $20 (or even more, in some large cities) each time they visit your practice.

No Handicapped Access

Not only is it the law that you must provide handicapped access to your practice, but it is good for business as well. Take a look at your practice and see if it is accessible to wheelchairs, patients with motor impairment, patients who are visually impaired, and patients who have hearing problems.

Once the Patient Arrives

Lukewarm Greeting

The doctor is almost certainly not the first person that your patients meet when they walk in your door. In fact, it is likely that they have spoken with at least one or two people in your office more than once, and will now meet at least two people *before* ever setting eyes on the doctor. Make sure that patients are greeted as if they are old friends, and that the receptionist has been expecting them and is happy to see them. If your staff has done the right things on the phone, patients will actually be excited to "finally meet" your staff and become part of the practice.

Unpleasant Reception Area

It has been said that patients should not go to a doctor who has dead fish in his or her aquarium or dead plants in the pots! The same applies to the reading material in the reception area. Magazines that are more than a year old do not indicate a practice that is current, fresh, or going to be helpful. We suggest that you regularly purge your reception area and exam rooms of magazines and print materials that are more than three months old. A nice gesture if you see a patient reading a magazine that is a few months old is to offer to give it to him or her. It is an easy way to keep the old magazines out of the office.

It is also critical that your reception area looks and smells clean, and that the furniture and fixtures are in good repair. Your reception area should look more like a living room than an office.

Outdated Equipment

If your exam tables have plastic that is torn or rusted legs or stirrups, you are sending a terrible message to your patients. The same applies to your equipment. One of us (NHB) is a urologist, and it is considered standard state-of-the-art to have a flexible cystoscope. Having a rigid instrument certainly indicates that your practice is antiquated, and using equipment that is less than state-of-the-art may indicate that the doctor is not up to date with his or her clinical skills.

Dirty Restroom

What goes through your mind when you are on an airplane and pull down the tray on the back of the seat in front of you and find coffee stains and dried food from the previous passengers on the tray? You just might be concerned about how the airline conducts maintenance and repairs on the planes' engines. The same thoughts go through your patients' mind when they go into the restroom and find a full wastebasket, paper towels on the floor, spilled specimen cups, and no toilet paper. This is a reflection on your practice's hygiene and sends a message that may be a barrier to entry to your practice.

You Are in a Rush

Have you conducted patient satisfaction surveys? If so, what are patients saying about the doctors in the practice? Do the doctors appear to be always in a hurry? Do the doctors answer all of the patients' questions? Do the doctors stand during the entire patient encounter with their hand on the doorknob? If any of your patients answer yes to these questions, you are creating a barrier to entry. The patient may be there, but you will fail to "close the sale." And the patient will seek care elsewhere. Like any other skills, interpersonal skills can be learned.

BARRIERS TO PREVENT EXIT

Let's get back to our metaphor of the castle. Are you creating such an incredibly positive experience for patients that they would never think of leaving the practice? This is the kind of defense you want to have so that patients would never think of exiting the practice. Let's look at some examples.

Signs Clearly Marking the Practice

Make sure that the signs identifying your practice are clearly visible to any patient looking for your office. This includes the building, the directory inside the building, and next to the front door of the office.

Robust Web Site and Use of Social Media

If your Web site is more than an online version of your brochure and allows the patients an opportunity to interact with the doctor and the practice, you will have built a barrier to exit. Patients are expecting their doctor and practice to have an Internet presence. They are expecting to be able to obtain information on their medical problems with up-to-date educational material. They expect to be able to make an appointment online. They expect that they can have their prescriptions refilled with an online request. These electronic interactions are desirable, and some will soon be mandated by law, so now is the time to get started.

E-Mail

These days, most patients have an e-mail address and would like to communicate with their doctors using this technology. Patients are just as busy as physicians and are not interested in playing phone tag with their doctor. If they have simple questions, they would like to be able to have them answered without having to make an appointment. A doctor who encourages e-mails from his or her patients is building an exit barrier. This topic is complex, however, with significant privacy and malpractice implications, so be sure to check with your IT consultant and/or legal counsel before agreeing to e-mail with patients.

Patient Record Access Portal

Patients want to have copies or access to their medical records. We live in a very mobile society, and patients do not always stay in one location. If they are away from their physicians, they want to be able to show their healthcare information to a new provider or an emergency department doctor, or just have the security of knowing that they own their data and records. The day is gone where patients have to beg for copies of their records or pay $1.50 per page to have them copied and mailed. Providing a patient portal makes your practice special and creates one more obstacle for the patient to leave your practice.

Same-Day or Next-Day Appointment

When patients have a medical complaint, in their opinion it is something that needs immediate attention. If you are able to accommodate emergencies and urgencies the same day a patient calls the office to request an appointment, you will have constructed a barrier to exit. This also applies to any new patient who calls the office for an appointment. You will endear yourself to this new patient, and he or she won't look for an excuse to leave your practice. Give patients easy access to your practice, and you will have devoted and loyal patients.

Welcoming Receptionist

The first introduction to your practice is the receptionist. The receptionist provides the *only* opportunity to create a positive first impression. If the receptionist is a happy person who likes his or her job and makes the patient excited and enthusiastic about coming to the practice, you will have a nice blockade for exiting the practice. If there is no glass partition or frosted window between the reception area and the back office, you will create a patients-first atmosphere in your practice.

Short Wait Times

Patients have a short fuse when it comes to waiting for their medical care. Anything longer than 15 minutes is unacceptable today. The best way to get a handle on the wait times is to do a time and motion study, and record the time the patient was to be in the office, the time in reception area and the exam room, and the time that the patient waited to see the physician. If a patient's wait time is longer than 15 minutes, you will have demonstrated a lack of respect for his or her time, and you will have built a bridge rather than a barrier to exiting the practice.

Post-Discharge Phone Calls

Seldom do patients receive a call from the doctor or practice after they have had a procedure or after discharge from the hospital. Every patient who has a procedure or is leaving the hospital has a question(s) about their medications, their dressing, the dos and don'ts, and their follow-up appointment. The practice that calls the patient at home demonstrates the extra attention that its patients are receiving and is building a huge barrier to exit. And a side benefit to you is that this process dramatically reduces the volume of incoming phone calls from patients.

State-of-the-Art Technology

Patients who see that the practice has an electronic medical records system and uses electronic blood pressure cuffs and thermometers will assume that the clinical skills of the doctor are also in the 21st century.

Paid Parking

It is such a nice perk to offer to pay for patients' parking or offer a discount stamp for the parking lot in or near your office building. It's one more barrier to exit.

One-Stop Shopping

Patients who come to the office and are able to get their lab testing and imaging performed in the same place will be thankful for this service. It takes so much extra time to go to the off-site laboratory or imaging facility. You will really hit a home run with your patients if their workup can be conducted on their first visit. For example, a woman sees her doctor for a routine breast examination. If the doctor finds something on the examination and can immediately do an ultrasound and a biopsy during that same visit, he or she goes a long way toward alleviating the patient's anxiety by reducing the wait time for a diagnosis and treatment. This is even more the case if there is a pathologist in the same office who can immediately read the slides.

Insurance Assistance

Insurance forms can be very confusing. Offices with staff members that help patients with their paperwork and spend time explaining the insurance process have another arrow in their barrier-to-exit quiver.

Translators

We live in a multicultural and multilingual society. If you have patients that speak languages other than English and have an onsite translator, you will be able to endear yourself to these patients, and they will often send their friends and family members to your practice. This is especially true in communities with large immigrant populations. Spanish, Korean, and Russian communities are particularly close-knit, and are grateful for healthcare providers that speak their languages.

Unique Services

Have you looked at the services, procedures, or technologies that are offered by your competitors? Are you differentiating your practice from that of your competitors? If not, you are missing an opportunity to build an exit bridge. Take a look around and see what niches are out there. Remember there are riches in the niches!

Bottom Line: Barriers can be positive or negative. A negative barrier is an obstacle to enter the practice. Make every effort to identify and remove them. A positive barrier is a fence that prevents patients from leaving. Build and strengthen these barriers to exit. If you look at your practice as a castle and eliminate the negative barriers and fortify the positive ones, you will be on your way to having a very successful practice.

CHAPTER 13

Seven Deadly Sins of a Medical Practice

NEIL BAUM, MD

The seven deadly sins of medical practice may not consign you to the flames of hell, but committing any of them will definitely affect your practice's success and profitability. The practice will suffer if: (1) the doctor is not accessible to patients; (2) you do not check your online reputation frequently; (3) you do not evaluate denials and submit only clean claims; (4) you do not take steps to make sure your practice shows up on the first page of a Google search; (5) you do not pay attention to overhead and staff turnover; (6) you do not start the day on time; and (7) you do not protect the practice against embezzlement.

1. THE DOCTOR IS NOT ACCESSIBLE

The number one complaint that patients have regarding their healthcare is gaining access to the healthcare provider and long waits in the reception room or exam room to see the doctor.

The Affordable Care Act has added over 20 million Americans into the healthcare system, but there has not been an appreciable increase in physicians to care for these additional patients. Consequently, the schedules of most practices are clogged, and patients cannot get speedy access to needed medical care.

The problem of access can be ameliorated by using physician assistants (PAs), medical assistants, and other ancillary providers. Recruiting new partners, using PAs and nurse practitioners (NPs), and seeing more patients in a workday are some ways that have been used in the past. For the most part, that does not solve the problems affecting most physicians and most practices. The typical clinic encounter model traditionally has been to simply increase the number of patients seen by limiting the time for each patient as well as having the physician start earlier or leave later or requiring additional overtime.

One model worth considering is the shared medical appointment (SMA). The SMA is designed to facilitate patient access while preventing physician burnout due to repeating the same clinical advice to patients with the chronic conditions encountered on a daily basis. In the SMA model, several patients meet in a unique setting that allows patients to interact with others with the same condition or diagnosis. This innovative appointment type allows a 90-minute encounter with a prescreened group of patients, usually numbering from 6 to 10 people, who may discuss difficult problems.

The SMA can be applied to appointments for many chronic conditions, such as diabetes mellitus, obesity, chronic obstructive pulmonary disease, congestive heart failure, and various organ-specific cancers (e.g., prostate, lung, breast).

Another option that is gaining traction in the marketplace, especially among millennials, is telemedicine. Although telemedicine has been part of the healthcare system for nearly 20 years, many doctors—as well as patients—are skeptical about its implementation. Barriers to early adoption of telemedicine include cost of equipment, logistics of incorporating telemedicine into the workflow in the office setting, state laws that make telemedicine more difficult to implement, legal issues of offering telemedicine across state lines or obtaining licensure to practice telemedicine, and, finally, obtaining payment from payers for providing telemedicine.

2. NOT CHECKING YOUR ONLINE REPUTATION

Nearly every business, including medical practices, lives and dies by online reviews. Healthcare consumers are not much different when it comes to selecting providers. Many, if not most, patients these days prefer to have another patient's opinion on a doctor or a physician group or a hospital before scheduling a first appointment, particularly for treatment of any kind of serious, chronic, or potentially life-threatening condition.

The many review websites where patients can express opinions include RateMDs (www.ratemds.com); Vitals (www.vitals.com); Zocdoc (www.zocdoc.com); Healthgrades (www.healthgrades.com); UcompareHealth.com (www.ucomparehealth.com); Citysearch (www.citysearch.com); and Yelp (www.yelp.com).

Any positive comments or compliments must be captured at the time of service, such as when the patient is in the exam room. In my practice, we use a kiosk from ContextMedia (Figure 1) and have the patient complete a two-minute survey on the spot about his or her experience in the practice. This also provides a good place to leave a testimonial about their positive experience in the practice.

FIGURE 1. Patient survey kiosk.

3. NOT EVALUATING DENIALS AND SUBMITTING ONLY CLEAN CLAIMS

Medical billing is a complex, ever-changing industry, and the amount of information that a typical billing claim contains is staggering. With patient information, insurer information, provider information, and physician information, there is tremendous room for error.

Add to that the complexity of diagnosis and procedure coding, and getting paid becomes an even greater challenge. With over 14,000 ICD-10 diagnosis codes; over 3000 ICD-10 procedure codes; continuously updated CPT, HCPCS Level I and HCPCS Level II procedure codes; and all of the possible (and impossible) combinations among them, it's a wonder that the system operates as efficiently as it does.

And of course, for the claim to be approved, each piece of information must be accurate. Claim scrubbing is a process of validating the combination of data on a health insurance claim. This validation covers two key areas: (1) patient/insured/provider/insurer data; and (2) the actual services performed by the practice and submitted to the payer as documented in diagnosis, procedure, modification and revenue codes.

Claim scrubbing can reduce and eliminate simple data errors that would result in denials and rework, but it also watches for more complex issues such as mutual exclusiveness, any comprehensive component, and medically unlikely procedures. Specialty practices that rely heavily on diagnostics can efficiently test their documentation of medical necessity. Users get alerts for every charge transaction that is contrary to current Medicare coverage rules and have the opportunity to correct them before submission.

Never forget that a denied claim means that someone is holding your money. The longer the entity holds your money, the more your cash flow will suffer, and you will not be as productive as you should be.

4. NOT BEING ON THE FIRST PAGE OF GOOGLE

Nearly 2 billion people around the world have social media accounts. Social media initially was a method for people to connect with friends and family; now it is considered (among other things) a necessity for a successful healthcare practice. The goal of any social media campaign is to be on the first page of Google or any of the search engines that are commonly used by the public to find healthcare providers and medical information. There are methods you can use to arrive on the first page of Google, which will translate to more patients and better relationships with your existing patients.

The Internet is a powerful tool for physicians, and social media plays an important role in the changing healthcare environment. Seven out of 10 Internet users access health-related information from the Internet, and patients are increasingly going online to research their doctors. The public is buying cars, finding financial planners, and finding other healthcare professionals such as dentists and podiatrists on the Internet and not in the Yellow Pages. Therefore, it is imperative for doctors to understand the search engine process and how they can achieve that first-page status on Google—and even the Holy Grail of Internet marketing, the #1 position at the top of the Google page. There is a process for search engine optimization that every doctor and practice can use to achieve the topmost placement on Google, Yahoo, Yelp, and HealthGrades.[1]

Remember—if you aren't on the first page of Google, you and your practice are going to be invisible to the potential patients you want to attract to your practice.

5. NOT CONTROLLING OVERHEAD AND STAFF TURNOVER

Nothing can torpedo staff morale and add to costs more than employee turnover. A few nonmonetary motivators that can enhance staff morale include the following:

- **Conduct regular staff meetings.** There is no better way to bring your staff together than to have creative staff meetings that produce positive changes in behavior, which translate to enhanced quality of care for your patients. Start by circulating an agenda at least two days prior to the staff meeting. The meeting should have a note taker who records what takes place at the meeting and what action steps are to be taken when the meeting is over. The note taker prepares a "to do" list and circulates the assignments as soon as possible after the meeting ends.
- **Dole out lots of recognition.** Napoleon said he could conquer the world if he just had enough red ribbon to give out as rewards and recognition. In my practice we have ABCD awards—or "**A**bove and **B**eyond the **C**all of **D**uty." My credo is *praise in public, pan in private.* When I catch an employee doing something right, my office manager or I send a thank you note to the employee's home address, making sure that it arrives on Saturday. I have a nice way to say "thank you" to employees who go the extra mile and exceed our patients' expectations of our practice. I write a "Thanks a Million" check (Figure 2). You will be amazed how appreciative employees are that you not only recognized their superior service, but that you took the time to put it writing. I think this written recognition raises the bar for outstanding service from other employees as well.
- **Surprise the staff.** Whenever you can provide an unexpected perk for your staff members, you can be sure that they will appreciate the gesture. For example, two employees were absent for a week. In spite of being shorthanded, we were able to function at our regular speed and

Neil Baum, M.D.
3525 Prytania St., Suite 614
New Orleans, LA 70115
(504) 891-8454
_____ 19____

PAY TO THE
ORDER OF _____ $ __THANKS__

THANKS A MILLION

BAUM'S BANK OF GRATITUDE
WIZ'S BRANCH

FIGURE 2. Thanks a Million check for employees.

capacity without affecting the quality of care we provided our patients. To thank the staff members for their extra effort, I arranged for a massage therapist to visit our practice on Friday afternoon at 4:00 PM, and everyone received a 15-minute massage as a way of saying thank you.

Encouraging your staff to develop team spirit makes good business sense. When your employees have a personal investment in problem-solving and decision-making, they will go the extra mile for the patients and the practice.

6. NOT STARTING ON TIME

There is no greater sin than beginning the day by seeing patients in the clinic 30 or even 60 minutes after their designated appointments. This not only aggravates patients, but unsettles the staff, because employees now have to start making excuses to patients.

In the near future, physician compensation is going to be tied to patient satisfaction. Nothing can negatively impact a patient satisfaction score more quickly than to start seeing patients more than 15 minutes after their designated appointment.

Of course there will always be delays that are reasonable and justified. But it is never permissible for the doctor to routinely arrive 10 or 15 minutes after he or she is supposed to start seeing patients and then start reading e-mails and returning routine phone calls.

Not starting on time is a deadly sin that can be avoided with a little attention to detail and making it a habit to prioritize putting patients first.

7. NOT PROTECTING AGAINST EMBEZZLEMENT

It is estimated that approximately one in six physicians will be the victim of embezzlement. This often comes about due to a lack of business training, because few doctors receive any education about the business of medicine during medical school, residency, or fellowship.

The best protection is prevention. I suggest performing a background check on all potential employees, which includes a credit check and a criminal record check on all employees who will handle money.

It is also important that you value your employees and make sure they know it. Be sure your employees are paid at competitive wage levels. To get an idea of what the current pay standards are, survey local offices yearly or refer to the practice payroll benchmarks.

Provide usual and customary benefits for your locale. Employees whose pay and perks are comparable to area norms may be less likely to feel they deserve more than they're getting and will be less like to "help themselves." Be familiar with your state's labor laws regarding exempt versus non-exempt employees, and pay overtime in accordance with your state law.

Many physicians do not learn the basic principles of accounting control. As a result, it is too easy for staff to take money. Most embezzlement in medical practices is carried out by someone working alone, so the two key principles are these:

- No one person should have control over the entire cash transaction process.
- Duties involving money should be distributed to two or more people. That way, collusion would be required for embezzlement to occur, which is less likely.

A policy should be in place where the same staff person should not open the mail, record the checks, balance out at the end of the day, post the payment, make the bank deposit, and reconcile the bank statement. Even in a small office, these tasks can be divided between two or more staff members.

I also recommend that the doctor perform unannounced random spot checks by matching the daily scheduled patients against posting and deposit slips.

Bottom Line: Avoiding these seven deadly sins is important for any medical practice. I do not mean to imply that the list is limited to seven sins. I know there are others that are also important to avoid. However, this a good point of departure for any successful medical practice. In a future article, I will discuss the seven virtues of a medical practice.

REFERENCE

1. Clarke A. *SEO 2017: Learn Search Engine Optimization With Smart Internet Marketing.* Simple Effectiveness Publishing, 2016.

CHAPTER 14

Attracting Referrals: Think Outside the Box

NEIL BAUM, MD, AND CANDIS DAUGHERTY, BS

Traditionally, physicians have looked to other physicians as their primary source of patient referrals. Do not forget, however, that there are other professionals who can serve as excellent sources. Any effective marketing plan will identify the professionals and organizations that have the potential to refer patients. By pinpointing common areas of interest and approaching these other practitioners, you can create a need for your services or expertise. Most nonphysician professionals are eager to have physicians see their clients and patients. However, it is necessary to communicate with these nonmedical professionals about their clients, which requires written or spoken communication to these referral sources. Additionally, nonmedical professionals and organizations are eager to have physicians address their associations and share educational material with their members. They also are eager to refer patients to physicians who respect them professionally as peers.

For example, podiatrists see many patients with diabetic foot problems; therefore, a talk by a primary care doctor or an endocrinologist on contemporary management of diabetes would be of interest to that group. This is also an opportunity to discuss methods to improve communication between physicians and podiatrists. A presentation from a physician to a group of podiatrists might include indications for referral from podiatrists to medical doctors. You might consider providing the audience with a copy of suggestions for referral to your practice. Your follow-up note should contain contact information including your cell phone number and back line number to allow the podiatrist easier access to your practice.

Following any meeting with nonmedical professionals, send a letter to all who attended, thanking them for the opportunity to speak at one of their meetings and inviting them to your office if they were ever in the area.

Numerous benefits may result from these presentations:

- You can expect two to three referrals a month from podiatrists—which is two to three referrals you would not have received had you not contacted the podiatrists for a presentation. Also, there is the potential for the podiatrists themselves to become patients.
- An editor of a podiatric publication will certainly appreciate an article written by a physician to include in the journal.

None of these opportunities would have come about had you not approached the podiatrists about talking at one of their meetings.

Also consider reaching out to chiropractors. In addition to the dozens of patients with chronic back pain that each chiropractor sees, they also see substantial numbers of patients with medical conditions that may need a referral to a medical doctor. Reputable chiropractors do not treat medical conditions with spinal manipulations or adjustments; they are happy to send them to a physician who will appreciate the referral and be sure to send the patient back to the chiropractor.

Interest in alternative methods of healing and complementary medicine is on the rise. An ever-growing percentage of patients are choosing alternative methods of healing or doctors and practitioners of complementary medicine. This reality has not been lost on the mainstream medical community, and many allopathic physicians now collaborate with chiropractors and acupuncturists, among others. Large cancer centers have established departments of integrative medicine, seeking to take advantage of the large sums of health care dollars being spent on alternative remedies and herbal medicines.[1]

The smart physician would be wise to develop contacts with reputable alternative practitioners, because millions of Americans now seek healthcare from a full range of such practitioners. If you are able to intelligently inform your patients about complementary remedies and their reasonable use, instead of discounting alternative remedies altogether, you are more likely to retain that patient. You become a resource instead of an adversary.

An article in the *New England Journal of Medicine* pointed out that Americans made an estimated 425 million visits to providers of nonconventional therapy in 1990. This number exceeds the number of visits during that year to all U.S. primary care physicians (388 million). Expenditures associated with use of nonconventional therapy in 1990 amounted to approximately $13.7 billion, three quarters of which ($10.3 billion) was paid out of pocket.[2] The number of patients relying on alternative therapies has increased even more in the last 15 years. In 2002, a report in the *Journal of Integrative Medicine* stated that 62% of adults used some form of complementary and alternative medicine therapy during the past 12 months when the definition of complementary and alternative medicine therapy included prayer specifically for health reasons. When prayer specifically for health reasons was excluded from the definition, 36% of adults were found to have used some form of complementary and alternative medicine therapy during the past 12 months.[3]

The evidence continues to mount that an increasing number of our patients are seeing nontraditional healthcare providers. We must make an effort to communicate with these providers in a professional manner, and, as a result, we can achieve additional referrals to our practices.

TARGET YOUR MARKET

For years, orthopedists have had a symbiotic relationship with the legal profession, particularly the personal injury (PI) attorneys. Many orthopedists now communicate directly with PI attorneys and insurance companies to generate referrals. An orthopedic clinic in New Orleans has escalated its outreach efforts to include insurance claims adjusters. Ancillary income can be obtained when orthopedists identify attorneys and insurance adjusters as important targets for potential patients. The following anecdote gives an example of an orthopedist who marketed to nontraditional referral sources.

An orthopedic practice invited local attorneys and insurance adjusters to attend a seminar on "Common Orthopedic Injuries and Their Symptoms," "Determination of Disability," and "Role of Diagnostic Testing" conducted by the doctors, nurses, and insurance billing/coding experts in the practice.

The practice identified two more important authorizers of payment: risk managers and insurance rehabilitation specialists. The clinic's mailings extend to thousands of attorneys, insurance claims adjusters, rehabilitation counselors, and risk managers all over the southeastern United States. The clinic offers continuing medical, legal, and nursing education credits for its seminars.

The clinic has tracked its referrals and has found that marketing has attracted a substantial number of new patients. The clinic reports that tracking the number of referrals from third-party guarantors (i.e., attorneys and insurance adjusters) for the period following inception of the clinic's seminars until four years later revealed that referrals had increased to an average of 15% more than previous levels.

OTHER REFERRAL SOURCES

Nurses

Nurses and hospital employees are other important sources of referrals. It is common for consumers looking for healthcare providers to ask nurses for recommendations. Doctors who are kind, considerate, and attentive to their patients are frequently the ones who are suggested by nurses.

Several times one of us (NB) has been asked to speak at meetings of the American Operating Room Nurses Association, and a number of referrals are generated after each presentation. If you are a surgeon, consider giving an in-service instruction. Whenever you are going to perform a new procedure, go to the hospital and give a talk to the operating room nurses. This accomplishes several goals:

- It makes the nurses knowledgeable assistants when you do the procedure;
- It reduces the anxiety they usually feel when assisting with a new procedure or operation; and
- It lets them know that this doctor is on the cutting edge, performing the newest procedures.

Whenever you have an opportunity to speak to nurses, always leave handouts. Just as with other speaking engagements, provide additional information to anyone who requests it. As a result, you can expect additional referrals from the nurses.

Pharmacists

Pharmacists are another group from whom patients frequently seek advice. Therefore, it is important to become an ally of the pharmacists in your community. For example, before you start prescribing a new medication, call (or have your office call) the local pharmacists and make sure they have the medication available.

You can also protect your patients from receiving confusing advice if you stay in touch with your pharmacists about nontraditional uses of established medications. For example, in the past one of us (NB) prescribed the mild antidepressant imipramine for mild stress and urge incontinence. In one case, the pharmacist told the patient that the medication was not used for incontinence but for depression. That meant there was a need for some explaining—to both the patient and the pharmacist. The problem was solved by photocopying the journal study showing the efficacy of imipramine for both urge and stress incontinence. By sending along the information about the medication with each patient, the pharmacist became educated, and several phone calls to explain the rationale for prescribing it were avoided.

You can also send articles to local pharmacists about your areas of interest and expertise. For example, one of us (NB) wrote an article on the use of transdermal scopolamine to treat bladder instability, which was an off-label use for that anti-nausea medication. The pharmacists in my community were thus knowledgeable about this new use. (Transdermal scopolamine is still not approved for use for that purpose.)

Pharmaceutical Representatives

Don't forget pharmaceutical representatives as another source of referrals. Not only are these men and women able to provide you with educational materials and sample medications, but they are also capable of generating good public relations for your practice. If you have a well-run practice, they will often mention it to other physicians and potential patients. If you want to endear yourself to the drug representatives, see them in a timely fashion. That is their "hot" button, and they really appreciate it if you do not ignore them or keep them waiting.

Other Referral Sources

Other possible sources for referrals include oral surgeons, dentists, and orthodontists. Neurologists interested in treating headache can communicate with dentists who have patients with temporomandibular joint syndrome. Psychiatrists can communicate with psychologists, sex therapists, social workers, and the clergy.

Ophthalmologists can work with optometrists. Orthopedists can look for referrals from chiropractors. Rheumatologists can connect with manicurists as women who visit a manicurist often have problems with the joints in their hands. And dermatologists can solicit referrals from barbers and beauticians. Once you do a little "out of the box" thinking about referrals, you can see a wider range of possibilities for your marketing.

FROM ALTERNATIVE TO COMPLEMENTARY

Not too many years ago most medical doctors scoffed at the mention of patients visiting chiropractors, acupuncture specialists, or homeopaths. Now that patients are seeking out these practitioners, medical science is taking a second look at these practice patterns. If physicians can overcome old notions of what constitutes the healing arts, there may be some fruitful collaboration in store for both types of practicing professionals. Not only are consumers willing to pay out of pocket for alternative medicines and treatments, but insurance companies are agreeing to pay for certain kinds of alternative medicine.[4]

CAST YOUR REFERRAL NET USING THE INTERNET

Have you Googled yourself or your practice lately? With pandemic fears and social distancing mandates in place, more people are utilizing the Internet for information. Are your online reviews positive or negative? Have you responded, within HIPAA guidelines, to your reviewers? The vast majority of patient complaints are related not to medical care, but customer service. When patients are frustrated because of rudeness, inattention, or long waiting times, today's response is to vent frustrations online with the click of a mouse. Even with the best intentions and actions by the best staff, a bad review of your practice is inevitable. However, responding to those reviews in a timely and courteous manner can demonstrate that your practice is making every attempt to rectify a patient's negative experience. Most patients will recognize that no one is perfect, not even medical doctors!

Replying positively and promptly to a negative review is often the best way to overcome the repercussions of a less-than-stellar review. In many cases, frustrated and angry patients just want to be heard. Acknowledging the patient's experience and responding in a positive manner not only will reflect well on your practice, it may even save the loss of a patient. In a best-case scenario, the reviewer may even remove the negative post or amend their review.

Keep in mind that simply searching for directions in Google Maps will reveal your Google ratings. If you have no stars or a low number of stars, patients may think twice about calling your office for an appointment.

Your online presence must be constantly monitored, either by yourself or by someone within your practice. Furthermore, always ensure the online responses to reviews are HIPAA compliant. Google Reviews are the most commonly used platform for those actively seeking reviews, but do not neglect to monitor other sites such as Yelp, Healthgrades, Vitals, and other online review sites.

APPROACHING POTENTIAL REFERRAL SOURCES

Some suggested ways to approach nontraditional sources for referrals include the following:

- Agree to meet "on their turf," at least the first time.
- Find common areas of interest and emphasize them.
- Show respect for the professions of nonmedical colleagues, even if you do not completely agree with their approach. In the past, this was much more of a problem, with physicians discriminating against osteopaths, orthopedists against chiropractors, and ophthalmologists against optometrists. In today's world of decreasing reimbursements and shrinking patient bases, we cannot afford to be provincial. It is time to expand our worlds—and expand our practices by doing so.
- Demonstrate the benefit of sharing patients and referrals. Not only will you increase your network of potential referral sources, but so will your nonmedical colleagues.
- Provide your referral sources with something new, interesting, and educational. You have an opportunity to increase your awareness and understanding of their professions, and vice versa.
- Promise to provide written documentation on a regular basis.
- Make every effort to refer patients to the specialties or professions of your nonmedical colleagues.
- If all else fails . . . feed them!

Bottom Line: By moving "outside the box" of traditional referral patterns, you can garner additional patients. All it takes is a little innovation and a little time. Whatever your niche, there are professionals who can feed you referrals—ophthalmologists with optometrists, orthopedists with chiropractors, rheumatologists with manicurists, dermatologists with cosmetologists and massage therapists—the range of possibilities for marketing is vast. Take the time to consider nonmedical professionals who could potentially make referrals to your practice and build a plan to connect with them.

REFERENCES

1. MD Anderson's integrative medicine. www.mdanderson.org/documents/patients-and-family/diagnosis-and-treatment/care-centers-and-clinics/Integrative%20Medicine%20Center/IMC-nutrition-WTE.pdf.

2. Puchalski L. The use of alternative and complementary medicine in radiology today. *Radiol Manage.* 2000;22(1):51-55.

3. Barnes PM, Powell-Griner E, McFann K, Nahin RL. Complementary and alternative medicine use among adults: United States, 2002. *Seminars in Integrative Medicine.* 2004;2(2):54-71.

4. Overbay A, Hall M. Insurance regulation of providers that bear risk. *Am J Law Med.* 1996; 22:361-387.

CHAPTER 15

Effective Scheduling Using Sacred Time

NEIL BAUM, MD

According to Tom Peters, the guru of excellence,[1] there are two secrets for success:

1. Find out what the patient wants and give him or her more of it; and
2. Find out what the patient doesn't want and avoid it.

Patients' number one complaint regarding healthcare is the delays they experience waiting to be seen by their physician. Languishing in the waiting room has been reported to cause more patient dissatisfaction than any other aspect of medical care, including fees.

One of the easiest ways to manage your schedule is look at what is currently taking place in your practice. This can be easily accomplished using a time and motion study (Figure 1). I suggest you conduct this study for just a few days once or twice a year. The time and motion sheet can be placed on the paper chart or added as a template to the electronic medical record. Doctors will be amazed at how much time patients are spending in their offices and how little of that time is spent with physicians. Sometimes patients are in the office for two hours and only get to spend five minutes with the physician. This most definitely does not leave them with a warm fuzzy feeling when they leave the office. This disparity between time spent in the office and time spent with the physician does not result in a positive experience for the patient and has the end result of tarnishing the reputation of the entire profession.

SACRED TIME

What are some solutions for dealing with the inevitable delays that will take place in any office? Nearly every medical practice has one or two urgent situations or emergencies that must be worked in every day. Most of the

Time and Motion Study	
	Time patient arrived in the office
	Time patient taken to the exam room
	Amount of time spent with the provider
	Time patient left the office
	Total time in office / total time with MD

FIGURE 1. Time and motion study.

time, patients with an emergency are just told to come to the office and that they will be worked into the schedule. This wreaks havoc with the schedule and delays patients who have designated appointments at the end of the day, because when the worked-in patient is fit in ahead of them, they often experience a significant delay in seeing the doctor. Another scenario occurs when a referring doctor calls a specialist and asks if his or her patient can be seen on the same day. Again, these patients often are told to just come to the office and that they will be worked into the schedule. There also are times when the need to see additional patients quickly can be anticipated: for example, flu season; back-to-school physicals at a pediatrician's office; or end-of-year requests for appointments so patients won't have to pay deductibles so quickly in January. Finally, most doctors can anticipate additional patients on a Monday morning when patients who developed problems over the weekend and went to the emergency department are requesting follow-up appointments on Monday morning.

To avoid the problems that arise with emergencies, urgencies, or work-ins, you can create a few 15-minute time slots. In my practice these slots are at 10:30 AM and 2:45 PM. Patients with urgencies or emergencies are told to come at those designated times or at the very end of the day. These slots are referred to as "sacred time" and cannot be filled until after 8:30 AM on that day. I have yet to encounter a patient or referring doctor who won't accept that scheduling option. Now the patient with a scheduled late morning or late afternoon appointment can be seen in a timely fashion.

I rarely have a day that those sacred time slots are not filled with urgencies or emergencies. On the odd occasion where the time slots are not used, the time can be spent returning phone calls to patients, completing patient charts, or dictating notes.

Finally, if you want to make your schedule effective, make an effort to be an on-time physician. This means starting every day on time, not arriving 10 to 15 minutes late for the office clinic and hoping to catch up later in the morning. So many physicians arrive a few minutes late, look at their e-mail, or do a few minutes of paper work, and as a result start 15 or 20 minutes late. This is the surest way to have significant delays in the office from which you can never recover. If you want to see patients on time, then you also have to be on time for your staff.

Bottom Line: The reality is that few physicians have the ability to make changes to healthcare policy. However all of us have the ability to be an on-time physician and solve the problem of patients waiting to see the physician. One solution is to provide sacred time slots time each day to see urgencies and emergencies.

REFERENCE

1. Peters TJ, Waterman RH. *In Search of Excellence: Lessons from America's Best-run Companies.* New York: Harper Collins; 2004.

CHAPTER 16

The Ten Never Evers of a Successful Practice

Neil Baum, MD

1. Never turn your back on your patients in the examination room.

Communication is enhanced when people are face to face with each other. That does not happen when the doctor spends the majority of time looking at the paper chart or the computer screen. Whenever possible, there should be no barriers between the doctor and the patient. Figure 1 shows a patient/physician/computer configuration that is to be avoided. Figure 2 shows a preferable arrangement where the doctor can look at both the computer screen and the patient. Experts say lack of eye contact is the biggest problem that results from having to input information into a computer. Eye contact establishes trust and a bond with patients, and a lack of it can be alienating. It also takes away the physician's opportunity to read body language and get other nonverbal cues from patients.[1]

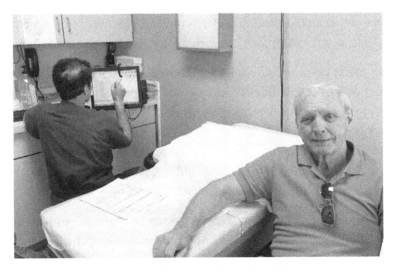

FIGURE 1. Doctor having his back to the patient. This is a never ever.

FIGURE 2. Doctor facing the patient. This is preferred.

A study performed at the University of California, San Francisco, analyzed data from patient–doctor interactions between 2011 and 2013. Each appointment was videotaped, and patients were contacted after the visit to assess satisfaction with the interaction. The study reported that doctors who spent less time typing on the computer scored much higher in patient satisfaction, achieving excellent care ratings 80% of the time. Doctors who spent more than one-third of the time looking at the computer instead of the patient achieved an excellent rating less than half the time. The researchers noted that high computer use by a clinician was linked to lower patient satisfaction and less rapport between patients and physicians.[2]

This problem can easily be solved by using a scribe. The scribe takes the history of the present illness, the review of symptoms, and the past medical history. The scribe then conveys his or her findings to the doctor, who enters the exam room to ask a few questions and perform the physical exam. The findings are entered into the computer by the scribe. As a result, the doctor can focus on the patient and does not need to ever touch the computer or look at a computer screen.

Another suggestion is to use the computer screen to educate patients about their health—for example, by showing a graph marking changes in his or her blood pressure over time, or showing trends such as cholesterol or prostate-specific antigen levels.

2. Never put your hand on the doorknob of the exam room when speaking to a patient.

Nearly every doctor has had the experience of reaching for the doorknob as the encounter with the patient comes to an end, only to have the patient bring up a question or a new complaint. You have probably already closed the patient's paper chart or electronic record. The fact that you have put your hand on the doorknob indicates that you have terminated the encounter and that you have moved on, at least psychologically, to the next patient. There is a very simple solution: before standing up to leave the exam room, ask the patient, "Have I answered all of the questions that you have regarding your visit today?" Or you can simply ask patients, "Anything else?"

Another "never" similar to the doorknob phenomenon is for the doctor to look at his or her watch. Again, this indicates boredom and readiness to terminate the encounter. If you think this does not matter, remember the town hall-style presidential debate in Richmond, Virginia, in 1992, when then-President George H.W. Bush infamously checked his watch during a question from the audience, then stumbled through his answer. It seemed that President Bush wanted to get this debate over with—that his heart wasn't in it. Many pundits believe this was the turning point of the campaign and cost him the election. The same can said for doctors: they can lose patients' attention and, perhaps, their confidence, if patients believe the doctor is paying more attention to his or her watch than the patient.

3. Never allow pharmaceutical reps to have access to the office when you are seeing patients.

What message are you sending to patients who have been patiently waiting in your reception area when someone with a briefcase walks to the front desk and asks to see the physician and then is escorted immediately into the "inner sanctum" to see the doctor? The message is loud and clear: that the pharmaceutical representative or the salesperson is more important than patients. This should never, ever be the situation. Patients should receive priority, and pharmaceutical representatives should be scheduled before or after patients are seen. In my practice, *no* pharmaceutical representatives are seen during patient hours. They can come before I start seeing patients, at lunch time (without the necessity of buying the practice lunch), or at the end of the day. It did not take long to institute this policy, and all of the pharmaceutical reps quickly got the message and did not interrupt patient visits.

Another benefit of this policy is that the reps become much more focused in their visits and in their presentation of their products. No longer do they spend valuable time asking about my vacations or my family; rather, they start right in by talking about the features and benefits of their products or asking how they can help me in my practice with their products.

4. Never make patients use a phone tree.

A phone tree is helpful for the receptionist, who does not have to triage the call and route the caller to the proper person in the office. However, the phone tree is not user friendly. Nothing is more irritating to a patient who wants to make an appointment, speak to a doctor, or discuss his or her bill than to hear "Press 1 to continue in English" and "Listen closely to our list of options, as they may have changed." It is easy to understand why practices use such automated phone systems: they are cheaper and more efficient than hiring more people to handle all the callers. Generally speaking, it is a bad idea to agitate your patients who perhaps already don't feel well. There is no better way to get poor patient satisfaction scores than to use a phone tree and place a patient on hold. Whenever possible, I suggest avoiding a phone tree in a medical practice. Also, avoid putting the phone on answering service during lunch hour. Patients may use their own lunch hour to call the doctor, and you want be available to your patients between noon and 1:00 PM. In my practice, each employee takes one day to eat at his or her desk and answer the phone during the lunch hour.

5. Never updating your website once it is created.

Too often, practices will make an electronic version of their brochure and think they have a website. That may have worked 20 years ago, but today the public expects much more. They are looking for current content and for an interactive website where they can ask questions and receive feedback or responses to those questions or comments.

Search engines look at your website for frequency of content updating. If you want to rank high on the Google search—i.e., the first page of Google—you must contribute new content on a regular basis. My goal is to provide new material at least every two weeks. In order to demonstrate currency of content, you keep your content up to date and ever relevant. I suggest that you write content that informs, engages, entertains, and collects information, such as the visitor's e-mail address. I also recommend including keywords that your patients might be using to find information on the Internet that may land them on your website. Finally, you want to be sure to include a call to action, which is intended to get the reader to connect from your website to your practice and actually convert the searcher from a viewer to a patient in your practice.

6. Never reprimand or correct an employee in front of patients.

Being reprimanded in front of patients is very embarrassing to the employee and does not demonstrate to patients that you have compassion and care about your employees. I find it best to mention to the employee that you would like to discuss some issue or matter later in the day and then meet with the employee with the office manager or the human resources person in the practice to discuss the problem and its impact on patient care.

7. Never fail to return calls to patients in a timely fashion.

"Timely" is going to have different meanings to different doctors. In my opinion, a timely response is within 24 hours. You send a negative message when patient calls are not returned. Of course, many calls need not be returned by the physician—but someone in the office needs to make contact with the patient either by phone or by e-mail. For example, if you promise the patient a report or result of a lab test or an imaging procedure and you do not have the result, it is important to call the patient and let him or her know that you have not received the report and that the patient has not been forgotten. This conveys to the patient that nothing has fallen through the cracks and that you remain on top of the situation.

8. Never be late for starting to see patients.

A physician shows disrespect for a patient if that patient has to wait 30, 60, or even 120 minutes past the scheduled appointment time to see the doctor. I know of doctors who arrive in the office 15 or 20 minutes after their first scheduled patient and then check their e-mail or even make a few non-urgent phone calls, with the result that they start seeing patients 30 to 45 minutes after the designated start time. Occasionally, of course, there are acceptable reasons why a patient may be kept waiting. While there is always the possibility that an emergency has caused an unusual delay, most practices that keep patients waiting do so even when there are no pressing emergencies. There is no better way to build a good reputation for your practice than being labeled as an on-time physician. That is certainly one of the perks that concierge doctors offer their patients—that is, ready access and not waiting an excessive amount of time to see the doctor. Whenever I see a patient who is upset about having had to wait, I will tell him or her that there will be no charge for the visit because of my delay. I feel that my reputation is worth more than the $75 office visit. I even recall introducing myself at a social event where the person said, "I heard about you, Dr. Baum. You are the doctor that didn't charge a patient who had to wait!" Isn't that reputation worth more than $75? Of course it is.

My take-home message: None—or very few—of us can change the healthcare system, but all of us can be more sensitive to our patients' time. There is no better way to do this than to see your patients on time.

9. Never fail to apologize when you have made a mistake.

Doctors, after all, are human, and we do make mistakes. I believe that a mistake is an opportunity to offer an apology when one is warranted. Every mistake offers an opportunity for improvement in your process of caring for your patients. An apology demonstrates that you are a caring doctor who empathizes when a patient has an undesired or unanticipated result.

10. Never answer your cell phone when you are in the exam room with the patient.

Even those doctors who feel they must carry their cell phones at all times should keep them in silent/vibrate mode and make every attempt not to permit interruptions when with a patient. I have a policy that only callers from the operating room, the emergency department, or the intensive care unit are permitted to contact me on the cell phone when I am seeing patients. In those rare instances, patients seem to understand the urgency of the situation and allow me to take the call. In all other instances, the phone goes unanswered.

Bottom Line: Ideally, we would all like to provide every patient with a favorable experience. However, this is not always possible. In this article,

I have provided some guidelines regarding actions to avoid. Following these guidelines will ensure that nearly every patient who passes through the portals of your practice has a positive experience and will provide you with stellar patient satisfaction scores.

REFERENCES

1. Reddy S. Is your doctor getting too much screen time? *The Wall Street Journal.* Dec. 14, 2015. www.wsj.com/articles/is-your-doctor-getting-too-much-screen-time-1450118616

2. Ratanawongsa N, Barton JL, Lyles CR, et al. Association between clinician computer use and communication with patients in safety-net clinics. JAMA Intern Med. 2016;176:125-128.

CHAPTER 17

How to Write Easy-to-Read Healthcare Materials for Blogs and Websites that Result in New Patients

RON HARMAN KING, MS, AND NEIL BAUM, MD

Most physicians and others in the healthcare professions have spent their entire professional lives writing for medical and professional publications. Few of us, however, have training or the skills necessary for writing medical content directed toward our patients and potential patients. Medical concepts and language can be complex. Our current patients and potential new patients need easily understandable health information regardless of age, background, or reading level. We offer three guidelines and resources to help you create easy-to-read health materials that will generate new patients and also retain your existing patients.

STEP 1: PLAN AND RESEARCH

Know your target audience. Consider the reading level, cultural background, age group, and English language proficiency of your intended audience. Who would you like to read your health materials? Next think about the objectives and outcomes of your content. What do you want your target audience to do as a result of reading your materials? For example, if your objective is to show the proper use of a Kegel exercise app to women with stress urinary incontinence, emphasize the outcome of their proper use and the likelihood that the patient will no longer be incontinent. A sample sentence might be: "Following the directions for your condition of loss of urine may help you to not rely on adult diapers!" We can assure you that will capture the attention of all women who suffer from stress incontinence.

STEP 2: ORGANIZE AND WRITE

Now that you have selected your audience, consider it carefully when writing. Cultural, age, and gender differences may have an impact on your content. For example, the writing style and graphics may be different for a brochure for teens about sexually transmitted diseases (STDs) than for adults over age 50 for whom you want to provide information on STDs.

Keep the language within the range of a 6th- to 8th-grade reading level. A number of readability checkers are available online. The Flesch-Kincaid reading ease score is the most widely used readability checker (https://readable.io). These readability checkers serve as a guide so that your writing will be easy to read and understood by your targeted audience.

Use the words your readers are most likely to be familiar with. By using the keywords that your users use, you will help them understand the copy and will help optimize it for search engines. We suggest that you ask patients who have accessed your site what words they used in the search bar of Google or any of the other search engines. Keep a record of these keywords and use them in the titles of your articles and in the first sentences, which will make your material come to the attention of the search engines and help with your placement on the first page of Google—or even the "Holy Grail," number one on the first page of Google.

Grab your readers' attention in the first few sentences. Make those sentences stand out by using compelling, clear language. For example, a website trying to encourage men in the New Orleans area to obtain a PSA test might begin as: "Nearly 30,000 men will die from prostate cancer each year. That's half of the capacity of the New Orleans Superdome. Most men will not die from prostate cancer if they get an annual blood test called the PSA test, or prostate-specific antigen test."

Structure the material logically. Start by stating or defining the topic. Include the most important points about what you want people to learn. Then write the body of the material. Finish with a summary of the material and restate the key concepts. It's the old tell 'em what you are going to tell them. Then tell 'em and finally tell 'em what you told them. It worked for Aristotle more than 2000 years ago and it still applies to today's writing for websites and blogs.

Include specific action steps users can take, and emphasize the benefits of taking action. For example, proper use of erectile dysfunction drugs can make you and your significant other very happy.

Examples and stories help engage readers. We suggest that you tell a story about a patient; however, it is imperative not to mention the patient by name or make any reference to the patient such that the reading audience might be able to identify the patient. Just keep HIPAA in mind, and you won't go afoul of the Office of Inspector General!

Write your draft, then review and edit several times. Remove words, sentences, or paragraphs that do not help the reader understand the concepts. For website and blog writing, brevity is always best. We suggest an ideal length of 400 to 700 words—any longer, and the reader is likely to "click off" and leave your page.

Consider incorporating Web-accessibility best practices. An accessible website helps people with reading and learning disabilities. (For more information on Web accessibility, see the WebAIM.org site.)

Language and Writing Style

Avoid medical jargon unless it is clearly and succinctly defined. Find alternatives for complex words, medical jargon, abbreviations, and acronyms. At times there may not be an alternative, or you may want to teach patients the terms because their healthcare providers will be using them. In those cases, teach the terms by explaining the concept first in plain language. Then introduce the new word or words. It is also helpful to provide a simple pronunciation guide. For example, "Urine is stored in the bladder and kept in the bladder by a muscle, the urine sphincter or sfink-ter, until it is socially acceptable to empty the bladder contents into the toilet."

Be specific about the advice you give. For example, if you are instructing a man following a vasectomy, instead of writing "Don't lift anything heavy," say "Don't lift anything heavier than a bag of groceries, or about 15 pounds."

Use varied sentence length to make the material interesting, but keep sentences simple. A general guideline is to limit most sentences to no more than 10 to 15 words. I suggest limiting each paragraph to no more than five sentences.

Make it conversational. Use words like "you" instead of "the patient." A personal voice can help engage readers as if you are actually speaking to them. Where appropriate, use bulleted lists instead of blocks of text to make information more readable. Use the active voice. Direct language helps people associate concepts with actions:

- **Active:** Caesar used his vacuum erection device today for a treatment for erectile dysfunction.
- **Passive** (which should be avoided): The vacuum device was used by Caesar today.

Be consistent with terms. For example, using "drugs" and "medications" interchangeably in the same document can cause confusion.

When possible, say things in a positive way. For example, say "Drink less caffeine" instead of "Don't drink lots of coffee."

Visual Presentation and Representation

- Use illustrations and photos with concise captions. Keep captions close to images.
- Avoid graphs and charts unless they are essential to convey the concepts. If you do use them, make sure they are simple and clear. We suggest that any graph in a blog or website article have only two lines, because many lines, as might be found in a medical journal, can be very confusing to the non-medical reader.
- Balance the use of text, graphics, and clear sections, or "white space." Try for about 40% to 50% white space.
- Use sans serif fonts such as Arial, Verdana, Tahoma, or Helvetica. Sans serif fonts are considered easy to read even at smaller sizes.
- Use boldface headings and subheadings to separate and highlight document sections, as in this article.
- Justify the left margin only. This means the left margin should be straight and the right margin should be "ragged."
- Use column widths of about 30 to 50 characters (including spaces).

STEP 3: EVALUATE AND IMPROVE

As you are starting on your blog and website writing, we suggest that you test your materials on a few patients or a sample group from your target audience. Testing during the writing process can help ensure your audience understands your materials. Evaluate the feedback you get and revise your materials if necessary. For more information, see the list of resources at the end of this article.

Bottom Line: Writing for lay audiences is not always something that comes naturally to physicians. However, if you follow a few of these suggestions, you can attract readers and convert web surfers to paying patients. Follow this three-step process and you will soon see your Google search soar to the top, with patients soon following from the Web to the telephone calling to make an appointment with your practice.

RESOURCES

Centers for Medicare & Medicaid Services. Toolkit for Making Written Material Clear and Effective, Part 6. www.cms.gov/Outreach-and-Education/Outreach/WrittenMaterialsToolkit/index.html?redirect=/WrittenMaterialsToolkit/.

Flesch-Kincaid reading ease score. https://readable.io.

National Institutes of Health. Clear and simple. www.nih.gov/institutes-nih/nih-office-director/office-communications-public-liaison/clear-communication/clear-simple. See especially Part 5, Pretest and Revise Draft Materials.

Web Accessibility in Mind. WebAIM. https://webaim.org/

CHAPTER 18

Effective Writing that Attracts Patients

NEIL BAUM, MD

In Frank Luntz's book *Words That Work: It's Not What You Say, It's What People Hear*,[1] he offers "Ten Rules for Effective Communication." This article was inspired by Luntz's book and explores the rules he suggests lead to successful communication. Luntz can be contacted through his Web site at www.luntzglobal.com.

Rule #1. Use small words. In general, you don't want to use words that will require a dictionary for your audience to understand your message. Most people don't have dictionaries on hand, and fewer still will bother to look up the meaning of your words. Try to use verbiage that can be understood by someone with a tenth grade education. Avoid medical jargon unless you define the term.

For example, if you are writing about urinary incontinence, don't use words such as *detrusor* or *external sphincter*. Instead, use a balloon analogy for the bladder and the stem of the balloon compressed by the thumb and first finger as the muscle that provides continence.

Rule #2. Brevity: use short sentences. Avoid long, meandering, complex sentences that require the reader to remember a few things to reach the end of the thought. Say one thing, period. Then say the next. Brevity is the basis of good speaking and writing.

For example, the sentence "Treating women with overactive bladder using Kegel exercises and biofeedback allows women to overcome the urges and the embarrassment of losing urine and having to depend on panty liners, pads, and even diapers" is far too complex. This message could be simply stated as, "There are simple techniques that can keep a woman dry without the use of medication." Whenever you can simplify a comment or statement without deviating from your message, do so.

Rule #3. Think billboard, not story board. Your message, particularly the titles of your content, must attract the reader in just a few seconds. Think of your title as a billboard on the highway. The billboard has only a few seconds to provide a message to the driver and his or her passengers to take the next exit for food, lodging, or shopping. Your titles should also attract the reader's attention very quickly, or that reader will leave your Web site or blog site in a nanosecond.

For example, a title like this one—"Urinary Incontinence—Diagnosis and Treatment"—is not likely to generate viewer interest or motivate that viewer to read the article and go to your Web site. A better title might be "Incontinence—When It Gets Wet Down There." But best of all is "Incontinence—You Don't Have to Depend on Depends!" I know this because I have tested all three titles on a blog site, and the first title generated very few comments or patients calling for an appointment. The third one, however, generated hundred of readers and led to several dozen becoming patients in the practice.

Rule #4. Consistency matters. If you are attempting to brand yourself or your practice, consistency is key.

Rule #5. Novelty: offer something new. Readers are easily bored, and you can capture their attention if you give them something new. Often the best approach is to offer a new twist on something already in their minds. Give your patients something that gives them a brand new take on an old idea. The combination of surprise and intrigue creates a compelling message.

If there is a new treatment or idea that can help patients solve their problems, you will engage their interest. If the treatment or product has been used and endorsed by movie stars or other luminaries, you will be able to capture their attention.

Rule #6. Sound and texture matter. Make use of alliteration, metaphors, and onomatopoeia. The sounds and texture of language should be just as memorable as the words themselves. A string of words that have the same first letter, the same first sound, or the same syllabic cadence is more memorable than a random collection of sounds. Write the way Winston Churchill spoke: "We shall fight on the beaches, we shall fight on the landing grounds, we shall fight in the fields and in the streets, we shall fight in the hills; we shall never surrender."

Rule #7. Write like you really care about the patient. Think about tuning into station WIIFM (or What's In It For Me). When you can think like a patient and offer content that has value, you will generate action and attraction. Remember: people will forget what you say, but not how you make them feel.

Using patient testimonials is the best way to demonstrate that you care and have solved their problems. For example, if I'm talking about a drug or procedure for urinary incontinence, and I have had a patient report to me how I have changed her life and have made it possible for her to socialize without having to "depend on Depends," I relate how that patient gave me and my nurse a hug, offered to write a testimonial for my Web site, and appeared with me on TV as we talked about the new treatment and how it changed her quality of life.

Rule #8. Visualize. "Paint a vivid verbal picture."[1] To support this advice, he argues that "the slogans we remember for a lifetime almost always have a strong visual component,"[1] something we can see and almost feel. "Snap, crackle and pop" needs no explanation that we are talking about a specific Kellogg's cereal.

For example, if I am writing about benign enlargement of the prostate gland and the symptoms that the enlargement produces, I will describe a balloon that represents the bladder with the stem of the balloon representing the urethra. My fingers compressing the stem of the balloon correspond to the obstructing prostate. I then write and create a picture of poor force and caliber of the stream, failure of the bladder to completely empty the urinary contents, and the negative impact that this has on middle-aged and older men. The more word pictures that you can paint with your writing, the clearer will be your message.

Rule #9. Ask a question and provide a solution to the patient's problem. Ask a question that links to you and your practice. In competition against Jimmy Carter during the 1980 United States presidential election, Ronald Reagan asked Americans, "Are you better off today than you were four years ago?" This question—so simple, so memorable, so personal—was more powerful than any essay or fact-based argument Reagan could have made, and perhaps, more than any other factor, led to his victory. Ask, "Are you having a problem with access to your physician? Want to be seen the same day you call for an appointment?" If you can deliver on that promise, you will have a very busy practice.

Rule #10. Provide context and explain relevance. Nietzsche said, "He who has a why to live can bear almost any how," and I immediately thought of those words in relation to this rule.

In Luntz's words, "You have to give people the 'why' of the message before you tell them the 'therefore' and 'so that.' Without context, you cannot establish a message's value, its impact, or most importantly, its relevance."[1]

But don't lose sight of the importance of seeing things from the reader's perspective. When explaining "the why," it is critical that you don't make the mistake of explaining why something is important to *you*; instead, you have to succeed at explaining why it's important to *your reader*. Only then will you be a valuable resource for a patient's healthcare.

For example, if your discussion is about blood pressure and high cholesterol, then you want to describe why this is important to take action on and control. Both of these—hypertension, and hypercholesterolemia—are silent diseases until they cause heart disease, kidney disease, erectile dysfunction, or a stroke. After giving the reader the "why," you can capture their attention and give them the "how" to correct the problem.

Bottom Line: Writing for patient readership is entirely different from writing for colleagues, journals, or medical publications. If you can write a compelling message in language that is easily understood by your readers, you can attract patients to you and your practice. Just follow a few of these rules.

REFERENCE

1. Luntz F. *Words That Work: It's Not What You Say, It's What People Hear.* New York: Hachette Books, 2007.

CHAPTER 19

Titles Are Terrific: Creating Titles that Will Attract Attention

NEIL BAUM, MD

You have written a blog or an article for the local health and fitness magazine, but no one comments on the article—you don't feel that people or the audience you are trying to attract is reading it. Do you know that a compelling headline is the key to attracting attention, and even more importantly, to holding that attention and keeping the viewer's eyeballs on the blog or your website? This article gives you suggestions for writing killer headlines that work.

We are largely driven by self-interest, and our brains are wired to look out and listen for any message that pertains to us. If your headline identifies a target group specifically, then that group, if they have an interest in your message, will take notice.

Highly specific approaches work much better to draw attention and create belief than generic and vague statements that can come across as untrustworthy. For example, rather than say, "Treatment for Incontinence," try, "Treatment for Incontinence: How Not to Depend on Depends."

Think about Station WIIFM, or "What's in it for me?" Above all, there has to be a payoff. Your readers need to know what is in it for them, or why should they care and continue to stay on your blog or your Web site?

Chris Garrett, a guru on the business of new media and online business (who can be reached at www.Chrisg.com), provides ideas and suggestions on creating titles that can attract viewers and keep them viewing your material.

The great advertising genius David Ogilvy said, "It has been found that the less an advertisement looks like an advertisement, and the more it looks like an editorial, the more readers stop, look and read."1 This has to be a goal of every blog writer. We need to make our material have the feel and look of editorial and not a sales pitch for our areas of interest or expertise.

Garrett suggests that without a compelling headline, you will not attract attention, and your article will not spread as easily. If you do write a killer headline, you will get more clicks and more bookmarks, and your readers will be compelled to share it with their friends and contacts.

Garrett recommends that your title grab the attention of the viewer. This can be done using a statistic, a claim, a fact, a jingle, or a rhyme, or best of all, indicating a benefit.

It is important to be as specific as possible. Highly specific approaches work much better to draw attention and create belief than generic and vague statements that can come across as untrustworthy. Rather than say, "Get great results" try, "New treatment reduces risk of cancer recurrence by 75%."

Make an effort to create curiosity. "Are you having a problem in the bedroom? If so, below are suggestions to put energy into your love life." It is well known in the media that the topic of sex has an allure and will almost guarantee viewers wanting to get more information.

Another suggestion is to provide powerful benefits. Does the headline offer a solution to their problem? If so, you can be sure that your title will take the viewers to the next level, which is reading the rest of your blog and hopefully picking up the phone and making an appointment (or, if you have a well constructed Web site, making an online appointment from there).

CATEGORIES OF MEDIA HEADLINES

Breaking News

New discoveries in healthcare or stories about celebrities and politicians with certain medical conditions are always hot topics for blogging. For example, in July 2013 there was an announcement that fish oil could be a promoter of prostate cancer. My blog entry on this topic, "Something Fishy About Fish Oil and Prostate Cancer," was of interest to many men who were taking fish oil to protect against heart disease. I received dozens of comments about that blog post, probably because it was so current.

Goals

Your blog will be read if you offer a way to achieve a goal, or to be attractive and healthier. One topic that generates lots of interest is fertility and infertility. A recent report noted that sperm counts have been decreasing in the past decade and may be impacting the fertility rate. My blog entry "Where Have All the Young Sperm Gone? Decreasing Fertility of the Millennial Man and Tips to Improve Your Chances of Having a Baby" attracted a lot of attention.

Problems

The flipside to the goal is the problem. Fear sells just as well as positives; just ask the newspapers. *Cancer* is a buzz word that also attracts attention. Any title that offers a new method of diagnosis, prevention, or treatment will be effective.

How-To

How-to articles share a technique to achieve something practical and beneficial. Offer to provide the steps to create something in reality. For example, *How to Win Friends and Influence People* is the best title of all. It has worked to sell millions of books and has been translated into dozens of languages. A healthcare example of a how-to would be "10 Steps for Preventing Urinary Tract Infections."

Entertaining

Social media provide an opportunity to express your sense of humor. Viewers want to know your personality, and you can make a dry medical article entertaining, fun, and even humorous. For example, "Cunnilingus and Throat Cancer—Fact vs. Fiction" was a blog entry when Michael Douglas declared in front pages of newspapers and on the nightly news that oral sex was the cause of his throat cancer.

Bottom Line: Titles that work trigger an emotional reaction. Remember we do not just want "interest," we want the reader to take an *action*—which means becoming a patient in your practice. You can do this by writing terrific titles.

REFERENCE

1. Ogilvy D. *Ogilvy On Advertising.*New York: Random House. 1985.

CREATING TITLES

Chris Garrett offers several formulas that you can use to create terrific titles. He suggests using the following "fill in the blanks" headline formulas:

1. Do You Make These _____ Mistakes?
2. The Secrets of _____
3. What _____ Can Teach Us About _____
4. Everything You Know About _____ Is Wrong
5. How _____ Made _____ and You Can Too!
6. If You _____, You Can _____
7. Finally, No More _____
8. At Last! _____
9. Learn How Millions of _____ _____
10. How to Get More/Better/Cheaper _____

Reprinted with permission from Chris Garrett, Chris Garrett on New Media, www.Chrisg.com.

CHAPTER 20

Lessons Learned from the Restaurant Industry: What Outstanding Waiters and Waitresses Can Teach the Medical Profession

NEIL H. BAUM, MD, AND JEFF J. SEGAL, MD, FACS

One of us (NHB) will never forget the young woman who took the orders of five people without writing anything down and correctly placed the food in front each patron. The waitress also did a few things that made our evening memorable. As a result, her tip was 25% of the bill. In this article, we will describe what the best waiters and waitresses do to increase their tips and how this might apply to the delivery of outstanding healthcare with stellar patient services.

STATE YOUR NAME

Every employee and even the doctor should clearly state their name and title when they meet a patient for the first time. This even applies to the receptionist who answers the phone. There's a world of difference between "Doctor's office, please hold" and "Good morning. This is [name of medical practice]. My name is [name of receptionist]. How may I help you?" In the former, a negative first impression is created; and as a result, the patient may not keep the appointment and may go elsewhere for his or her medical care. The latter phone response is polite and clear, and makes the patient feel that the office and doctor are there to serve patients and not the other way around.

ONE SIZE DOES NOT FIT ALL

In the restaurant industry, diners want their needs met. At a minimum, that means getting the food to the table in timely fashion with zero errors. Sometimes the diners want the waiter's opinion on the wine, the specials, or the desserts. Sometimes the diners are interested in engaging in social banter with the waiter. Every group of diners is different.

There are times when one of us [JJS] responds to the ubiquitous "Do you have any questions?" with "Do you know what Avogadro's number is?" The purpose is not to quiz the waiter on Chemistry 101. It's to set the tone for the evening that social banter is OK and to make the table memorable enough to receive high-priority service. Incidentally, a surprising number of waiters do indeed know what Avogadro's number is.

But a waiter's small talk is not appropriate when business people are in the midst of a tense negotiation, or a husband and wife are in a heated discussion one inch away from a nuclear meltdown. At that point, discretion is the better part of valor. Top off the water, deliver the food, and get out of the way.

As a doctor, know when breaking the ice with engaging banter makes sense. It makes sense when you first meet a patient and hope to learn a bit more about his or her background. It's more appropriate with elective care than urgent or emergent care. On the other hand, when you've been given the task to explain the options to a new patient who just learned that his or her diagnosis is cancer, you will have the patient's full attention for just the first few sentences. At that point, every word must count, and you don't have the luxury of chit chat.

An experienced doctor, like an experienced waiter, knows how to deliver the right amount of information mixed with the right amount of social interaction to each person.

BE AUTHENTIC AND BE TRUE TO YOUR PATIENTS

It is important to notice that waiters at both the International House of Pancakes and a Ritz Carlton restaurant can do well financially. But the work at each entity is dramatically different. At IHOP, it's a low-cost, high-volume, quick-turnover process. At the Ritz Carlton, it's a high-cost, low-volume, slow-turnover process. Diners understand this implicitly when they sit down. Their expectations are based on the reputations of the respective entities. Waiters who deliver service at or above this zone of expectation will be tipped well.

Every doctor's practice is different. Some, like concierge practices, are high-cost, low-volume practices. Patients expect Ritz Carlton-like service.

Other practices are focused on convenience. Some high-volume pediatric practices, for example, enable slots for same-day appointments with the understanding that the child might not see his or her usual doctor that day, but the child will definitely see a doctor, and the problem will be diagnosed and treated.

Some doctors' practices are a hybrid of IHOP and Ritz Carlton. The key to making this work is to set minimum expectations up front, then do your best to exceed them.

BE HONEST WITH YOUR PATIENTS

When a waiter says there are two specials—the grouper and the tuna—you might ask, "Which is the better dish?" If the waiter says, "They're both good, it just depends upon your taste," you've received no real response to your question. Perhaps they're both tasty, but any additional information to help break the tie might be helpful. It's often a breath of fresh air when a waiter states, "I personally don't like the grouper. It's been on the menu for a while, but it's rarely ordered. And often when diners order the grouper, it's overcooked. But that's just my opinion." That's code for order the tuna.

In healthcare, patients are looking for answers and guidance. The more you hedge, the less confidence they have in your ability. As a spine surgeon, you can offer patients physical therapy or surgery for a herniated lumbar disc. After describing the risks and benefits of each path, a patient might say, "This is all very confusing. What would you do?" If you say little more than "Each patient is different; it's really up to you," most patients will perceive that response as below the bare minimum. You can and should qualify that each patient is different and that your tolerance for risk might be very different than that of the patient. But the patient wants the question answered.

Perhaps you can state that based on your experience, 70% of your patients choose surgery, and 30% choose physical therapy. The reason some patients typically choose surgery is their window of time to be out of work is narrow. And the reason other patients typically choose therapy is because they experienced a known risk with a different surgery in the past. You're not telling the patient paternalistically what to do. You helping the patient ask the right questions to make a better decision for himself or herself. Like successful waiters, doctors should give straightforward, honest answers.

IF YOU MAKE A MISTAKE, OWN UP
TO IT, AND MAKE IT RIGHT

When one of us [JJS] dined at a high-end restaurant for lunch, patrons who arrived later received their food before those at the author's table, who had been waiting longer. The waiter explained that there was a mix-up in the kitchen, the food would be out shortly, the meal was free, and there would be 50%-off coupon that could be applied at a future visit. Mission accomplished, anger dissipated, and loyal customer created. And the tip was still on the full amount.

As a doctor, it's inevitable that service errors and lapses will occur. For example, you may be running an hour late, you may have forgotten to return a call, or you may have inadvertently double-billed a patient. Fix the problem. Make it right. Then go above and beyond patient expectations. This is what outstanding waiters and waitresses do. If the food delivery is delayed, the staff will often provide a free drink or comp the guests a dessert. This often ameliorates the problem, and the guests feel that the restaurant takes ownership of the problem.

Medical practices can do the same thing. Some practices surprise patients with a $10 Starbucks card if a patient has to wait too long. Other practices might write off a small amount if there's been an embarrassing clerical error. (Of course, this practice needs to be squared with state and federal regulations and any insurance contractual obligations.)

One of us (NHB) will tell a patient who has a legitimate complaint that there will be no charge for the visit. Now some will say, "You can't do that." Let the truth be told, you can treat a patient for free. What you can't do is waive the copay but bill the insurance company. That is illegal, and you can run afoul of the Office of Inspector General. What is our take-home message? If you underdeliver, own up to it, make it right, then overdeliver at your soonest opportunity.

Bottom Line: Let's not forget that we, too, are in a service industry. We have an obligation to provide outstanding service just like the restaurant industry does. We have to make every effort to ensure that every patient has a positive experience with the practice. When we do that, we don't have to worry about the Affordable Care Act or any other governmental intervention, as we will have a plethora of patients who appreciate outstanding care and are willing to pay for it.

CHAPTER 21

The Shared Medical Appointment: A Proposed Model of Medical Appointments

Eugene Rhee, MD, MBA, and Neil Baum, MD

The shared medical appointment (SMA) is designed to facilitate patient access while preventing physician burnout due to repeating the same clinical advice to patients with the chronic conditions encountered on a daily basis. The SMA enables patient group interaction in a unique setting that allows for patients to understand other patients' problems and journeys with the same condition. This innovative appointment type allows for a 90-minute encounter with a prescreened population of patients to discuss difficult problems.

The typical clinic encounter model has traditionally been to simply increase the number of patients seen by limiting the time for each patient as well as having the physician arrive earlier or leave later. SMAs seek to think outside the box in an era where providers must explore new, innovative solutions.

THE SHARED MEDICAL APPOINTMENT: SOMETHING NEW?

SMAs actually started in Kaiser Permanente in Northern California, originally developed by Edward Noffsinger, PhD. Notably, other practices around the country, including the Cleveland Clinic, the University of Virginia, Wake Forest University, and Kaiser Permanente in San Diego, have all adopted SMAs.[1]

The providers, in a group setting, perform a series of one-on-one patient encounters during a 90-minute block to manage, educate, and treat a common medical problem in a group setting. Patients benefit with access to the medical provider and receive significant education with fellow patients who suffer from similar medical conditions. The medical provider boosts access and productivity without increasing clinic hours or costs. This is a 90-minute experience in which the patients feel that they are receiving personalized attention, merely in the presence of others, and are rewarded with extensive education about their medical problems without feeling rushed. This is not a group therapy session, nor is the SMA intended to be a class. Each patient learns from the interaction of the provider with other patients with similar medical problems. In fact, patients are comforted by the idea that they are "not alone" and derive a more personalized experience interacting with similar patients.

The SMA model can be applied to appointments for many chronic conditions, such as diabetes mellitus; obesity; chronic obstructive pulmonary disease; congestive heart failure; and various organ-specific cancers, such as prostate, lung, and breast.

HOW IS THE SMA EXECUTED?

Traditionally, a return appointment takes up a 15-minute slot. Ten patients seen in a morning clinic will typically use 2.5 hours. With a 1.5-hour SMA, the same 10 patients can be encountered, for a net gain for the provider of one hour. One medical provider with one medical assistant is all that is required.

The patients are clearly offered voluntary appointments in the SMA through two options:

1. During the initial consultation, the physician suggests to the patient that his or her common condition can be addressed in a group setting that is less rushed and offered as a subsequent appointment type.
2. A specially trained receptionist offers the patient an option to see the provider in a group setting. This receptionist has a clear ability to assist in access for the patient with a quicker and more desirable appointment slot, provided that the inclusion criteria for the type of patient offered a SMA are met. For example, a patient returning post-prostatectomy needs a follow-up visit every three months for one year. That patient is given an option to follow-up in a SMA so he can compare his progress with that of other patients.

FIGURE 1. Effective seating configuration for a shared medical appointment.

It is important that the patient understands this is an option and that individual appointments may be made as well.

SMAs are 90 minutes in length. It is imperative for the success of the SMA that the appointments start on time. Conference rooms or reception areas are often used. If the latter, it may be useful to schedule the SMA as the first or last appointment of the day with the reception area closed while the SMA is in session.

Before the appointment, patients complete an interim medical history form. Spaces are provided on the form for questions, issues, and prescription refills. For each SMA medical problem, inclusion criteria are established. The receptionist and nursing staff gather all necessary laboratory results for each patient. The electronic medical record system provides the perfect opportunity to use this system in a way that is efficient for the office.

FORMAT

We suggest limiting the enrollment to 10 patients. The chairs are configured so that the patients sit in a semicircle (Figure 1). Nametags are distributed to personalize the event. The medical staff checks-in the patients and has them sign the confidentiality agreement. The provider initiates the introductions and discussion outlining the plan for the SMA. Patients are urged to join the discussions. The provider briefly introduces the common diagnosis and explanation with the aid of a short presentation. Each patient is discussed within the group. There is no need to rush the discussion as all patients are hearing about similar problems and advice.

Because issues overlap and are rarely repeated, each subsequent patient takes less time. By the time the last patient is encountered, most have only brief questions and concerns. All patients have benefitted from in-depth discussion beyond what could be achieved during the traditional 15-minute follow-up appointments. Ten patients have been cared for during a 90-minute block, with the physician improving his or her efficiency and gaining an additional hour of provider time.

CONFIDENTIALITY CONCERNS AND COMPLIANCE

Because patients in SMAs self-select, they are typically comfortable in the presence of other patients. A confidentiality form states that they agree to discuss their own medical history in the presence of others and to not disclose the contents of the SMA to others outside the meeting. We have found that patients take this disclosure very seriously. Some individual patients may need a physical exam, which the provider performs at the end of the SMA with the nurse taking over the rest of the group. It is extremely important that the patients have an opportunity to complete patient satisfaction surveys as a means to document quality (Figure 2).

Providers typically bill for the individual services as documented in the progress notes. These visits are usually billed as level 4, with code 99214, or level 3, with code 99213, depending on the complexity of the actual care provided for established patients. Medicare generally pays for group visits if there is some one-on-one time with the physician. Practices should contact local carriers and other insurers about their policies for new and established patients.

"Check with your carriers to ensure they actually reimburse. Some carriers are still a little bit resistant," said Roland Goertz, MD, former president of the American Academy of Family Physicians. "You don't want to set all this up and then find out you don't get paid."[2]

RESULTS

It has been reported that 85% of the initial SMA patients opted for another SMA, and 79% of the patients rated their visit as "excellent."[3] At Kaiser Permanente, the excellent rating was 96% for the first 100 patients that

Shared Medical Appointment (SMA)
Patient Satisfaction Survey

Our program success for the Shared Medical Appointment (SMA) depends on you! We want your experience with the Shared Medical Appointment to be as positive and supportive as possible. Your anonymous feedback will help to ensure that these goals are met. Please take a few minutes to let us know how we're doing.

Please rate your Shared Medical Appointment (SMA) encounter on each criteria using the scale provided.

	Strongly Disagree	Somewhat Disagree	Neither Agree nor Disagree	Somewhat Agree	Strongly Agree
I found SMA to be an acceptable way of receiving medical consultation.	1	2	3	4	5
I found the check-in process to be easy.	1	2	3	4	5
I was able to communicate well with the healthcare provider.	1	2	3	4	5
I clearly understood I had an option of individually making an appointment.	1	2	3	4	5
The provider was able to address my real concerns as a patient today.	1	2	3	4	5
My ability to understand my medical problem was improved by the SMA.	1	2	3	4	5
My healthcare provider was familiar with my medical history.	1	2	3	4	5
The environment worked well today for me.	1	2	3	4	5
Overall, I was satisfied with the provider today.	1	2	3	4	5
Overall, I was satisfied with the SMA.	1	2	3	4	5

Any comments, problems, or suggestions on how we can improve the SMA are welcomed here:

FIGURE 2. Shared medical appointment patient satisfaction survey.

attended a SMA at Kaiser Permanente San Diego (unpublished data). Key factors for this level of satisfaction may be improved access, visits that are not rushed and allow greater one-on-one interaction, and appointments that start and end on time. However, the single most important factor may actually be what is so unique about the SMA: the ability to be heard by many, a simple yet powerful concept in social media.

SMAs may initially be viewed with skepticism from colleagues, staff, administrators, and patients. It is imperative that this start as a small pilot program with only a few dedicated "champions" initially (provider, medical assistant, and receptionist). After a six-month trial has passed, productivity numbers are analyzed for each provider involved and compared with the last year's production for that particular provider. Other potentially interested doctors may accompany the SMA doctor to explore whether this is a viable option. Additionally, other patients who have been a member of the SMA may be used to facilitate the group. The SMA will only work with the support of the staff, including the SMA receptionist who schedules these appointments. Considerable decision-making is necessary to understand who should be offered an SMA, and the receptionist can follow a script and format as part of his or her initial training.

The SMA appeals to the physician as patient satisfaction increases and the monotony of the traditional return appointment is lessened. The physician experiences fewer problems with the schedule in the morning or afternoon, and enjoys a pleasant experience in the clinic, honing his or her presentation skills as well as individual clinical acumen.

Bottom Line: It is time for a major paradigm shift in the delivery of American healthcare. It is no longer necessary to take care of only one patient at a time with the doctor being eyeball-to-eyeball with the patient. Using modern techniques such as robotic surgery, we can operate on patients without even touching them. We can treat patients from a great distance by using telemedicine. And now we can treat a group of patients all at the same time with the SMA.

The results of patient surveys indicate favorable patient satisfaction scores with SMAs. We can provide quality medical care with this approach to healthcare delivery. The SMA improves the efficiency of healthcare and productivity of practitioners, allowing doctors to see more patients in a short period of time. It is a win for the patients, a win for the staff, and a win for the physician. Who could ask for anything more?

REFERENCES

1. Noffsinger E. *Running Group Visits in Your Practice*. New York: Springer; 2009.
2. Elliott VS. Group appointments can serve both patients and practices. *American Medical News*. February 19, 2011; www.amednews.com/article/20110919/business/309199969/5/.
3. Bronson DL, Maxwell RA. Shared medical appointments: increasing patient access without increasing physician hours. *Cleve Clin J Med*. 2004;71:369-370.

CHAPTER 22

Creating Value for Your Patients—From the Perspective of the Patients

RON HARMAN KING, MS, AND NEIL BAUM, MD

Marketing requires the answer to only three questions: (1) Who are your patients?; (2) What do they value?; and (3) How can you give patients what they value better than any other similar practice in the community or in the region?

It really comes down to the promise of delivering on your promise to provide the best experience for your patients, one that stands head and shoulders above that available from any other practice. It comes down to what the patient perceives and thinks about his or her experience with the practice and with the doctors in the practice.

Two interactions are vital to the success of your encounter with the patient. The first is to control the most enjoyable component of the encounter with the practice and improve the least enjoyable aspect. For almost every patient, the most enjoyable component is typically the human interaction with caregivers— not just the physician. Caregivers can include not only clinicians but also administrative staff. Social media research shows consistently that how patients are greeted and treated outside the exam room can be far more important in determining patient satisfaction than the quality of their clinical care. It also is necessary to identify and improve the *least* enjoyable aspect of the encounter. In the Internet age, it is remarkably easy to determine the less enjoyable aspects. One way is to provide online customer satisfaction surveys to patients after their clinical visits. Another is to simply read a provider's reviews on the various "rate-your-doctor" websites. In assessing the reviews, the singular objective is to look for patterns and themes in a collection of reviews rather than in a small handful. If complaints consistently repeat the same source of frustration, the practice has useful information to act upon for improving the value of the patient experience.

The second most important interaction is the end of the experience—understanding what the patient was feeling at the end of the interaction with the practice.[1,2] These sentiments often are what drive patients to review their healthcare experiences on other websites.

Patients may receive different types of value from your participation in their medical care. If you can understand what the patient perceives as that received value, then you can make every effort to deliver what the patient deems important.

There are four value components that should be understood by every practice:

- Functional value;
- Monetary value;
- Social value; and
- Psychological value.

This article discusses the first two components as the "hard" values of the patient's point of view, setting aside the latter two "soft" values for another discussion.

FUNCTIONAL VALUE

Functional value is what the patient feels is being done to solve his or her medical problem. For example, if the patient presents with a headache, the functional value is what the doctor can do to relieve the pain and discomfort.

To tailor your practice to the needs and wants of your patients is to understand what aspects of value are important to them. If you can do that, then you will have fulfilled the overarching feature of providing what is important to the patient. Now you can anticipate favorable patient satisfaction scores, improvement in your online reputation, and happy patients, making life pleasant for the doctor and the staff.

Achieving high value for patients must become the overarching goal of healthcare delivery, with value defined as the health outcomes achieved per dollar spent. This goal is what matters for patients and unites the interests of all actors in the system. If value improves, patients, payers, providers, and suppliers can all benefit, while the economic sustainability of the healthcare system increases.[3]

Value should always be defined around the customer. Because value depends on results, value in healthcare is measured by the outcomes achieved, not the volume of services delivered. Volume is old school, and an antiquated method of reimbursement.

Patients often seek out healthcare for a single, primary reason: they are sick, they don't feel well, they are in pain, or they fear having a disease or condition that prompts them to seek medical attention. The doctor or practice that understand this and is capable of fulfilling the patients' functional needs will have satisfied and contented patients. In a urology practice, there are several conditions that prompt a patient to seek immediate help: kidney stones and back pain; scrotal pain; inability to urinate; blood in the urine; and fever and chills accompanied by urinary symptoms. To be certain that the staff understands these urgencies and emergencies that require immediate attention, there should be a sign in front of the receptionist listing those conditions that must be seen within the day or those conditions or situations that mean the patient must be sent to the emergency department.

Another component of functional value is access to care. Patients may place a higher premium on access to care than on other offerings or promises that the practice makes. For example, some patients are willing to pay several thousand dollars more for their healthcare if they are assured that they can have prompt access to the practice and the doctor(s). This concept, *concierge medicine*, meets that functional need that patients desire. There certainly is a segment of the population that is willing to pay additional fees if they have the doctor's cell phone number and know that if they have questions or need to be seen, they can have immediate access to the doctor.

Access to care is so important that it has created a new industry of urgent care centers. These are not emergency departments but facilities where patients can walk in, be seen quickly, and have basic laboratory and imaging studies performed.

We would like to suggest a concept that we have found useful, "sacred time." This is a time slot left empty in the middle of every morning or afternoon so that patients with an emergency or urgency can be seen on the same day that they contact the office. We suggest a 15- to 20-minute time slot every day that can be used to accommodate these patients who are in need of immediate care.

MONETARY VALUE

Monetary value is simply the price that the patient must pay for your services. Of course, there are patients who shop for the cheapest price. You may not be interested in catering to those patients who are only price conscious, but before you turn them away, consider knowing what your prices for your services are so that you are able to give that information to those who are price shopping.[4]

We are all motivated to reduce spending, and this can be accomplished by increasing price transparency. It is no secret what a consumer pays for an airline ticket, a hotel, or a dental appointment. Therefore, physicians can no longer hide behind price obfuscation. It is soon going to be mandatory to publish the prices that doctors charge or those prices that a patient would pay for medical care. The end result of price transparency is certainly going to be an increase in competition in the healthcare arena and will certainly result in lowering prices overall.

The overarching goal of price transparency is to provide patients with the cost of care that includes total and out-of-pocket costs for episodes of care including the doctor, the hospital, and even the costs of the medications that they will be expected to purchase. Granted, given the reality of enormous variances in insurance plans and coverage, this can be a difficult goal to achieve. One technique is simply to provide an example clearly marked as such, along with adequate disclaimers that final charges are subject to individual insurance plans. Nonetheless, patients are impressed by the effort toward transparency and certainly understand and accept the complex realities of the American healthcare system.

Expenses vary even for relatively common procedures. For instance, in New Hampshire, in 2008, the average payment for arthroscopic knee surgery was $2406. In other areas of the country the cost for same procedure could range from $3717 to more than $11,617. In Massachusetts, the median hospital cost in 2007 for an MRI of the lumbar spine, performed without contrast material, ranged from $450 to $1675.[5]

Because patients usually are in the dark regarding the price of medical care, publishing price information could both narrow the range of fees and lower prices, in part by permitting consumers to engage in more cost-conscious shopping and selection of lower-cost providers and in part by stimulating price competition on the supply side, forcing high-priced providers to lower their prices in order to remain competitive. Proponents argue that consumers have price information and compare costs when purchasing just about any other good or service (imagine buying a car, a house, or a computer without knowing its price). Come on, doctors: healthcare should be no different. In the authors' own experience, we have seen practices see sudden surges in new patients after merely posting information about their fees on their websites. Surprisingly, it is not about price, but transparency—by no means were the fees the lowest in town. Rather, the candor of the act was enough to earn trust from strangers.

In defense of not revealing the cost of care, healthcare does differ from other consumer goods in a few important ways. First, most patients are insured, so in the past they paid very little out-of-pocket cost for their medical care, which dramatically weakens or eliminates their incentive to choose a lower-cost provider. Second, patients are concerned about the quality of their care as well as its cost, and it is much more difficult for a patient to assess the quality of medical care than that of other goods. Patients, unfortunately, may rely on cost as a proxy for quality. The belief that higher-cost care must be better is so strongly held that higher price tags have been shown to improve patients' responses to treatments. It is possible to think of this phenomenon as the Mercedes effect—a more expensive car creates the perception of added value, even though there may not be hard evidence of any added value at all. Moreover, the lack of independent information on the quality of care may reinforce patients' tendency to rely on physicians for advice about where to receive their care, and patients may be unwilling to go against a clinician's advice in the interest of saving money. Finally, determining the cost of medical care is different from determining the cost of other goods and services, because it is often hard to know in advance what exact combination of services a patient will need. For this reason, the average price for a particular procedure or service, which is the most readily available information, does not capture a patient's actual cost of care and may be a misleading indicator of true cost differences.

Price-transparency initiatives will have to address several major challenges if they are to have the desired effect. First, it is not clear which prices to report: although average unit costs (e.g., the price of an MRI of the knee) are the most readily available, personalized, episode-level costs would be more meaningful to patients (e.g., the price that an enrollee in a Blue Cross Blue Shield preferred-provider organization would pay at a particular hospital for a knee replacement, including all related doctor's visits, tests, facility charges, and anesthesia services). Moreover, meaningful information about quality must be delivered alongside prices so that patients can make decisions by comparing care choices on both dimensions.

Finally, and most fundamentally, consumers must be engaged in considering price information in their decisions to use medical care. Consumers with health plans that require them to pay a higher share of their medical expenses (e.g., enrollees in high-deductible plans and those with substantial coinsurance) have more at stake in their decisions and should be more cost-conscious shoppers. Procedures that are elective, for conditions that are not life-threatening, and that can be performed in various settings, also may be most appropriate for price comparisons. There is evidence that consumers will "shop" for prescription drugs, a less complex type of medical care, when they bear the responsibility for a significant portion of the cost of their care.[5] Targeting transparency initiatives toward these consumers and toward less complex procedures could increase their impact. It may also be necessary to explain to patients the factors that could account for differences in the price per service or episode of care, so that they do not automatically associate higher prices with better care.

It is difficult to defend the obscuring of healthcare prices. The challenges associated with leveraging price transparency to moderate overall healthcare spending, however, may explain the limited role that this tactic has played in healthcare reform proposals. Attempts to increase cost-conscious shopping and reduce spending through price-transparency programs are appealing, however, because these efforts can be implemented without disrupting current payment systems and because market-based approaches to healthcare reform generally enjoy broad political support.

Outside the medical world, nowhere has this approach proven more successful than for the nation's busiest domestic airline, Southwest. Its *transfarency* (a term the airline coined to describe a unique approach to treating customers the way they expect and deserve to be treated) advertisements and marketing position have clearly earned the trust of passengers sufficiently to make the carrier the most successful in the country. Although it is too early to tell what the outcome of experiments with increased transparency in healthcare will be, the urgent need to reduce cost growth in healthcare is probably incompatible with permitting the current level of price variation to continue. How long are payers and policymakers willing to wait to see whether market-based transparency initiatives will work before moving to other, potentially more onerous, polices, such as increased regulation? That is the question.

CONCLUSION

Let's be honest and forthright. No healthcare provider can say publicly, objectively, and with unassailable evidence that his or her medications, treatments, or diagnostic skills are better than the doctor next door, down the street, or in the region. Therefore, the successful doctor will have to differentiate his or her offering to patients by creating higher value. By increasing value to patients, you make your practice more attractive, drive improvement in outcomes, employ a happier staff, and, ultimately, become a happier and more successful doctor.

REFERENCES

1. Wolf JA, Niederhauser V, Marshburn D, LaVela SL. Defining patient experience, *Patient Experience Journal.* 2014;1(1):Article 3. http://pxjournal.org/journal/vol1/iss1/3.
2. Robinson J. What is the patient experience? Business Journal. September 30, 2010. www.gallup.com/businessjournal/143258/patient-experience.aspx.
3. Porter ME. What is value in health care? *N Engl J Med.* 2010;363:2477-2481.
4. Sinaiko AD, Rosenthal MB. Increased Price transparency in health care — challenges and potential effects. *N Engl J Med. 2011;*364:891-894.
5. Arthroscopic knee surgery cost and arthroscopic knee surgery procedures. NewChoiceHealth.com. www.newchoicehealth.com/arthroscopic-knee-surgery-cost

The Most Common Patient Complaints that the Front Office Receives and How to Manage Them

Lynn Homisak and Neil Baum, MD

Doctors report that about one in six patients are "difficult." That translates to three or four unpleasant visits with patients each day.[1] The majority of these complaints can be successfully managed by a receptionist who has the skills to understand the processes taking place throughout the practice. This article will discuss the top 10 most common complaints that a patient is likely to bring to the front office and how the receptionist can successfully manage the complaints and attempt to keep the patient happy and satisfied.

TOP 10 COMPLAINTS

1. "How much longer do I have to wait? Don't you people know how to schedule?"

Avoid this response: *"It's not us! We can't predict patients with emergencies, but we get them all the time, and they have to be seen! Besides that, patients come in with more problems than they tell us, and that backs us up even more. I always have to wait when I go to MY doctor too!"*

Suggested scripted response: *"I understand your frustration, and I apologize, Mrs. Jones. We do appreciate your patience. We do the best we can to keep our day on schedule. Sometimes we get emergencies or are presented with unexpected conditions that require immediate care. While these interrupt our flow and disrupt our schedule, it's critical that we address them. I hope you know that we would do the same for you. What we can do is reschedule you* *for the first morning appointment next time to avoid any potential backup caused by these situations."*

Commentary:

1. Apologize; express your concern and the value of your patients' time, and take responsibility for what happened. Never place blame on "them" or "they," whether they are patients, the doctor, or the other staff.

2. It's important that you empathize with your patients and not test their patience. Using the same lame excuse (e.g., "We had an emergency") wears thin if overused. If you HAVE a lot of emergencies, make allowances for them in your schedule.

3. For the most part, patients expect to wait short periods of time. It's the consistent or prolonged lateness and a lack of communication or knowledge of your policies that aggravates them.

4. Triage patients; schedule enough time to treat ALL their conditions.

5. Don't make comparisons with other offices; instead, be the exception.

6. Most importantly, if you *repeatedly* run late, stop trying to put a bandage on the problem and *fix it!*

2. "Why did you take him/her first? I've been waiting here longer than he/she has!"

Avoid this response: *"Yes, I know, but her appointment was before yours."*

Suggested scripted response: *"Yes, I realize that, Mr. Smith. Do you realize that you arrived early for your appointment? We make every effort to take patients according to their scheduled appointments; not based on when they walk in. You are always welcome to come in early and relax; and if we can see you then, of course we will. Thank you for your patience. I'll be calling you in very shortly."*

Commentary:

1. Avoid confrontation altogether by verbally acknowledging to the patient who arrives earlier than his or her scheduled appointment **at the time the patient arrives**, so there is no misinterpretation of your actions.

2. There are only a few instances where you can justify taking a patient who walks in earlier than another when in fact his or her appointment is later (and none of them excuses keeping a patient who arrived on time waiting):

- You had a cancellation, and a patient arrives in time to fill the opening in the schedule;
- You have an empty room, and the doctor is standing in the back waiting anxiously for the next patient to arrive; or
- You can begin prepping the patient in a special room reserved for him or her without interrupting the schedule.

3. "All I came for is to have this simple issue looked at. Why do I need to fill out all this paperwork?"

Avoid this response: *"First, it's our policy; but secondly, if you don't do it, we won't get paid by your insurance company."*

Suggested scripted response: *"I know it seems like the paperwork is irrelevant, Mrs. Jones, but it actually plays a major role in the quality care that we provide. You see, the body is like a machine, and our goal is to make sure it operates at top performance. As part of your professional health team, we understand that it's in your best interest to provide a comprehensive health history so we can make sure everything remains in excellent working order. Getting small symptoms checked now may prevent large problems later."*

Commentary:
1. Focus on what's important for the patient; not what's in it for you!
2. Responses should be about providing quality care and working as a professional team with all the patient's medical specialists, as opposed to "the insurance company requires it" or "it's our policy."

4. "Why do I have to see the nurse practitioner or the physician's assistant and not the doctor?"

Avoid this response: *"The doctor is too busy to see everyone. That's why we had to get someone in to help. If you don't like the new physician's assistant/nurse practitioner, we'll reschedule you to see the doctor, but that means you'll have to wait a long time for another appointment!"*

Suggested scripted response: *"Mr. Smith, you should know that the doctor would only choose someone to take care of our patients who is professionally trained and fully qualified. Our nurse practitioner/physician's assistant is an excellent care provider, and I'm confident you will like him/her. The doctor has asked us to schedule you with him/her this time to allow you to be seen* *quickly with suitable time for your condition. Afterwards, they will discuss your care. If you ever feel you need to see Dr. Brown, he/she will be here for you. Either way, you will be well taken care of!"*

Commentary:

1. A consistent approach by all team members is essential.
2. Communicate! Most issues are resolved if patients are aware of who is seeing them as opposed to feeling "shuffled off" to another (unfamiliar) practitioner without their knowledge.

5. "Why do I have to come in the office to review the test results? Can't you just give me the results over the phone?"

Avoid this response: *"No, we can't. The doctor needs to see you."*

Suggested scripted response: *"Only the doctor is qualified to evaluate the results. It's important that we schedule an appointment so that he/she has the proper amount of time to review and explain the findings. I assure you, you will have a much clearer understanding that way. I can offer the next available opening."*

Commentary:

1. Offer an explanation . . . don't just say no.
2. If patients don't understand *why* it's important for them to be present, they will just assume that you want (and may even accuse you of wanting) to give them the appointment to get another copay/office visit out of them.

6. "I didn't know I needed a referral. What's the big deal? Why can't the doctor just see me, and you can get the referral later?"

Avoid this response: *"The big deal is sometimes we can't get one after we've already treated you, and then we can't bill you either. Besides, it's not our job to get the referral; it's yours. If you don't have a referral with you, you can't be seen today."*

Suggested scripted response: *"We are not allowed to see you without a referral, Mrs. Jones. If we do, we are breaking the rules of your insurance contract, and the insurance company will hold you responsible for the payment. We don't want to see that happen to you."*

Commentary:

1. Make your conversation patient interest-based; in their best interest—not the receptionist's interest.
2. While it's not necessarily your "job" to get the referral, assisting your patients (if need be) the first time around can be interpreted as good customer service.
3. An educated patient is a more compliant patient, so use this time to also educate and instruct your patients in the importance of knowing their insurance benefits so your good deed does not become an expected habit.

7. "Oh, you can fit me in; I'll only be five minutes!"

Avoid this response: *"Are you kidding [laughing]? Nothing takes our doctor five minutes. Besides, he/she will start talking to you, and that's how our schedule gets backed up!"*

Suggested scripted response: *"Mr. Smith, while it seems that only five minutes are necessary, Dr. Brown is very thorough. In order to give you the quality care you deserve and have come to expect from him/her, it would be best to make an appointment that allows for an adequate examination. [Offer first available appointment.]*

Commentary:

1. Don't relinquish control of the schedule.
2. Refrain from remarks such as, "It's *never* just five minutes!"
3. Don't make fun of or blame the patient for asking.
4. Don't disrespect (especially *voice* disrespect) for the doctor.

8. "I am a personal friend of the doctor's. I'm sure he/she would say to put me on the schedule today."

Avoid this response: *"Everyone thinks they're a personal friend of the doctor, and then I get in trouble when I try to squeeze them into the schedule. I'll tell you what: let me put you in for [date and time], and I'll try to call you when we get a cancellation. OK?"*

Suggested scripted response: *"As a personal friend, I'm sure the doctor will want to spend quality time with you. The best opportunity for that would be an appointment on [date and time], and I will be happy to call you if we* *have a change in the schedule before that. What is the best number where I can reach you?"*

Commentary:
1. Validate their importance.
2. Always offer to get them in sooner if there is a change in the schedule.
3. Never say, "... when we get a *cancellation* ..." Better to say, "... if there is a change in the schedule."
4. Replace "can't" and "try" with more positive words like "can" and "will."

9A. "Sorry I'm late." (first offense)

Avoid this response: *"No problem. Have a seat. We'll be right with you."* or *"Well, now you have to wait!"*

Suggested scripted response: *"Yes, I see that. Is everything OK? Let me take a look at the schedule and see if we can still take you today, Mrs. Jones. As a result, you may have to wait. Would that work, or would you prefer to be rescheduled? In the future, a preemptive call could possibly help us adjust our schedule to accommodate your lateness; otherwise, we will have to reschedule you."*

Commentary:
1. Don't lie. If you have no intentions of "being right with them," don't use the phrase loosely.
2. If possible, try to be accommodating to first offenders, but use this as an opportunity to educate your patients about your appointment policy—without actually using the word "policy."

9B. "Sorry I'm late." (repeat offender)

Avoid this response: *"No problem. Have a seat. We'll be right with you."* or *"Well, now you have to wait!"*

Suggested scripted response: *"I'm sorry, Mr. Smith, as previously advised, it will be necessary to reschedule your appointment."*

Commentary:
1. Be firm, but be polite.
2. Don't make threats; you will initiate confrontation. Chances are the reason patients keep coming late is because: (1) no one ever says anything to them; or (2) they know your office always runs late anyway.

3. Triage the patients' condition. Do they need to be seen immediately or can they wait?

4. Don't give them a choice by saying, "Can we reschedule you to another day?" Instead, take control, and offer them your first available date and time.

10. "You people have a lot of nerve sending me a bill. I'm not paying it, and you can tell that to the doctor."

Avoid this response: *"You had the services, didn't you? This bill is your responsibility!"*

Suggested scripted response: *"I see that you were billed, and I'd like to try to understand more about it so I can help you. I'd like to review your account. Would it be possible for me to call you back in about an hour?"*

Commentary:

1. Don't try to match wits, and don't be defensive. It's not about *you*. Your offer to help will put things on a better track; and taking an hour breather will give you time to research the details while the patients have a chance to calm down.

2. If you say you're going to do something, be sure you *do it*, or you will jeopardize your credibility and that of the practice.

3. If you can't help them, find someone who can.

4. Refrain from starting sentences with "you"; they sound accusatory.

CONCLUSION

There isn't a practice that doesn't have front desk issues and problems with patients. Many of these problems are associated with monetary complaints. It is vital to the success of the practice that the receptionist resolves the problems with the patient at the point of interaction, which is at the front desk. Using some of the scripts suggested in this article will help you successfully resolve these potentially cataclysmic situations.

REFERENCE

1. An PG, Rabatin JS, Manwell LB, Linzer L, Brown RL, Schwartz, MD, for the MEMO Investigators. Burden of difficult encounters in primary care: data from the Minimizing Error, Maximizing Outcomes Study. *Arch Intern Med.* 2009;169:410-414.

Is Your Glass Half Full or Half Empty? Your Decision May Impact Your Practice

NEIL BAUM, MD, AND LYNN HOMISAK

How you view the level of the liquid in the glass is up to you. You can blame your circumstances on bad luck, or you can see the situation as an opportunity to improve your station in life and make the stumbling blocks stepping stones to success. Abraham Lincoln lost six consecutive elections before being elected as the 16th President of the United States. He didn't see the obstacles that included depression, loss of a child, and marital discord as a blind end. He saw what mistakes were made and what he needed to do to improve his electability.

The same is true with a medical practice. You can approach insurance companies for contract negotiations and get rejected multiple times. Those rejections may mean only that the insurance companies don't have accurate data and history to make a decision in your favor. Don't take multiple rejections personally. Rather, reassess your situation, and take steps to change the offering to make it more attractive. Seeing the glass as half full will make all the difference and make it more likely that you will achieve the outcome you desire.

Take-home message: You can point your finger and blame others but remember that when you point a finger at others, three fingers are pointing back at you. You have to take responsibility for the situation, see the glass as half full, and make the changes necessary to achieve your objectives. See obstacles as stepping stones instead of stumbling blocks.

THE GLASS IS HALF FULL

Those who see the glass as half full have made every effort to remove all negativity from their lives. If you want to have a half-full glass, you must divest yourself of all negative people who are not encouraging and enabling your success.

For example, if you have lunch with a group of doctors who are complaining and talking about how terrible their practices are, you can be sure their negativity will spill over into your life and your practice. We suggest that you make every effort to avoid these doctors who are sucking the fluid out of your glass. Surrounding yourself with like-minded physicians and others who are positive is likely to improve your attitude about your own glass.

Take-home message: Having negativity in your life prevents you from living and achieving a truly positive existence.

Look for the positive in every aspect of your life. Remember in every person and in every situation, there is something good. If you look for it, you will find it.

For example, if you have to terminate a dishonest employee, consider all the circumstances of that situation, and find something positive about the event. Examine what happened when this person was hired and what signs you might have missed that would have revealed problematic conduct. When unusual behaviors were noted by staff members, did you take action, did you listen to their comments or advice, will you learn from this experience? This simple exercise could improve your surveillance and oversight so you can recognize these signs earlier the next time.

Take-home message: There is almost always a silver lining to be seen in every event and with every person. Look for it, and your glass will appear half full.

THE GLASS IS HALF EMPTY

If an optimist sees the glass as half full and a pessimist sees the very same glass as half empty, it's not really about *what is*; rather, it is about the *perception* of what is. More specifically, it's about attitude; the feeling or psychological response, based on genetics and life experiences, that motivates us to place importance (or unimportance) on things. Some might question whether or not seeing the glass half full or half empty really has any bearing on our outlook in life or does it mean (as the late George Carlin once said), "We just need a bigger glass!"? And what does this all have to do with management, anyway?

Silver linings can be seen if we choose to look for them. But how do you convince a pessimist to make those choices? Unfortunately, the outlook of pessimists does not include silver linings, and their "misery over hope" preference affects not only their lives, but also the lives of everyone around them.

For example, assume that both an optimist and a pessimist receive a substantial wage increase. The optimist rejoices and views this raise as a recognition of and reward for his or her hard work. The optimist expresses happiness and is motivated to strive to do even better. The pessimist, when given this same wage increase, turns it into a self-made nightmare. Instead of feeling rewarded, the pessimist thinks, "Great; now they'll expect me to work harder!" or "Great; now I suppose I'll have to wait *another* two years to get another raise!" or "Great; now everyone will scrutinize me because I got a raise and they didn't!" The pessimist creates and wallows in his or her own cesspool, and there is just no pleasing him or her.

Pessimists will always try to drag you down into the proverbial quicksand because misery loves company. According to the law of attraction, like energy attracts like energy, so as positive as we like to think we are, there are many times we get sucked into a pessimist's negativity just by being around this type of person. Luckily though, this theory applies to both good *and* bad energy. And if you recognize that, then you can better deal with (or minimize) negativity by "acting" as opposed to "reacting." Instead of letting pessimists drag you in or leaving them there to drown in their own pessimism, reach down to grab their hand and help pull them up. Often, these individuals don't even realize that what they say or do affects others in a negative way, so it's okay to point out to them that their actions are making you feel negative, as long as you focus on the behavior, not on the person.

Take-home message: People who continue to "think" negative, will always "see" things as negative unless there is a more predominant force that can shrink that pessimistic attitude and help those individuals see their world in a different light.

Focusing on the negative is a choice, and that is probably what American writer and clergyman Charles R. Swindoll thought when he was quoted as saying, "Life is 10% what happens to you and 90% how you react to it."[1] As human beings, we are given the ability to choose, which is what separates us from animals.

For example, you wake up to a beautiful sunny day. Your coffee is perfect. Your cereal is snap-crackle-and-popping. There's no traffic on the way to the office. And when you arrive, your staff greets you with a big smile. You are thankful to have a full day of patients on your schedule and think to yourself, "Life is good!" Then it happens. As your team prepares for a productive day by reviewing the schedule, almost immediately, everyone's eyes focus on the 4:00 PM slot to find that it is occupied by none other than the complaining, exasperating, never-can-please-her Mrs. Stormcloud. Can you relate?

You can sense from the grimaces, loss of focus, and mood swing in the room that the dance of anticipation has begun before she even arrives. Attention suddenly shifts from the 39 lovely, appreciative, positive patients on the schedule (who staff members know will shower them with compliments, appreciation, gifts of homemade goodies, and smiles) to the one negative patient who will find fault with every aspect of her office visit. The dreaded patient is not due until the end of the day, and yet, the staff members will carry the negativity with them all day long. It's hard to imagine that *one* negative has the power to outweigh 39 positives, but it does—if we *choose* to allow it. The same way we *choose* to see the proverbial glass half empty instead of half full.

"The Story of the Two Wolves" is one told to a young Cherokee boy by his grandfather about a battle that goes on inside us all. "One wolf," he said, "is evil. It is anger, envy, jealousy, sorrow, regret, greed, arrogance, self-pity, guilt, resentment, inferiority, lies, false pride, superiority, and ego. The other is good. It is joy, peace, love, hope, serenity, humility, kindness, benevolence, empathy, generosity, truth, compassion, and faith." The grandson thought about it for a minute and then asked his grandfather, "Which wolf wins?" The old Cherokee simply replied, "The one you feed."[2]

This point is frequently emphasized (by LH) during her presentations as she shows the audience a white piece of paper with a one-inch-diameter black dot in the middle. She asks the audience members what they see. Some of the responses include, "a black dot," "dark, black hole," or "black circle." Rarely will anyone say they see the white paper. I think this comes as no surprise because the color black usually carries with it a negative connotation (blacklist, black humor, black plague), and it is especially prominent when contrasted with white, which represents goodness and purity.

Take-home message: If you feed negativity, it will continue to grow. Although human nature can sometimes lead us to focus on the black negatives in our lives, when we do so we neglect to see, and thus miss out on, the positives.

Is your office environment negative? As a doctor, if you were to come into contact with a patient whose symptoms suggest a staph infection, you'd want to immediately take action by treating it with appropriate antibiotics to either stop the bacteria or at least prevent it from worsening. You'd do this because you know that it's highly contagious, and it spreads quickly. Yet when similar symptoms surrounding your own version of "staff" present in the medical office, many times they go undetected, undiagnosed, and, sadly, untreated! It's because the latter infection is developmental, and the TLC that it requires cannot be written on a prescription pad or filled by a pharmacy.

Jen, for example, works in a medical office and has been there for more than 10 years. She complains to everyone that her job is boring and hard. She is caught all too often staring at her watch, counting down the minutes until she leaves. And then, finally, it's Friday at 5:00 PM. Her coworkers know it's the moment she's been waiting for, so they smile and wish her a happy weekend. She leaves them not wearing a smile, but a frown. 'What's the problem, Jen?" one asks. "Isn't this what you waited for all week?" Before she can even stop to appreciate the moment, Jen responds, "Yeah, but only two more days, then it's back to the rat race!" Why is Jen so anxious to leave work? Is it because she is unhappy there?

Psychologists and researchers from around the world have all concluded that happy workers are productive workers.[3] While you are not expected to *make* your employees happy, as their leader your role is to help create an environment that *allows* them to be both happy and satisfied. Staff members look to you to set the tone; it starts at the top. If you walk in like Debbie or Donald Downer, it transfers to them and to your patients.

Take-home message: If you want to be inspired by your staff, your doctors, or your colleagues, be their inspiration. Complement your own attitude by surrounding yourself with like-minded personalities and people who think as you do, and you will have created an environment that you are most comfortable in. At the same time, learn to be accepting of others by understanding that not everyone will see the glass or life at the same level, but that difference is not necessarily wrong. As different as people are, so are attitudes.

The reality is that doctors have a choice and can face a set of circumstances and situations that can be interpreted as either positive or negative. We are reminded of a story of a shoe manufacturer who sent a salesman to Australia to sell shoes to the Aborigines. After a very short period of time, the salesman returned and told the boss, "Not a chance to sell shoes in Australia; as none of the Aborigines wear shoes!" The owner of the company sent another salesman, who was known for his optimism, and he returned and reported to his boss with excitement and enthusiasm, saying, "Boss, what a great opportunity we have in Australia; none of the Aborigines wear shoes! All I have to do is tell them how comfortable the shoes will feel, how nice they will look on their feet, and how they will prevent diseases and infections of the feet." Three questions to ask:

1. Which one of the two salesmen is likely to sell more shoes or any other product he is asked to promote and sell?
2. Which one would you hire if you were in human resources or were looking for a partner and you had a chance to hire the optimist or the pessimist?
3. Most importantly, which one are you?

Are you seeing the glass as half full or half empty? The choice is up to you. You can see the decrease in reimbursements, the increasing overhead costs that impact most practices, and the increase in competition coming from complementary and alternative medicine as a problem or an opportunity. We can assure you that if you see these situations as opportunities, you are likely to find creative ways to improve the situation and perform the equivalent selling more shoes to the Aborigines.

Finally, remember attitudes are contagious. Make sure yours is worth catching.

REFERENCES

1. Good Reads. Charles R. Swindoll Quotes. http://www.goodreads.com/author/quotes/5139. Charles_R_Swindoll.
2. First People—The Legends. www.firstpeople.us/FP-Html-Legends/TwoWolves-Cherokee. html.
3. Williams RB. Are Happy Workers More Productive? Success.bz. www.success.bz/articles/2429/are_happy_workers_more_productive.

————————— **CHAPTER 24 BONUS FEATURE** —————————

FIVE ADDITIONAL TIPS FOR MANAGING/ COMBATING/MINIMIZING NEGATIVITY AT WORK

1. Show genuine appreciation for tasks that are performed well. In fact, spread the compliments around fairly and generously to all staff members. We always like to encourage doctors and managers to put four quarters in their left pocket each morning as a reminder. Every time they give a compliment to someone, they can move one quarter from their left pocket to their right. At the end of the day, all four quarters should be in their right pocket. Soon, compliments will freely roll off your tongue, and you won't need the quarters to remind you!

2. Don't automatically reject ideas presented by employees and/or coworkers. Allow and *encourage* their input for the betterment of the workplace. Giving them the opportunity to take part in decision-making policies will provide them with a sense of belonging and ownership in their work.

3. Set up a "negativity shield" by addressing any signs of low morale, gossip, low performance, and unacceptable behavior immediately before it has a chance to fester or spread. Taking this approach may send a message to others that "positive only" vibes are allowed.

4. End all staff meetings on a high note by having everyone share one nice thing (about a coworker, their job, a particularly pleasant patient, something complimentary that a patient said, or an unexpected gift received) so that everyone leaves the meeting feeling "up!"

5. We are all human, and we all have good and bad days, but try to recognize when you yourself are the one spreading (or contributing to) the negative feelings. Be aware of your words, actions, tone, body language, and defense mechanisms. Take a time out and don't give in or "react" to your own negative thoughts. Others will mirror your behavior.

CHAPTER 25

Managing the Chronically Late Patient

NEIL BAUM, MD

"I'm late! I'm late! For a very important date!"
—*The White Rabbit, Alice's Adventures in Wonderland, Lewis Carroll*

Lewis Carroll wrote about the tardiness of the White Rabbit in *Alice's Adventures in Wonderland* in 1865. The problem of tardiness is older than the White Rabbit, and lack of punctuality plagues every profession and human interaction. Unfortunately, in the medical profession, patients who arrive late for appointments cost the practice not only in lost productivity but also in deterioration of staff morale. Solving the problem is usually within your grasp, and no practice has to tolerate the chronically late patient.

CREATE AN OFFICE POLICY REGARDING LATENESS

The practice should establish a concise, written policy regarding arriving late for appointments. It should clearly state the position of the office and the physicians. The policy should advise patients to arrive early to complete their paperwork or to complete the paperwork online to facilitate their office visit. Patients should be told that if they arrive late—and state a reasonable time such as 30 to 45 minutes—that they will be seen at the end of the day or will have to reschedule their appointment.

IT STARTS AT THE TOP

There is no hope of having patients arrive on time for their appointments if the doctor is chronically late. "As ye sow, so shall ye reap" (*Galatians VI*). That biblical saying also applies to doctors. You can't expect patients to be on time if the doctor is chronically late. The doctor has to set the example for the staff and patients. You have to make a commitment to be an on-time physician before you can demand that patients also arrive on time.

If you are chronically late, identify the issues and problems that affect your arrival in the office on time. For example, if delays in making rounds first thing in the morning routinely make you run 15 minutes late for clinic patients, then you will need to start 15 to 20 minutes earlier at the hospital. You can also determine what time to start rounds by looking at your hospital list and making a conservative estimate of how long rounds will take. Give yourself a cushion of 10 to 15 minutes so that you arrive at the office early instead of late.

Announce to your patients that you are committed to being an on-time physician. Post a notice in the reception area informing patients the doctor is making every effort to see them on time, and would like to request that patients arrive a few minutes *before* their designated appointment so they can check in and be taken to the exam room in order to be seen on time.

Also, if you running late despite your best efforts, it is a nice courtesy to have the receptionist announce the delay to the patients in the reception area, and give them the option of waiting or rescheduling.

OVERBOOKING: A NO-NO

I don't suggest overbooking as a solution to dealing with chronically late patients. If everyone shows up on time, this will result in significant delays in seeing your patients. This is not a desirable situation and can tarnish your reputation.

LISTEN TO THE EXPLANATION OF THE DELAY

Many patients have an explanation for their delay, and it behooves the front office staff to listen to the reason—it just may be legitimate. For example, if an older patient is dependent upon a family member to bring him or her to the office, you can't hold that against the patient. It then becomes necessary to have a discussion with the family member who is doing the driving. Certainly, the patient who is usually on time should be given some consideration for the occasional lateness.

However, you don't need to see chronically late patients when they arrive late for their appointment. They can be moved to the end of the line or seen at the end of the day. A chronically late patient should not be put ahead of a patient who arrived on time. This is a disservice to the patients who are on time.

HAVE A "FACTS OF LIFE DISCUSSION"

When I encounter a chronically late patient, a conversation takes place between the receptionist or the office manager and the patient that goes something like this:

Receptionist: You were scheduled for 2:15, and it is now 3:15. Is there a reason for the delay?

Patient: I got caught in traffic.

Receptionist: Let me ask you a question. If you had an airline ticket for a flight from New Orleans to Atlanta, and the flight left at 2:15, what time would you arrive at the gate for the departing flight?

Patient: Probably 2:00 or 2:05.

Receptionist: We are no different than the airlines. We make every effort to see patients on time, and we expect that you are going to be on time. When you come late as you have on multiple occasions, you are taking the time slot of a patient, and that slot can't be filled when you are late. As a result, you have left a vacant appointment slot that could have been filled by someone else if you would have let us know about the delay.

Patient: I'm sorry. I will try to be on time next visit.

Receptionist: We have no option but to see you at the end of the day or reschedule your appointment. If you make any future appointments, we will schedule you as the last appointment of the day so there will not be a problem filling your time slot if you are late. If the problem continues, the doctor will have no other option but to ask you to find another physician to take care of you.

CHARGE THE PATIENT

Charging patients a fee for being late has been tried for decades without success. It is very difficult to collect these fees and certainly will antagonize the patients. Giving patients a warning that they will not be seen or will be moved to the end of the schedule if they are late is enough of a penalty and can prevent patients from being repeatedly late.

If you decide to charge a patient, it is necessary to inform the patient of the late charge before you can levy the fine. Often, merely posting a notice in the reception area about charging patients if they are late encourages them to be on time.

DISCHARGING THE CHRONICALLY LATE PATIENT

The chronically late patient demonstrates a lack of respect for the physician and the practice's time. This becomes an expense and a liability to your practice. After a patient is late two or three times, you might give the patient appointments only at the end of the day. If the violations continue, then sending a letter suggesting that the patient obtain his or her healthcare elsewhere is certainly appropriate. In most states, you have to give the patient two to four weeks to find another physician and provide the patient with a copy of his or her medical records.

Bottom Line: Doctors need to be efficient and productive. We cannot tolerate patients being chronically late, which creates problems for the staff and for patients who arrive on time. Developing and implementing a policy regarding lateness goes a long way to solving the problem of the chronically late patient.

CHAPTER 26

Productivity Improvement: Three Steps to Move from 25% to 90% Productivity

Jon A. Hultman, DPM, MBA, CVA, and Neil Baum, MD

PRODUCTIVITY MEASUREMENT USING RELATIVE VALUE UNITS

Today, the most common productivity measure being used to compare physician productivity is the number of work relative value units (wRVUs) generated. The advantage of this method is that determination of wRVUs is independent of dollar amounts generated and is unaffected by collections. Although the wRVU method is not perfect, it enables a comparison among physicians of: (1) the relative times they require to perform a service; (2) the technical skills and the physical effort expended by each physician; and (3) a cognitive effort score as determined by each doctor's management of complex diagnoses. Using wRVUs, two physicians who provide the same services over the same time period would generate the same number of RVUs, regardless of fee schedules, type of insurance, or collections. These wRVU factors, along with operational costs, will be used to determine the multiple for converting wRVU productivity to compensation. Operational costs are the key reason that compensation of two equally productive doctors may vary from clinic to clinic.

Using measurements produced by the Medical Group Management Association (MGMA) for comparing the productivity of two physicians on its database—one in the 25th percentile of productivity and the other in the 90th percentile—we find the former to be generating 4848 wRVUs, whereas the latter is generating 8682 wRVUs. In other words, the doctor in the 90th percentile is almost twice as productive as the one in the 25th. Because of such differentials, two physicians with the same education and

165

training who are working in the same clinic could be receiving significantly different levels of compensation.

Comparing wRVUs from the lowest to the highest on various databases, we have seen productivity numbers vary from a low of 1700 to a high of 14,000. Those physicians generating 14,000 wRVUs seem to be almost superstars to those who generate far less. Although some factors impacting individual productivity may be related to inherent skills or "gifts" possessed by individual doctors and might be difficult for others to duplicate, upon seeing the size of this range, one is likely to ask, "What can make one doctor so much more productive than another?"

Many tools can be used to increase productivity. The good news is that most of these can be learned and are under a doctor's control. The bad news is that these tools are not easy to implement—if they were, every doctor would be utilizing them, and the wide range of productivity would narrow. Measuring productivity will remain relevant in the future regardless of insurance type, payment model, or practice type due to the predicted physician shortage, increased demand from an aging population, and the emphasis on patient access to healthcare. Even "pay-for-quality" models are aided by increased productivity: many of the factors that improve productivity also improve quality because they simplify processes and reduce the number of errors.

PRODUCTIVITY ENHANCEMENT

Let us examine a few ways to improve productivity, with an understanding that all will require additional learning.

Efficiency

The most effective way to improve productivity is through efficiency, which is focused on improvement of the workflow employed in a practice's operational and communication processes. Few doctors understand what "efficiency" actually is. They do not recognize the amount of time wasted by inefficient workflows—those that employ numerous tasks and handoffs performed in "traditional," series processes. Workflow studies show that staff or doctors are "waiting for something" or are performing unnecessary "extra" tasks more than 50% of the time.

For example, a patient who has had testing performed by Dr. A is then referred to Dr. B, a specialist. To avoid duplication of services and additional costs, the specialist wants to review the tests previously performed. When the patient arrives in the specialist's office without the reports or the disks with results of the testing, it could take 30 to 45 minutes to obtain a signed consent for release of records, contact the referring physician's office, and wait for a phone call or a fax of the report. However, if the patient had been informed when he or she initially called for an appointment that the visit would be expedited if he or she obtained copies of the studies and any subsequent report and brought them to the office at the time of the first visit, this simple step alone could save several hours of wasted staff and physician time.

This type of inefficiency results in an incredible amount of lost time that not only reduces productivity, but necessitates additional staff—which, in turn, increases costs without increasing productivity.

Physician Extenders

Equally effective is the use of "physician extenders" to leverage a doctor's productive time. As with the use of efficiency principles, extenders enable a physician's tasks to be performed in parallel. The presence of physician extenders is one of the reasons that the productivity of doctors working in large groups typically is significantly greater than that of those practicing solo or in small groups.

For example, one of us (NHB) uses a scribe. This is one of the most effective methods to enhance the efficiency of any medical practice. The scribe shadows the physician and takes notes either in the electronic chart or by hand. Another benefit of the scribe is that the doctor no longer has to input data into the electronic medical record (EMR), thus freeing the doctor to have more face-to-face contact with the patient.

Technology

The effective use of technology can improve the workflow of every process, whereas ineffective employment of technology can do exactly the opposite. One key area to focus on is avoiding input errors—that is, the ones at the front end of processes. Finding and fixing these errors at a later time is far more costly than putting a plan in place that continuously reduces errors from the beginning of the patient encounter. This means, for example, the patient has a current insurance information card and the receptionist accurately inputs the information into the EMR. This also applies to accurate

CPT and ICD-10 coding. A mistake of one letter, number, or period can result in denials and costly delays in receiving reimbursements.

Another technology productivity booster is the use of patient portals. Patient portals can reduce the number of staff necessary in the business office, creating an opportunity to shift more staff to the clinical area—the place where care is actually delivered. Simple things, such as the opportunity for patients to access their own lab results, send messages, request prescription refills, or schedule appointments on their own, substantially improves efficiency, because all of these tasks typically interrupt doctors and staff and require a great deal of their time. When these portals are put in place, not only are costs and patient waiting times lowered, but quality is higher. One way to imagine the long-term advantage of this tool is to compare booking a flight online versus booking one as it was done 20 years ago (e.g., through a travel agent). Today, a customer can compare prices, book a flight, select a seat, and print out a ticket—all without speaking to a person or waiting in line. Similarly, when a patient in a medical practice books an appointment by phone, checks in at the front desk, fills out forms, and asks questions upon arrival, the process is slow and tedious. These and dozens of other tasks can be handled much more efficiently using modern technology to reengineer workflow in ways that make the tasks both more convenient for patients and less time-consuming for staff.

Although there are more ways one could improve productivity, the three listed above offer the opportunity to easily move a physician from the 25th productivity percentile to the 90th. These three methods of improvement are also interrelated: efficient processes and the effective use of technology enable a shifting of staff from business to clinical areas, and this, along with utilization of physician extenders, who spread greater volume over the same fixed costs, have a direct impact on productivity as well as quality of care and service.

Bottom Line: Times have changed, for both the clinical aspect of healthcare and the financial and business aspects of managing a practice. Nearly all employed physicians are going to be evaluated and compensated on the basis of their productivity. Using these three techniques can significantly enhance your wRVUs, your productivity, and even your compensation. So if you are going to continue to work, you must continue to enhance your productivity. You and your practice will be glad you did.

CHAPTER 27

Strategic Planning: A Practical Primer for the Healthcare Provider: Part I

Neil Baum, MD, Erich N. Brockmann, PhD, and Kenneth J. Lacho, PhD

Entrepreneurs are primarily concerned with recognizing profitable opportunities and seizing the initiative to take advantage of that opportunity.[1] Once seized, success without competition is relatively easy. However, success breeds competitors and requires a different skill set for further survival and ultimate economic success. To survive in today's fast-changing healthcare environment, the primary care physician needs management skills in addition to entrepreneurial skills already held.[2] This article provides primary care physicians with a practical primer to strategic management. We present the strategic management process using a fictional private medical practice located in an urban environment.

PURPOSE

Entrepreneurs pour their hearts and souls into new ventures for years hoping for that elusive pay-off.[3] Perhaps they have heard of strategic management but haven't really had time to pursue it as a process. Few know much about strategic management, and fewer still have ever participated in the process. And unlike in larger organizations that may have strategic management departments, the onus for everything in smaller, start-up organizations falls to the owner/manager/physician.

Therein lies the purpose of this article—to remove some of the mystery associated with strategic management. And we hope we'll be able to provide some practical guidance toward taking the next step in managing an ongoing business. A summary of the strategic planning process and a list of suggestions for conducting the process are provided. We think you will find that the process is pretty much common sense and easier to accomplish than originally perceived.

The importance of strategic management to a business can be summed up with the old saying, "If you don't know where you are going, any road will take you there." Prudent use of the information contained in this article will help ensure that you and your company will find the road to success and will continue to follow it year after year.

THE STRATEGIC MANAGEMENT PROCESS

Your first step in learning the strategic management process should be to put yourself at ease. Although the term "strategic management" invokes a grandiose technique that may seem larger than life, it is, in fact, little more than an exercise in proactive time management. It's all about how to achieve what's important when faced with conflicting demands and limited resources. Second, don't get caught up in the hype of strategic management. Too many organizations go through the motions but lose sight of the intent. These companies are ridiculed in mainstream culture such as in the Dilbert comic strip—often, when you want a plan bad enough, you get a bad plan. Remember that the intent of strategic management is to set up your company for future success.

Planning is the first phase of strategic management, followed by the implementation phase. We concentrate on the planning process here by showing how things *should* progress while giving some practical examples.

Mission

Your mission is your starting point. Just as important as knowing where you are going, you need to know where you are starting from—where you are today.[4] A good mission statement provides an introduction to your company and tells readers what you're doing and how you're conducting business. Clearly state your company's name, location, major product/service offering, major customer(s), and source of competitive advantage. Think of yourself trying to answer the following questions: Why am I in business? What am I doing? How am I going to make any money?

For illustration, assume a fictitious single physician, Dr. Smith, who opened his own general practice, The Smith Clinic. Smith provides general clinical services in an urban downtown office and provides surgical procedures in a major hospital located across the street from his practice. A good mission statement would be:

> The Smith Clinic provides a nonthreatening, comfortable setting for patients in the uptown area who desire preventative and acute treatment of medical discomfort or concerns. We will see you at your scheduled appointment time or quickly as a walk-in. By the time you leave our office, you will know what you need to do to address your condition. If further treatment is necessary, it will be arranged prior to your departure. Our success rests on our ability to provide all patients with accurate and timely diagnoses and treatments better than our competitors.

After reading this mission statement, one can easily picture what the business does. It would be difficult to develop a similar understanding if the mission was simply "To make money" or "Keep people healthy." In a capitalist economy, it's a goal of most businesses to make money. The issue at hand is to structure and position your company so that it has the best possibility to make more money than the competitors.

Vision

Once you have defined the current state of your business with your mission statement, you then need to define where you're going. Your destination will be described in your vision statement. We can all remember President John F. Kennedy's vision of "A man on the moon by the end of the decade" and Martin Luther King's vision of "I have a dream." Both are simple yet extremely powerful.

A good vision statement need not be as powerful as those above, but it should be useful. The business's vision statement should paint a clear picture of the company in the distant future—one that can easily be visualized. In general, vision development should be easy for an entrepreneur. After all, the vision is simply a representation of the opportunity that was recognized and led to the formation of the business in the first place.

A vision is often less defined than the mission and more goal-oriented. Visions provide a unifying motivation for the organization. The time frame is flexible, but three to five years is a reasonable goal. A good vision should inspire and motivate everyone at the company. Building on Smith's example, a decent vision could be, "When experiencing or even thinking about medical concerns, The Smith Clinic is the first choice that comes to a mind for how to answer questions quickly and accurately." This vision provides sufficient direction for managers at Smith's to use when setting priorities.

Now that we know where we are (i.e., the mission) and where we want to go (i.e., the vision), it's time for a reality check. The owner/manager needs to evaluate his or her company relative to competitors to see what needs to be done to make sure that the company will reach the desired future. This issue is addressed in the next part of the process and has two steps. We start by looking inside the business with an *internal* evaluation of what the company has and then look outside at the *external* environment to see how the company compares to competitors in ways that are useful in attracting customers (i.e., be competitive).

Internal Evaluation

Internal evaluation involves some serious soul-searching. You need to look around and take inventory of everything that you have at your disposal. Put yourself in Smith's shoes, and the inventory should include everything he has: people, buildings, desks, chairs, waiting rooms, examination rooms, consultation rooms, computers for electronic health records, and so on—these are resources. Now look at what's being done with those resources: greeting patients, registering patients, examining patients, maintaining records, consulting, cleaning, and sterilizing—these are activities.

The internal evaluation process should provide a very detailed description of the business—what it has and what it does. The more detail the better. In fact, the soul-searching session will be more effective if you can remain objective and refrain from assigning adjectives during this identification phase. To illustrate by building on Smith's example, one resource could be the clinic's address/location. Although the location may be a reason for success (e.g., ease of access, close to hospital, good parking), avoid any claims of "prime" location for the moment. Simply list everything; the list will be pared down and prioritized later.

Smith's resources would include: a physician with credentials from a particular medical institute; two nurses; a receptionist; 100 square feet each for a waiting area and two examination rooms (each with appropriate medical instruments and a computer with Internet access); a combination consulting space and general office for the owner; a lease on the property; and so on. Smith's activities would include: meeting and greeting patients; making appointments; examining patients; running tests; documenting results; communicating results to patients; preparing the examining room for the next patient; disposing of waste; paying the employees; paying the bills; and so forth.

The more detail you can provide, the better—because you have to evaluate each of these activities to see where you rank relative to competitors. We want to find out what Smith does better than his competitors. Furthermore, why should potential patients choose Smith over Brown, Jones, or Williams? This is the question we want to answer next, and the more activities we have in our description, the more options we have in our next step—external evaluation.

Bottom Line: Every practice, regardless of size, location, or specialty, needs to create a strategic plan. Getting started requires creating a mission, followed by creating a vision. In Part II, we will connect the internal analysis to the external analysis and show how everything fits together into your strategic plan.

REFERENCES

1. Baron RA, Ensley MD. Opportunity recognition as the detection of meaning patterns: evidence from comparisons of novice and experienced entrepreneurs. *Management Science.* 2006;52:1331-1334.
2. Ireland RD. 2007. Strategy vs. entrepreneurship. *Strategic Entrepreneurship Journal.* 2007; 1(1-2):7-10.
3. Mitchell RK, Busenitz L, Lant T, McDougall PP, Morse EA, Smith JB. Toward a theory of entrepreneurial cognition: rethinking the people side of entrepreneurship research. *Entrepreneurship: Theory & Practice.* 2002;27:93.
4. Ireland D, Hitt MA. Mission statements: importance, challenge. *Business Horizons.* 1992;35:34.

Strategic Planning: A Practical Primer for the Healthcare Provider: Part II

EXTERNAL EVALUATION—THE COMPETITORS

You need to identify your niche in the medical marketplace; this is what distinguishes you from all the competitors who are fighting for the same group of patients (i.e., the target market).[1] Your practice's intent should be to attract those patients instead of allowing them to freely seek out your competitors; this is critical to your practice's success. Simply put, you need to determine what the patients want. You then need to perform those internal practice activities that provide the bases for what the patients want, and you need to do so better than your competitors.

You will have to rely on marketing research to identify what your target patients want and how they decide whom to choose among various competitors. In Dr. Smith's target market, for example, the potential patients for all four competitors come from occupants of the office buildings in the central business district; this is consistent with his mission statement described in Part I of this article. Let's say that Smith hired a consultant to survey the potential patients to see what criteria they use when deciding where to address any medical concerns. The consultant identified three factors: easy access from the central business district; rapid diagnosis and correction of conditions; and minimization of return visits. Smith, who is familiar with the area around his clinic, identified three other medical clinics that might be able to satisfy those criteria: Brown's, Jones', and Williams'.

The task at hand is to make sure that Smith is able to provide at least one of the above three factors better than the other three clinics can. In other words, Smith wants to make sure he has a competitive advantage. Therefore, we need to evaluate each of Smith's activities relative to the corresponding activities of the other three competitors. The initial intent is to see which activities Smith's clinic performs better (i.e., its strengths) and where Smith's clinic does not perform as well (i.e., its weaknesses) relative to his competitors' performance. This comparison provides us with a common denominator against which we can make meaningful and valid comparisons.

We can now revisit Smith's activities and see if, and where, he has a competitive advantage. Recall that the patients' first decision criterion was convenience. After evaluating his location relative to those of the three competitors, Smith can see if more potential patients are within a three-block radius of his clinic than of the other clinics. Smith needs to come up with objective measures for defining "rapid diagnosis and correction of conditions," the second criterion. The third criterion, minimum need for return visits, might require an objective evaluator to examine the need for return visits.

Due to space constraints, we have limited our coverage of competitive advantage here. To be really useful, you should evaluate all of your activities against very specific measurement criteria in order to see where you rank relative to your competitors or industry standard.[2] You may find other areas that are not necessarily linked to the competitive advantage but where you need to improve your practice, such as reducing costs.

Our focus now shifts to longer-term considerations. What else is going on around your company that you haven't considered yet? How will those events change the way you are conducting the business in the long term?

OTHER EXTERNAL CONSIDERATIONS

Certain elements in the healthcare environment must be considered, because they will affect the general practitioner or primary care provider. One obvious element is the recently enacted Affordable Care Act (ACA). The near future will see testing of the ACA.[3] The ACA is not only about increasing healthcare coverage, but also about the way healthcare is delivered.[4] There are additional external elements to consider as well.

Technology is increasingly enabling care to be conducted over great distances between the patient and the doctor. Videoconferencing through webcams on laptops and mobile devices means that patients can interact with their medical providers over the Internet. Self-monitoring devices will make it easier for patients to monitor their own vital signs, monitor their blood glucose and cholesterol levels, and report their readings without having to physically make a visit to a healthcare provider.[5]

Patients will be encouraged to take better care of themselves (e.g., lose weight, quit smoking). Healthcare coaches provided by healthcare providers will be used to manage chronic medical problems.[4] Also there will be more emphasis on healthy living at the job site. Company-sponsored wellness programs are expected to increase.[3]

Structural changes will occur as consolidation of providers continues. Health systems and hospitals will continue to expand. Many medical groups, such as hospital health systems and physicians' practices, will merge or be acquired.[6] Development of urgent care centers and the provision of basic medical needs (e.g., shots) at retail drug chains and "big box" stores is going to continue. Legislation attempting to expand the scope of practice by such medical providers as dentists, nurse practitioners, physician assistants, optometrists, and others has been watered down or killed in many state legislatures.[7]

This brief description of the healthcare external environment reflects the transformation of healthcare in the United States. In this fast-changing environment, the primary care physician will have to monitor the changes and make strategic adjustments.

Now let's illustrate the impact of these environmental changes. Smith is not immune to changing regulations; these changes affect potential revenue and, therefore, profit. Smith is faced with two choices: (1) he can raise the prices for other services not directly affected by reimbursement rates; or (2) he can simply absorb cost increases and reduce his profit. In Smith's marketing research report, he should have noted that "price/insurance" was not one of the major decision criteria on the part of potential patients. Therefore, Smith could raise prices to compensate for increased costs without losing too many patients. Of course, there is some price level at which the other criteria will start to play less of a role; this needs to be considered during the marketing research process.

In general, we refer to external factors that can have a positive impact on practices as *opportunities* and the negative ones as *threats*. Because these opportunities and threats affect all medical practices, your practice's specific competitive advantage should allow you to benefit more than your competitors when all are faced with the same circumstances. Similarly, you should lose fewer patients than your competitors when all of you are faced with the same threat.

For instance, the aging population in general, together with the likelihood that people will work longer, affects general practitioners and primary care physicians. On the positive side (from Smith's perspective), increased age also increases susceptibility to illness and injury. A clinic that provides appropriate services quickly and efficiently will enjoy a correspondingly higher demand than one without such efficiency. On the negative side, corporate downsizings have reduced the total population of potential patients in the target area. However, since Smith enjoys a higher demand than the competitors, he will most likely lose fewer patients than the other three.

The evaluation of the general environment is the least well defined area in strategic management. Doctors and office managers must exercise creativity and be insightful in order to notice changes. In fact, it would really help if doctors could predict the future. However, since that's impossible, your next best bet is to stay alert to what's going on around you by scanning the environment. By paying close attention to such media, you become more sensitive to changes. Although you will not be able to actually predict a change, you may be able to notice subtle changes before your competitors. You can then take action before anyone else and give yourself a competitive edge.

PUTTING IT ALL TOGETHER IN A PLAN

It is now time to put these pieces together into a coherent and comprehensive strategic plan. The theme in any strategic plan is to fit all the pieces together. Ask yourself the following questions and then develop a to-do list of objectives that will set your company up for future success:

- Do I have sufficient resources to accomplish my current mission and achieve my future vision?
- Do I have sufficient strengths to ensure that I remain competitive?
- Do I have too many weaknesses such that they will overwhelm any advantages I may have?
- Are there enough opportunities and not too many threats such that I can achieve my future vision?

If you can answer "yes" to all of these questions, then your strategic management priority is to simply monitor the situation and note if anything changes. If you answer "no" to any of the questions, then you need to establish a detailed action list to correct the situation. Based on your understanding of where each of the pieces fit into the bigger picture, you can develop an action plan to correct the situation.

REACHING THE IMPLEMENTATION PHASE

Actually accomplishing the necessary tasks is the basis for the second phase of strategic management, the implementation phase. But until the necessary actions are identified, the plan can't be carried out. It is easy to see that strategic management is a philosophy or way of thinking and not simply a quick fix, as most want.

All too often we hear about putting out the fires, crisis management, and being reactive versus proactive. We "know" that we should plan; it's just too easy not to plan. Now that you have read this primer, we hope that you have a better understanding of the practical application of strategic management tools. Even more, we hope that you recognize how naturally strategic management fits with a commonsense perspective of running an ongoing business. Finally, combining an understanding that one should plan with the planning structure that strategic management provides, we hope that many will embrace the strategic management philosophy and enjoy a resulting positive influence on their bottom lines.

Bottom line: Strategic management is all about positioning your company relative to your competitors so that your performance will be better than theirs. This process is accomplished through discrete but interconnected steps where you identify resources and activities. You then compare your activities against your competitors' activities to see whose are better; these become strengths for the owner. Your strengths that correspond to what the customers want become your competitive advantage. You then use your competitive advantage, in the face of changing environmental conditions, to out-perform your competitors.

REFERENCES

1. Porter M. *Competitive Strategy: Techniques for Analyzing Industries and Competitors.* New York: Free Press; 1980.

2. Barney JB. *Gaining and Sustaining Competitive Advantage.* Reading, MA: Addison-Wesley; 1997.

3. KBM Group. Top 10 healthcare trends, 2014. KBM Health Services.http://content.kbmg.com/download/TOP_10_Healthcare_Trends_2014_Whitepaper.pdf.

4. DeVore S. The changing health care world: trends to watch in 2014. *Health Affairs Blog.* February 10, 2014. http://healthaffairs.org/blog/2014/02/10/the-changing-health-care-world-trends-to-watch-in-2014/. Retrieved 7/10/2014.

5. Hewlett-Packard Development Company. Top 5 healthcare technology trends for 2014. www8.hp.com/us/en/campaigns/healthcare/articles/2014-tech-trends.html. Retrieved 7/10/2014.

6. Valentine S. Top 10 healthcare trends to watch in 2014. January 2014. www.thecamdengroup.com/thought-leadership/top-ten/10-healthcare-trends-to-watch-in-2014/

7. Sanner A. Newly insured to deepen primary case doctor gap. The Advocate Baton Rouge, LA. June 23, 2013. http://the advocate.com/home/6323359-12 newly-insured-to-deepen-primary. Retrieved 6/23/2013.

CHAPTER 28

A Roadmap for Strategic Planning in the Healthcare Practice

ALLISON FRY, MBA, AND NEIL BAUM, MD

Medical practices and hospitals can survive without a strategy, but that is about all they can do. They will be like the proverbial duck that appears calm on the surface of the water, but, in reality, those practices and hospitals that lack a strategy will be paddling like hell underneath the water to remain afloat. Without a strategy, hospitals and practices will struggle to remain profitable or survive over the long term. In the United States, that's why hospitals are being bought out or even closing.[1] The same applies to medical practices that are being acquired by hospitals or are merging with other practices within the community. With a well-crafted, clear strategy, which is effectively communicated to all members of the practice or team, and then carefully implemented, the likelihood of success, profitability, and enjoyment from the healthcare profession is dramatically increased. Let us be clear, however: the process is not easy, and it does require considerable time, energy, and effort to successfully carry it out.

WHAT IS STRATEGY?

Strategy is a framework within which the choices about the nature and direction of the practice or hospital are made. It is the boundaries that determine what lies inside or outside the practice's or hospital's priorities. It is strategy that defines what services will be offered to patients in the medical practice and what services or products the hospital will offer to patients and doctors who use the facility. The strategy will define what patients the practice is going to attract and what payers they are or are not going to accept. The strategy also may prioritize geographic areas that the practice or hospital will focus on, such as what zip codes to market their services to. The strategic plan also defines the direction in which the practice or hospital is headed and how it might maintain an existing course or strike out in a new direction.

GATHERING INTELLIGENCE

Strong strategic planning is grounded in research, ensuring that the resulting direction is well-informed. To get started, it is important to create strategic questions that will guide the planning process in order to focus the data gathering. These questions will be high-level and will address fundamental decisions that will have to be made, such as "Should we expand our geographic footprint, and if so, where?" Other strategic questions may address services offered, the financial model, operations, growth, or other big issues facing the practice or hospital.

The data-gathering phase begins internally, by looking at information such as the practice's financial statements, patient base, operational metrics, services offered, and patient and satisfaction metrics, among others. It is important to look at both a current snapshot of the organization's status and trends over the past five years. Then dig into the details of any trend that stands out to in order to understand the key drivers. For example, if the profit margin has been decreasing over the past five years, is that decline due to the revenue side or overhead costs? If it is on the revenue side, is it due to decreased reimbursement rates, decreased productivity from practitioners due to an operations bottleneck (leading to fewer patients seen), or something else? Understanding the past trajectory of the practice and its current strengths and weaknesses is a key starting point for making sound decisions about the future.

At the same time, external intelligence is also critical. This includes data such as demographic changes in the geographic footprint of the practice, long-term trends in the healthcare system, and the competitive landscape. When analyzing the competitive landscape, it is important to consider organizations that may not seem immediately relevant, but that may provide an alternative for patients in some way. For example, a large practice may not consider the new "minute clinics" a competitor, but patients may go there for certain quick services, in which case the large practice would need to take these clinics into consideration in making decisions for the future. On the one hand, those quick services may be areas in which it is strategic to vie for the patients because it brings them into the office for other higher-paying services. On the other hand, these may be lower-priority services, and the large practice might do better by focusing on other services where it has a unique advantage. Looking at market share trends over time can also help inform where the competition may be gaining ground. External data can inform the opportunities and threats facing the practice in the future.

Once the key challenges facing the practice or hospital have emerged, it can also be useful to gather intelligence from other practices or hospitals that have been through these challenges to learn from best practices or mistakes. While direct competitors often do not want to share competitive information, there often are a few analogous organizations, either serving a different set of patients or located in other geographic areas, that may be able to offer insight. Additionally, when there are other practices or hospitals with whom the practice collaborates and which would benefit from stronger practices themselves, these organizations are also often willing to share their perspectives.

STRATEGY FORMULATION

The insights garnered from the intelligence-gathering phase are used to craft a strategic direction for the organization. Start by setting three to five key strategic goals. These goals may be offensive or defensive in nature, depending on the strengths, weaknesses, opportunities, and threats identified. For example, if the practice sees unmet need in its area, perhaps expanding its presence and increasing its market share in that specific area is a goal. However, if the market is saturated in its current area, perhaps expanding to new geographic areas is a goal. Or if a host of new competitors have emerged and patients have been leaving, perhaps a goal is to improve patient satisfaction. Retaining a customer generally consumes significantly fewer resources than acquiring a new one.

After setting the key, high-level goals, the next step is constructing directed initiatives that will enable the practice to achieve those goals. In response to the first example—increasing market share within the current area—perhaps the demographics are shifting, which is creating an opportunity to serve an entirely new segment of the market. If this is the case, an initiative may be to target certain populations as a means of acquiring new patients. If an inadequate number of exam rooms is revealed to be the cause of a bottleneck that is hindering practitioners' ability to see more patients, perhaps physical building expansion is a goal. For the second example—patients have been leaving the practice—understanding why patients have been dissatisfied can help guide appropriate initiatives. Are patients concerned about the quality of care? Or do they simply go somewhere else because it is more convenient or they feel more comfortable speaking a different language? Initiatives should have a specified timeline, which is sequenced based on any contingencies—that is, initiatives that must be completed before another can begin—and then prioritized based on maximum effectiveness at minimum cost.

Constructing a plan that is simple and easy to follow allows everyone in the practice to prioritize decisions and resource utilization to ensure the whole practice or hospital is moving in the same direction. In this way, strategic plans not only tell a practice what to do going forward, but also create boundaries, eliminating potential directions that may be a distraction from the core strategy.

PLANNING PROCESS

The strategic plan must be supported by the budget, including both revenue generation and expenses. On the revenue side, the strategic planning process can help the practice understand where the best opportunities for revenue lie and target those areas. This could take the form of addressing payers or rates, or targeting a different mix of clients based on their typical payers, or even targeting different services that have higher profitability rates than others. Whatever the goal, the revenue projections should reflect these priorities and should show an anticipated shift over time.

Resource allocation often is the place where tough decisions must be made. Because strategic planning eliminates some activities that are not a priority, costs may need to be cut in some areas to reallocate those resources to a new priority area. For example, if the plan is to target a new patient demographic, more resources may be needed in marketing. It is important to create a budget for each initiative, detailing the costs and timeline. Then incorporate these costs into the current budget, shifting resources from lower-priority areas to where they are needed to accomplish the strategic plan.

For a strategic plan to be successful, the plan and the budget—including both revenue targets and resource allocation—must be in alignment.

STRATEGY IMPLEMENTATION

The key to implementation is accountability. Even if everyone in the practice understands the strategic goals, if a decision is based on the goals but goes against personal incentives, staff will likely not make the strategic decision. Therefore, it is important to look at financial and personal (e.g., time or effort it takes to do something, efficiency) incentives to make decisions and adjust them to be in alignment with the new strategic plan.

It is also important to assign accountability for completion of a specific initiative to one person. That point person is responsible for ensuring that his or her specific initiative is accomplished on time and on budget. When accountability is assigned to a team, it can muddy the waters; so, if a team is responsible, appoint one team leader who is ultimately accountable.

Finally, for implementation to succeed throughout the practice or hospital, the plan must be communicated at all levels, and leaders within the practice must model how to act in line with the plan. What is expected of each team member must be made clear. It is then important to have everyone agree to the plan and agree to their role in seeing the strategic plan implemented.

MONITORING, REVIEWING, AND UPDATING THE PLAN

The purpose of planning is not just to create a strategic plan, but to accomplish the objectives. One way to know whether you have achieved your plan is to measure performance. Creating solid measures is just as important as developing a performance scorecard. Measures must include quantifiable performance statements.

Some of the different types of measures to consider for your strategic plan include the following:

- **Efficiency measures:** Efficiency measures include productivity and cost effectiveness, measured as ratio of outputs per inputs. Examples of efficiency measures might be how long patients wait in the reception area on average before being taken to the exam room, or how long patients wait to be seen by the doctor.
- **Outcome measures:** Outcome measures are the end result of whether services meet proposed targets or standards. They demonstrate impact and

benefit of activities. One example would be the percentage of patients who use the nutritionist in the practice and have achieved their ideal weight.

- **Quality measures:** Quality measures gauge the effectiveness of expectations and generally show trends in accuracy, reliability, courtesy, competence, responsiveness, and compliance. Examples of quality measures include the number of patient "redo's" after surgery within a specified time period, or the average number of days a patient waits to obtain an appointment for an urgent versus a routine appointment.
- **Project measures:** Project measures show progress against an initiative that has a deadline. The measure is usually stated as the percentage complete.

Sometimes the measures are obvious, such as:

- Number of new patients;
- Number of procedures performed on a monthly basis;
- Percentage of patients discharged from the hospital that have to readmitted within 90 days;
- Percentage improvement in patient satisfaction surveys;
- Percentage of claims denied by insurance companies;
- Percent reduction in employee turnover; and
- Percent reduction in account receivables (particularly in those accounts that are more than 120 days old, because those are not likely to be collectable).

Other times, the measures are less obvious, such as calculating a return on investment (ROI). This can be done in advance by looking at the budget and understanding how much an initiative is expected to cost and then calculating either how much additional revenue or cost savings are expected. The ROI is then calculated as the gain from the investment, minus the cost of investment, divided by the difference in the cost of investment. For example, if a marketing plan is expected to cost $10,000 and bring in an additional $30,000 in revenue from a new target audience over the next three years, the ROI is calculated as:

$$\frac{\$30,000 - \$10,000}{\$10,000} = 2$$

In this scenario the expected ROI is 2× over three years, and the practice or hospital can measure its progress on this initiative by comparing it with this expected rate. ROIs can also be useful to help prioritize initiatives; those initiatives with higher ROIs can be sequenced before initiatives with lower ROIs.

SUMMARY

Strategic planning in healthcare is essential for successful operations, expansions, and profitability. Shifts and changes in the healthcare industry affect virtually every sector, including private medical practices, hospital outpatient clinics, acute care or outpatient emergency centers, urgent care centers, and long-term-care facilities. In order to succeed, it is critical to have a strategic plan. A successful strategic plan allows physicians and other leaders to establish a roadmap for the future and gives those involved in caring for patients a direction to follow. It can also breathe new life and energy into organizations that have been like that proverbial duck, paddling like hell to make ends meet.

REFERENCE

1. Obamacare Forcing Rural Hospitals to Close. Newsmax.com. March 15, 2015. www.newsmax.com/Newsfront/obamacare-rural-hospitals-close/2015/03/15/id/630246/. Accessed July 7, 2016.

CHAPTER 29

Managing Pitfalls and Potholes of Medical Practices

KEN GOLDBERG, MD, DAVID F. MOBLEY, MD,
AND NEIL BAUM, MD

Doctors are not perfect, and problems are likely to occur. Our success, enjoyment of our profession, and even keeping burnout at bay depend on how we mange those potholes and pitfalls that will certainly come our way.

This article discusses six of the potholes and pitfalls that nearly every practice will experience at some time. The authors have a total of more than 120 years of experience in both private practice and academic practice and have enjoyed nearly every one of those years. We have, for the most part, successfully navigated our way through the potholes and pitfalls that have come our way. We wish to pass along our experience to you, and of course we welcome your own management suggestions for these obstacles that we all encounter at one time or another.

UNHAPPY PATIENT

If you recognize that a patient is not happy, either by his or her demeanor or from feedback from the nursing staff, it is possible to rescue the visit. If the patient is, indeed, unhappy, he or she should be returned to an examination room to discuss the problem, which may be all that is needed to ameliorate the situation. If another room, such as your private office, is available to discuss the issue, this can often be a better option than revisiting the exam room.

The key is to identify the issue or the problem. Most often, it is the result of poor communication; maybe it was a problem that was not identified or addressed. It certainly could have to do with the patient's expectation as to what he or she anticipated from the visit and the reality of what was experienced.

It is reasonable to offer an apology and ask, "How can I make this right?" In many cases it is something simple, such as not receiving a return call they expected. In such situations let them know you agree (if you do) and that you and your staff will do all possible to avoid such adverse events in the future. It is important to document what occurred in the patient's record. Some options that can go a long way to improve how the patient feels include waiving the fee for the visit, or offering a refund of the copay. Other options include asking the patient to return at no charge when there is more time, offer free follow-up appointments, or even provide some sample medication. Finally, let the referring doctor know that the patient was not happy with the experience in your office, and include your efforts to rectify the issues with the patient.

As with so much in medicine, prevention can be the key. At the close of each visit ask the patient in words to the effect, "Do we have a plan?" or "Does what I'm recommending make sense to you?" This way the patient has the opportunity to express their understanding and agreement—the "last word," so to speak.

REFERRING PROVIDER ERROR

Referring physicians often are not specialists in your field and may lack your particular expertise. They may not have performed the best study or prescribed the optimal medication. Their diagnosis may not be correct. It is important *not* to make disparaging comments about the care rendered by referring doctors, denigrate them, or offer to explain their reasons or actions. Sometimes the issue can be something as simple as not having the necessary documents to provide a diagnosis or plan. If appropriate, inform the referring physician about the encounter.

WHEN THERE IS A POTENTIAL FOR LITIGATION

A complication or a possibility of litigation needs to be identified in an honest but factual manner. Offer no excuses—but an explanation of what occurred, with an apology, is appropriate. It is important to be empathetic, caring, and available to respond to their concerns. It is imperative to document the conversation. Do not, under any circumstance, alter the medical records. It is important to notify the malpractice carrier. In the case of a significant issue, such as a complication, it is important not to refund or pay any medical bills without consulting an attorney.

THE DRUG-SEEKING PATIENT

As physicians, we are particularly aware of the extent of the problems of drug usage, drug abuse, drug overdosing, and drug-related deaths in the United States. The annual number of U.S. drug-related deaths currently exceeds 70,000. Opioids and benzodiazepines, as well as stimulants such as amphetamines, are the major sources of inappropriate drug use.[1]

Most physicians will encounter drug-seeking patients. Emergency departments (EDs) are reported to be a particularly vulnerable point of entry for these individuals, because many make repeated visits to the ED, often at many different hospitals. The physicians and nurses in EDs need to be able to recognize and identify drug-seeking patients by paying attention to the following:

- Requesting medications by generic or trade name, and often claiming that all other medications in the class fail to help or that the patient has severe side effects or other allergic reactions to the other medications;
- A questionable and vague medical history;
- Pain levels ("Doctor, it's an 11 on a 1 to 10 scale!") out of proportion to the physical findings, lab tests, or imaging studies;
- A history of "doctor shopping" or seeing multiple other physicians for the same problem, with no one able to discern a diagnosis;
- Excessive criticism of previous physicians;
- Manipulative and aggressive behavior;
- Chronically missing appointments;
- Requiring refills before the refill is due;
- Repeatedly coming to clinic without an appointment;
- Excessive flattery;
- Excessive or unnecessary phone calls;
- Trying to contact the "on-call" physician to prescribe the desired medication when the prescribing physician has declined to refill the medication;
- Requesting increasing dosages of medications;
- Unwillingness to consider alternative therapies;
- Claims of lost medications;
- Being more concerned and interested in the drug than in the condition for which the drug is allegedly being prescribed;
- Deteriorating home, school, or work life;
- Family discord; or
- Mild to moderate depression.

When we are faced with a drug-seeking patient, it is very important to obtain a careful history and perform an examination and testing as indicated. While obtaining the history, identify when the patient's medication needs started, what were the circumstances, was surgery involved, what medications have been used, and what was the patient's response to the medication? Did the patient try to stop taking the medication? What happened when the patient attempted discontinuing the drugs?

When a patient requests a medication with abuse potential, it often is appropriate to inform the patient that the medication is not indicated, or that you simply don't prescribe these medications. It is appropriate to recommend alternatives and to consider appropriate referrals to a pain management specialist.

In some situations, contacting the authorities may be appropriate. Depending on the situation, building security or even local police should be contacted. The U.S. Department of Justice has an online reporting form on their website.[2]

In an office practice with more than one physician, it is important to alert the other physicians and their staffs that a known drug abuser may try to contact them after hours and that you advise not filling requested prescriptions from such individuals. It is important that careful documentation of all encounters be performed, not only to provide an appropriate record of all discussions, but in case the patient should become litigious.

Drug-seeking patients are very common in most communities, and careful management with sensitivity and compassion is of paramount importance.

DIFFICULT PATIENT

Some patients start their encounter with a negative bias toward physicians and medicine in general. All of us in the healthcare profession have had the experience of interacting with a difficult patient. It doesn't matter if you are a pathologist, plastic surgeon, pediatrician, or primary care physician, you will have the experience of managing the difficult patient. Fortunately, difficult patients make up only a small percentage of the patients that we care for. Doctors report that about one in six patients are "difficult." That translates into potentially three or four difficult patients each day.[3]

Unfortunately, few of us have had any formal training on how to manage a difficult patient. It is something we have learned, or maybe not learned, by trial and error. Often, errors associated with managing a difficult patient can lead to undesirable consequences, complications, and even litigation.

First, most patients in the healthcare setting, such as in our offices or in the hospital, are out of their comfort zone. Even the most self-confident patient, when placed in a situation of uncertainty, may become uncomfortable, anxious, and even hostile when he or she does not know what to expect. The best way to avoid creating a difficult patient is to always explain what examinations and tests you plan to perform. This relieves the patient's anxiety and can make the patient much more mentally comfortable when confronted with a medical test, procedure, or diagnosis with an unfavorable prognosis.

Second, patients often are in a stressful situation. Remember, what is commonplace to each of us is probably a first-time experience for our patients. Take, for example, the history and physical examination. Patients will be required to reveal personal secrets and issues that they wouldn't share with their partners, best friends, or clergyman. Then they will commonly get undressed just a few minutes after meeting the doctor, put on a gown that seldom covers the entire body, and then be probed in areas of the body that have never been touched or explored before by another person.

Finally, health issues and fear of the unknown lower a person's threshold for anger, potentially precipitating a conflict and making the patient a management problem. Therefore, it is imperative that all of us in the healthcare profession, which includes receptionists, office managers, file clerks, and insurance and billing agents, as well as the doctors, nurses, and physician assistants, to be aware of the potential for patients to become anxious, uncomfortable, and psychologically disoriented in the medical environment.

Just as there are signs and symptoms associated with various diseases and conditions, there are signs that you may have or may create a difficult patient. First, listen carefully to the tone of voice. If the patient is speaking louder than expected or more rapidly than usual, then the provider must modulate and speak more slowly and softly. Watch the patient's body language. Look for signs of agitation such as wringing of the hands or tapping of the feet, which is a sign of impatience. Clenched fists and clenched teeth are signs that you are dealing with a difficult patient.

A patient who is in a defensive position, such as sitting with crossed arms, often will provide clues about the intense conversation that is about to take place. Pay attention to the breathing pattern. A restricted breathing pattern or sighing is an indication that the patient is upset.

Another warning sign of a potentially difficult patient is the doctor-shopper. If a patient has seen multiple physicians for the same complaint, just plan on spending more time with this patient. If a patient with this history is rushed, plan on having a difficult patient and poor patient satisfaction scores!

Allow the patient to complete his or her explanation of the medical problem without any interruption. During the average patient encounter, the physician often interrupts the patient after only 16 seconds![4] Make every effort to remain focused, listen to the patient, and do not interrupt until the patient is finished talking.

If possible, try to have your discussion with a difficult patient in a private location where it cannot be overheard by others in the office. Escort the difficult patient from the exam room to another secure location in the office so that you can talk in private and without interruption. If you can, sit next to the patient in order to avoid any barriers, including physical ones, separating you and your patient.

ABUSIVE PATIENT

We've all been there: the patient is rude, is demeaning, or even says sexually explicit things to you or to a staff member. What do you do when the patient crosses the line?

There are often explanations for abusive behavior by patients. Sometimes when a patient is in pain or has just learned of an ominous diagnosis, he or she may lash out at those who are helping them. On other occasions, this behavior may be caused by a medical illness, a psychiatric illness, or drug withdrawal. It may be a spontaneous or automatic response when a patient is out of his or her comfort zone. Although that may be how they're instinctively dealing with something, it does not make it acceptable. They may just need a little firm, but respectful, reminder that there are better ways to deal with difficult situations.

As a physician, you are still obligated to provide care for the patient. Most patients will cease the abusive behavior once you have drawn the line and requested to be treated more respectfully.

Although most abusive patients can be managed with the cease-and-desist approach just described, there are circumstances where additional responses are required. If, for example, a patient is cursing, threatening, or disrupting the care of other patients in the office, it is time to call security and have the patient escorted from the premises. On the rare occasion when patients hear that you are requesting security, they receive the message and their behavior takes an about-face and the behavior becomes quickly more civil.

Finally, if a patient is a repeat offender and not likely to change his or her behavior, then it is appropriate to terminate the patient from the practice. This consists of sending the patient a certified letter stating that the doctors in the practice will no longer provide care for the patient. The patient usually is given 30 days to find another physician. The letter should clearly state that medical care will be given only for emergency care.

All healthcare workers are likely to encounter aggression and, on occasion, violence. Practice design and policies as well as staff training can help manage these uncommon events.

Bottom Line: Every practice and every doctor is going to encounter problems caring for patients. Although the majority of patients are appreciative and grateful for the care we provide, there are occasions where kid-glove management, tact, and firmness must be used.

REFERENCES

1. National Institute of Drug Abuse. www.drugabuse.gov/related-topics/trends-statistics/overdose-death-rates, January 2019
2. U. S. Department of Justice. Drug Enforcement Administration. Diversion Control Division. RX Abuse Online Reporting: Report Incident. https://apps.deadiversion.usdoj.gov/rxaor/spring/main?executione1s1
3. An PG, Rabatin JS, Manwell LB. Burden of difficult encounters in primary care: data from the Minimizing Error, Maximizing Outcomes Study. *Arch Intern Med.* 2009;169:410-414.
4. Groopman J. *How Doctors Think.* New York: Houghton Mifflin; 2007.

CHAPTER 30

Pinball Wizard or Bowling Alley Marketing

NEIL BAUM, MD

In the late 1900s and early 2000s, the standard way to create a website was to electronically convert your trifold, colored, patient brochure and put it up on the Internet. This type of website is no longer an effective method of marketing and promoting your practice.

Traditional marketing resembles bowling: a practice uses traditional marketing techniques (the bowling ball) to reach and influence patients (the pins) (Figure 1). Mass media (the bowling alley) function as mediators for marketing content. Medical marketers throw the ball as hard and straight as they can, in the hope that it will hit the target. But the marketing journey isn't a straight line anymore and neither should your marketing be. Marketing today is actually more like a game of pinball (Figure 2).

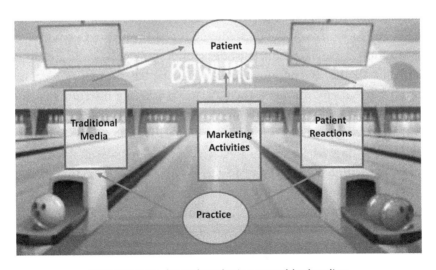

FIGURE 1. Traditional marketing resembles bowling.

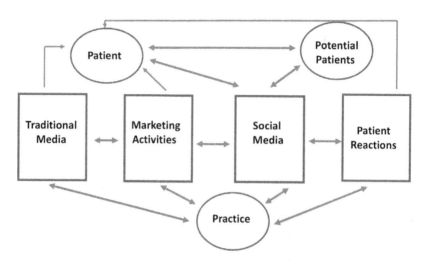

FIGURE 2. Marketing today is more like a game of pinball.

Social media has changed the picture. Marketing is now more closely aligned with a pinball machine. "Pinball marketing" is an environment in which marketing instruments (the balls) are used to reach patients (bumpers, kickers, and slingshots). In the new pinball environment, patients have much more control than they had in the old bowling alley atmosphere. Empowered patients receive regular messages and actively participate through social media by sharing their experiences with doctors and their practices. The "slingshots" and "bumpers" of social media further increase the unpredictability of the marketing dynamics by multiplying social media episodes and providing the basis for future pinball activities. To continue the pinball metaphor, the pinball machine is our current environment, the balls are marketing instruments, and the audience are the spinners, bumpers, and flipper bats that propel the ball away from the hole that ends the contact with that ball (Figure 2). Unlike bowling, where the "pins" had no power to make an impact, the audience in pinball marketing can actively take part, redirecting the ball or causing it to speed up, slow down, or even stop. But be careful not to shake the machine too vigorously or you will have the dreaded tilt message and your game will be terminated.

Since its introduction in 2006, Facebook has grown exponentially. By 2013, it was one of the top three websites, along with Google and YouTube. One out of seven persons on this planet is an active member of Facebook,[1] in spite of limitations to people under 13 years of age and the fact that it is not accessible in China, the world's most populous country.

This dramatic growth of social media has affected medical practices in ways we are just beginning to understand. This article offers an overview for those physicians and practices interested in digital marketing and how social media has changed the playing field between physicians and both existing and potential new patients.

We have to go where our markets are (e.g., email, Facebook, Twitter) and create relevant content, experiences, and platforms where they can engage with us.

As a marketer you can no longer simply roll a bowling ball and wait for it to hit your target—you must actively take part. You must interact with your existing patient or potential new patients. It is important to test multiple digital media options, run multiple campaigns, and measure those campaigns to see how audiences are responding to your content or your message. It is essential to identify what works and continue that marketing method, and also to find out what doesn't work and delete it from your marketing mix. The days of just having a webpage or a blog and considering that effective marketing are over. You must provide fresh content on a regular basis and you must have multiple social media outlets such as YouTube, Facebook, and Instagram.

Bowling is like playing American baseball or standing over a pot of water and watching it boil. Pinball, on the other hand, is played at high speed; you have to continually monitor and tweak the vast multimedia options, and you must take action based on your findings. But your job doesn't end after you've uploaded a new social media post or issued a new press release—you have to follow its course carefully, measure its impact, and then identify any trend or crisis.

If you don't move fast enough in pinball, you lose—and it's the same with healthcare marketing. Monitor your audience and be ready to respond to what attracts or deters your audience. There is a world full of potential patients who have access to social media platforms, where they can share both their positive and their negative experiences about a practice's services. Negative comments can quickly escalate into a crisis that threatens the success of the practice.

In this chaotic, interactive world, your marketing approach needs to move from bowling to pinball. This not only will help you recognize the increasing power of the consumer and embrace the cocreation of brand stories, but also will enable you to develop a deeper engagement with your market and your patients. When you see the value of a multichannel campaign and start understanding how each component complements the others, you will start to reach that top score!

If you are not connecting with your patients like a pinball player in this era of social media networking, then you will fail to connect to potential patients who may want to avail themselves of your services.

Your community of potential patients is the lifeblood of your social networking. It's essential to ensure that this community is full of potential patients who are actually interested in what you have to say or the services you wish to offer. You want to target those people in your community who are interested in you and your practice, not the fact that you friended them first and not the fact that you use a certain hashtag in your tweets. Those actions seldom result in new patients. One of the methods you can use to identify those targets is to consider psychographics.[2]

Psychographics focuses on the interests, attitudes, and emotions of a segment of potential patients—exactly the things practices need to understand to best promote their services to the particular segment of the population that the practice wishes to attract. To reach these ideal patients, you must know what or who they value most, where they get their medical education and medical information, and what content appeals to them.

Psychographics is like demographics on steroids. Psychographic information might include your patients' habits, hobbies, health-related experiences, and values. Demographics explain "who" your patient is, whereas psychographics explains "why" they become part of your practice.

Your message must be engaging to anyone who accesses your material. Your social media pipeline must be full of information that highlights the physicians and the practice. For example, if you write an article on your urinary incontinence program, and your title is "The Diagnosis and Treatment of Urinary Incontinence," that probably will not entice readers, even if they have incontinence, to read your article or to make an appointment with your urologic or gynecologic practice. However, a title such as "Urinary Incontinence—You Don't have to Depend on Depends!" is likely to attract readers to drill deeper into your message and perhaps contact your office, ask questions, ask for more information, and, hopefully, make an appointment. You are actually having an electronic conversation with a potential patient and you want to receive a response that starts the conversation. Remember that it's *social* media, and you must be social with it.

Today, in an Internet world and with social media having become ubiquitous, the bowling metaphor no longer fits. Now it's time to play pinball. Now medical practices release a "marketing ball" consisting of the practice brands and brand-building messages, which are then diverted or bounced around and often accelerated by social media "bumpers," which change the offering's course in chaotic ways. After the marketing ball is in play, those who are in charge of marketing and practice promotion attempt to guide the marketing with agile use of the "flippers," but, unfortunately, the ball does not always go where it is intended. Those who receive the marketing message now can respond, provide their opinion, decide to receive or reject the message, or ask for additional information. Also, potential patients can initiate their own discussion by bringing up topics that are important to them and look for the healthcare profession to respond. Marketing in the pinball era involves the player (the practice) launching the ball into play by feeding engaging and useful content into the game area, where it is moved around by those online. Occasionally, it will come back to us via email or through physician review sites that affect our online reputation. At this point, we can use the flippers to interact with patients and potential patients and pass the ball back into the social media sphere.

If our practice does not feed the social media sphere by flipping communications back, the ball will drop through the flippers, and the longer-term, two-way relationship between the patient and the practice will cease to exist.

Bottom Line: Practices have to start a conversation, listen to what the patients want, and then respond in a timely fashion. Medical practices have to learn how to maneuver the pinball in this new environment or the ball will slowly slide down between the flippers and be out of play—meaning the practice won't gain new patients or maintain the loyalty of existing patients.

REFERENCES

1. Hennig-Thurau T, Hofacker CF, Bloching B. Marketing the pinball way: understanding how social media change the generation of value for consumers and companies. *Journal of Interactive Marketing.* 2013;27:237-241.

2. Baum NH. Patient profiling using psychographics: demographics vs. psychographics and why culture matters most. *J Med Pract Manage.* 2020;35:234-236.

CHAPTER 31

Developing a One-Page Marketing Plan: Part I

Allan Dib and Neil Baum, MD

This article is the first of three parts on using the one-page marketing plan to enhance your practice's potential. This part discusses the Phase 1, the period before the patient actually enters your practice. Part II addresses Phase 2 of the one-page marketing plan, in which you receive leads from your marketing efforts, and shows you how to develop a system of follow-up and how to keep in touch with potential new patients. Part III will discuss how to create enthusiastic fans and how they help promote your practice.

Today, marketing in medical practices is ubiquitous. Who would ever have thought that great medical establishments such as the Mayo Clinic, Cleveland Clinic, and Kaiser Permanente would embark on marketing strategies for their institutions? Marketing aims to attract new patients to the practice and then provide them with a stellar patient experience, followed by establishing a system to keep the patient within the practice and make that patient into a raving fan. All of this can be accomplished using a one-page marketing plan.

Every profession, including healthcare, has a well-thought-out plan that is created, distributed to the staff, and followed meticulously. This is true in the airline industry, where pilots follow a flight plan, as well as in the military, when soldiers follow an operation plan. Marketing is not taught in medical school, and most physicians and office managers are clueless when it comes to marketing and practice promotions. We have seen many practices hire a marketing consultant who provides an assessment of the practice in a slick business plan that identifies the needs and wants for marketing the practice. This very expensive, multipage plan is put on a shelf and never looked at again and, more importantly, never implemented. The result is a waste of precious marketing dollars on a plan that doesn't work for the practice.

We suggest that if you create and follow a one-page marketing plan, you are likely to see more patients enter the practice as a result of this simple approach to medical marketing.

THE CIRCUS AND MARKETING

Historically, physicians have thought that marketing is just another word for advertising and requires an outlay of lots of money. Let's look, instead, at marketing as thinking about the circus coming to town. If the circus is coming to town and there is a sign saying, "Circus Coming to the Showground on Saturday," that is advertising. If the sign is on the back of an elephant that strolls into town, that's promotion. If the elephant walks through the town's flowerbed in front of City Hall and the newspaper writes a story about the debacle, that's publicity. However, if the mayor offers his observation of the elephant and laughs about the elephant, that's public relations. Now if the town's citizens show up at the circus and buy a ticket to see the show, that's sales!

The one-page marketing plan consists of nine elements, which are divided into three phases (Figure 1):

1. Identifying a target market and following up on any potential patients needing the services of the practice;
2. Providing the patients with educational materials before they enter the practice and have an outstanding experience; and
3. Ensuring that after the patients leave the practice they continue to return regularly, and, more importantly, become enthusiastic fans who tell others about the wonderful experience they had with the doctors and the practice.

Phase 1 is the period *before* the patient enters the service cycle. In Phase 1, the future patient doesn't know anything about you or your practice. If you can create an awareness of your practice, you have accomplished the first and very important part of the patient cycle. This phase is a magnet, or the "hook" that entices the patient to provide information about him- or herself and ensures that the patient will avail themselves of Phase 2 or when they become part of your practice.

During Phase 2, the potential patient becomes an actual patient and has their initial experience with the practice. If that experience is positive, the patient is likely to remain in the practice and will segue to Phase 3.

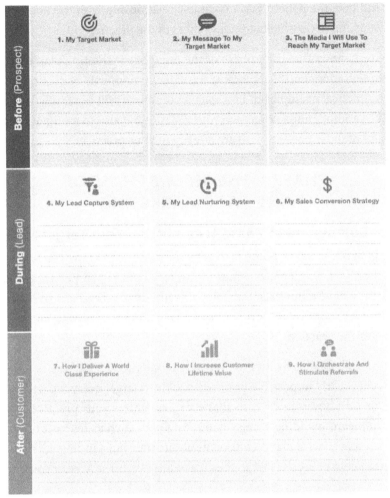

FIGURE 1. Marketing plan worksheet. Used with permission from SuccessWise and available at 1pmp.com.

Phase 3 begins after you and your practice have participated in the care of the patient and the patient has had a positive experience. You will want them to tell others about that positive experience. The patient has interacted with your staff from the time they made their initial phone call to the practice until the moment the doctor-patient encounter ends, they pay their bill, leave with educational material, and all of their questions have been answered. Your marketing has made promises of providing access to the practice, that timely follow-up will be achieved, and all of the patient's questions will be answered at the time of the visit. When those promises are fulfilled, the patient has a favorable relationship with the doctor and the staff and is very likely to refer others to the practice.

Figure 1 shows that each phase of the one-page marketing plan consists of three components. Let's look at the three components of the first phase with practical examples of how each component will hopefully lead not only to adding more patients to your practice but also to maintaining the loyalty of those patients who are already in your practice.

PHASE 1: THE *BEFORE* PHASE OF ONE-PAGE MARKETING

First Component of Phase 1: Identifying Your Target Market

The goal of the *before* phase is to get your patients to know you and your practice. When you create a message to reach out to prospective patients and they have demonstrated even a modicum of interest, you have to continue to connect with the prospective patient to motivate him or her to enter the practice.

This usually begins by identifying your target market. Let's be very honest—it is nearly impossible or unreasonable to target everyone with what you do and how you do it so that everyone enters your practice. Phase 1 also means avoiding a mass marketing plan such as television, radio, or newspaper with bland comments about your outstanding services, or claims about being the first in the area to offer such a service or treatment.

We suggest using the "PVP" approach to identify your ideal patient. This consists of *personal* enjoyment, *value* to the marketplace, and *profitability.*

Personal enjoyment is the enjoyment you have providing care for a certain type of patient. For example, if you are a primary care doctor, do you enjoy helping patients achieve their ideal weight and helping them with their diet, nutrition, and the use of supplements? If you are an orthopedic surgeon, you may have an interest in sports medicine and helping weekend warriors overcome the injuries incurred by middle-aged and senior patients who engage in sports. Another example is the urologist who offers treatment for middle-aged men who are experiencing difficulty with urination and erectile dysfunction. Each practice can find the area or niche that they enjoy, and identify a target market by doing so.

The value to the marketplace is the benefit of your service to your target market. For instance, if your target market is women with problems achieving pregnancy, you can be certain that your practice offers a very high value to the couple who are trying desperately to become pregnant.

Finally, you must determine the profitability of providing care and services for your target market. You want to avoid any target where the fees you charge are not worth the effort or the expense of your marketing programs. You want to avoid—at all costs—having a target market that is not profitable.

Next, you want to learn as much as possible about your target market. If your medical practice is dependent on referrals from other physicians, then you want to know as much as possible about your referring physicians. To this end, one of us (NB) has developed a simple worksheet called the "Baum 10" to learn the hot buttons of referring physicians (Figure 2). This brief survey of your existing and potential referring physicians can provide valuable insight into their practice and their private life.

Second Component of Phase 1: Crafting Your Message

The second component of the Phase 1 consists of crafting your message. Most marketing messages are boring, similar to all other messages, and ineffective. Most medical marketing doesn't address the needs and wants of the target market but instead lists platitudes that don't work to attract patients. Providing the practice logo and a laundry list of the diseases and conditions that are treated and the procedures that are performed is ineffective. We call this "me too" marketing that is likely the same as all the other practices in the community. So why are you wasting your precious time and dollars?

We recommend that you develop a unique service proposition (USP). What is it that makes you different and special and that distinguishes you from others who also are trying to attract the same kind of patients that you are reaching for? Let's look at the example of water—one of the most abundant commodities on earth. In contrast to many areas of the world, in our country, most tap water is free and safe to drink, yet millions of Americans are paying $1.69 or more for a liter of name-brand bottled water such as Evian, Fiji, or Smart Water. The price of bottled water is 20% more than the same volume of Budweiser beer, 40% more than the same volume of milk, and

The Baum 10

1. NAME_____ D.O.B._____

2. TELEPHONE NUMBER(W)_____ (H)_____

   FAX NUMBER:_____ E-MAIL:_____

3. ADDRESS (W)_____

      (H)_____

4. EDUCATION:_____

5. SPECIAL AREAS OF INTEREST:_____

_____

6. HOBBIES AND RECREATIONAL ACTIVITIES:_____

_____

7. MARITAL STATUS:_____ PARTNER:_____

8. CHILDREN:_____

_____

9. CONVERSATIONAL INTERESTS:_____

_____

10. DINING PREFERENCES:_____

ADDITIONAL NOTES:_____

FIGURE 2. The Baum 10 worksheet on referring physicians.

more than three times the cost of gasoline! Now that's the power of your USP: motivating people to pay more for water than what is available for free at the tap. What is the USP that will make you the Evian of healthcare?

Most of the choices we make—from the coffee shop we frequent for our jolt of java to the company that provides the medical supplies for our medical office—are based on a USP. Doctors may not even be aware of it, because subliminal suggestions, social media, and word-of-mouth marketing can be as contagious as a multimillion-dollar advertising campaign.

A medical practice is a business, and, in order to thrive, a practice needs brand recognition. In fact, if a practice doesn't take the time to build a unique brand, patients will seek care elsewhere and may form opinions of the doctors and the practice that may not be what the doctors or the practice were hoping for. Perhaps the practice has had the unfortunate situation of just one negative online review giving the practice a one-star rating, or the practice may have a negative label or bad reputation that can't be erased or prevented, such as long wait times, unfriendly front desk, and inability to get through by phone because of the phone tree. As in other businesses, the most successful hospitals and practices usually have a strong USP that clearly differentiates them from all others that provide similar services.

We recommend that you identify your USP and craft your message to your target market, emphasizing what makes your practice special and different. The goal of your USP is to answer the question, "Why would a potential patient prefer to become a patient in your practice rather than a similar practice in the area?" Most patients find out about your USP *after* they have become part of your practice. What we want to emphasize is that your USP is to be used to attract patients *before* they have entered your practice.

Third Component of Phase 1: Reaching Potential Patients Using Social Media

John Wanamaker, a media mogul, once said, "Half the money I spend on advertising [practice promotion] is wasted; the trouble is I don't know which half." That comment was made over 100 years ago, when tracking of marketing efforts was in its infancy. Today, we have readily available technology to quickly, inexpensively, and easily track our marketing effectiveness.

This usually cannot be accomplished in-house, especially in small to medium-sized practices that don't have a marketing expert on board. To determine the success of your marketing using website and social media analytics, you probably will need to hire an expert who specializes in medical marketing and is familiar with your target market and the media that you use to reach that market, whether that is print advertising, direct mail, Internet, or social media. If you are going to be successful in marketing and promoting your practice, you will want to get a return on your marketing expenditures.

Let us give you an example of measuring the return on your marketing investment. You consider a direct mail campaign and send out 100 letters. The cost of printing and mailing your 100 letters to potential patients is $300. Your response to those 100 letters was 10 potential patients—a 10% response rate. From the 10 who responded, only two called for an appointment—a 20% closure rate. Carrying out the calculation a little further, you acquired two new patients at a cost of $300, or $150 for each new patient from the marketing effort. If each new patient had medical services of $200, you made $50 for each new patient. If you are in primary care and the patient stays with you for ten or more years, the return on your investment is going to be huge, especially if the patient has a good experience and tells others about you and your practice.

Our take-home message is: rather than just getting your name out there, you'll do much better by concentrating on getting the names of potential patients in here, or in your practice.

Bottom Line: A successful marketing campaign *before* the patient enters the practice is based on three components:

1. Identifying the target market you are trying to reach;
2. Crafting the marketing message that will reach your target market; and
3. Choosing the right media vehicle to reach your target market.

Developing a One-Page Marketing Plan: Part II

This article is the second of three parts on using the one-page marketing plan to enhance your practice's potential. Part I discussed Phase 1, the period before the patient actually enters your practice. This part addresses Phase 2 of the one-page marketing plan, in which you receive leads from your marketing efforts, and shows you how to develop a system of follow-up and how to keep in touch with potential new patients. Part III will discuss how to create enthusiastic fans and how they help promote your practice.

In prehistoric times (probably the Paleolithic age), the man (most likely a male member of the clan or tribe) woke up every morning, collected his primitive weapons, and headed out to hunt for food. On a successful day, he would come back with a deer or antelope, and the family was able to eat. However, I am sure there were days when he returned empty-handed and the family might go hungry. There was pressure every single day to hunt successfully, because the survival of the clan depended on it—it was a constant battle.

Contrast the daily hunter with the farmer, when the hunter-gathers eventually became involved in agriculture. The farmer planted seeds, and the clan would wait weeks or months for the wheat, barley, or corn to become ready for harvesting. From planting to harvesting, the plot of land needed to be watered, weeds removed, and the crops tended to on a regular basis.

What does the hunter-to-farmer story, which is perhaps the most significant single development in human history, have to do with one-page medical marketing? Our observation, when it comes to practice marketing, is that most physicians behave more like hunters than like farmers. They take their trifold brochure, electronically convert the content, and then hire a high school student to paste it into a website template and declare, "Our practice has a website." Or the practice hires a marketing firm that has little or no experience in medical marketing to create a logo and write a newsletter and add some meaningless slogan like "state of the art technology"; claims to be a leader or expert in the area; sends the materials out for a few months; gets no follow-up from any potential patients who contact the practice for more information; and is disappointed and states, "Marketing doesn't work." Doing nothing more than "getting the word out" or "getting the practice name out there" is futile and a waste of time and money.

Most medical practices are clueless about the purpose behind practice promotion and effective marketing. These practices and doctors believe that marketing consists primarily of getting the word out, getting recognized, or creating a buzz about the doctors or the practice. If you ask doctors the goal of their marketing, they will state they are interested in acquiring more patients or performing more procedures. Successful medical practices that truly understand practice promotion describe marketing as keeping existing patients and attracting new patients who are interested in your area of interest or expertise. This kind of marketing is the "long haul" or "farming" approach versus the "instant" or "hunting" approach to practice promotion.

The successful practice identifies potential patients, enters them into a database, and then follows up with additional educational material on a regular basis or provides useful products that are a constant reminder of the practice so that when "the time is right" and the patient needs your services, your practice will be remembered, and they will call for an appointment and become members of your practice. Now your practice is building value that will serve as a magnet to attract new patients to your practice and will also keep your existing patients within your practice.

Early humans made progress by moving from being hunter-gathers to farmers. However, farming did require regular care and attention to the crops. The same applies to your practice promotion and marketing efforts. You can't create just one newsletter, one blog, or one social media submission and have the phone ring off the hook. Marketing requires constant and frequent offerings so that when the time comes for the potential patient to need your services, your practice and your name will be easily recalled, and you will have captured a new patient from your marketing efforts.

The next box to check off in your one-page marketing plan (see the first article in this series, in the May/June 2022 issue) is to create a database system to enable organized follow-up with any potential patients. For example, if you make a presentation to a lay audience, and you collect their names, address, and email addresses, then you have to have the information you need to connect with all of those people who were in your audience. The likelihood is that giving a single talk to a church group or a service club will result in a significant number of those in the audience becoming patients.

For example, you have a monthly support group for a medical condition that is in your repertoire or in your strike-zone of medical care. At any given time, or on average, 3% of those attending the program might be highly motivated and ready to call for an appointment. An additional 7% are very amenable to becoming a patient, and then there may be another 30% who are interested in your services but cannot pursue them now. Then there's the

30% who are not currently interested, and, finally, the reality is that another 30% just come to the meeting for the coffee and the cookies and will never be interested in becoming patients even if you didn't charge them. If you measure your marketing by new patients who contact your practice right after the program, the 3%, you are missing out on the other 97%. You have to be a farmer and continue to take care of your field, meaning those who may eventually need your services at a future date. You need a system that continues to reach out to those who you can possibly identify as potential patients. Now, by going from the 3% who are immediately interested to nearly 40%, you are multiplying the effectiveness of conducting a support group by 1233%. Now that's what we call a real return on your investment.

Therefore, it is imperative to keep track of your potential patients with a customer relationship management system. You will want all of your leads regarding potential patients to be entered into that system. The sidebar presents a list of software programs for healthcare practices that offer customer relationship management.

Next, comes nurturing your leads.

Most medical practices hrave an attitude of "one and done." They write a blog, add an article to their website, or send out a newsletter. Nothing happens after one or two attempts, and they decide the marketing does not work. The statistics on the success of nurturing your leads in all areas of marketing and practice promotion is that 50% of practices will give up after one contact with a potential patient; 65% will give up after two contacts; and 80% give up after three attempts.[1]

With each interaction with the patient, you have an opportunity to create a negative impression, a neutral impression, or a knock-their-socks-off mind-blowing impression. Most practices accept the negative or neutral impression. The really successful practices create a "shock-and-awe" approach so that whenever the patient needs the services that the practice offers, they will be quickly remembered and the patient will make that call to become a patients in that practice.

A shock-and-awe approach works best when a physical package is mailed to the potential patient. This provides information or surprises that are so distinctive that the recipient cannot forget where they came from and who was the sender.

Examples of a shock-and-awe package might include a book on a medical topic. This is even more meaningful if you have written the book. For example, if I give a program on impotence or erectile dysfunction, I send attendees a copy of a book I wrote on the topic. Of course, I could save on postage if I gave out copies to those in the audience right after an evening program on the topic. It is far better, however, to send a copy of the book a few days later. I usually distribute a sign-in sheet and tell the audience that if they sign the sheet with their name, home address, and email address, I will send them a copy of the book. Almost every member of the audience provides this information to receive a copy of the book.

Another present that is effective in the shock-and-awe package is a DVD or CD that introduces the doctors in the practice, gives a tour of the office, and provides testimonials from a few patients.

If you have written or been featured in articles that have appeared in the local or national news media, send copies to prospective patients, because this enhances your credibility. It is also effective to send papers or articles that you have written that appeared in professional journals, because they add to your perceived expertise.

The least effective items are scratch pads, pens, magnetic refrigerator calendars, or mousepads with the name of the practice, contact information, and logo. These are given out by other practices, usually at the point of service, and your trinkets will not stand out amongst the "tchotchkes" from other practices.

The best shock-and-awe packages contain a handwritten note from the doctor expressing interest in the potential patient and offering to be available and to answer any questions.

In summary, a shock-and-awe package should:

- Give potential patients an amazing and unexpected surprise that is valued by the recipient;
- Demonstrate your expertise in a particular medical area and that you are a trusted authority in your field; and
- Move the potential patient closer to picking up the phone and making a call to your office if they are in need of your services.

Our message is that a shock-and-awe package provides you with a huge competitive advantage. It's ethical, it's easy, and it's effective.

Finally, the second part of the one-page marketing plan requires conversion—not a religious change of faith, but moving those in the public sector to becoming paying patients. This requires winning the trust of the potential patient so that person calls and makes an appointment.

It is common for those not skilled at marketing to put their toe in the water before becoming fully immersed in the river. They often send out one or two newsletters from the practice, and when they fail to receive new patients from their efforts, they then cease all marketing endeavors. Our take-home message is that an attitude of "if you build it, they will come" may apply to baseball fields but not to marketing and practice promotion. A newsletter like all the others is screaming "me too," and you may be left competing on price, which is a losing marketing plan.

Let us illustrate our position with a true story about a virtuoso violinist, Joshua Bell, that emphasizes the importance of context. Joshua Bell is one of the best concert violin players in the world. As an experiment sponsored by *The Washington Post*, Mr. Bell wore a baseball cap and sunglasses and played for 45 minutes, on a 300-year-old Stradivarius violin worth $3.5 million, at a Washington, DC subway station during rush hour on January 12, 2007. More than 1000 people passed by Bell; however, only seven people stopped to listen to him play, and only one person recognized him. Just a few nights earlier, he had played at the Kennedy Center and the cost of each ticket was $100. When he played in the subway, he had a hat placed conspicuously to collect tips, where he received a grand total of $32. Here was a virtuoso who would receive $1000 per minute to play in front of a sold-out audience! (You can watch this amazing story of Joshua Bell in the Washington, DC, subway station on YouTube: www.youtube.com/watch?v=LZeSZFYCNRw.)

This is no surprise; the social context in which a behavior occurs affects how it is interpreted. Take the very same talented musician, playing the exact same music on the same violin—in one instance he earns $32 an hour, and in another context, he earns $60,000 per hour. What made the dramatic difference? I believe it was positioning.

If you think of yourself as a subway performer, your audience/patients will pay you accordingly. On the other hand, if you position yourself as a professional concert performer, you attract a totally different customer/client/patient and get paid accordingly. Our take-home message is that the public will accept you at your own appraisal of yourself.

If you believe you provide superior service, you have the possibility of positioning yourself at a much higher level. You can offer your service at a much higher price and also attract a higher quality of patient. I don't suggest that you try to compete on price, because there will always be someone who will charge less than you do, and then you will have reduce your price even more and ultimately the quality of your service will deteriorate.

We want you to think in terms of providing value to your patients. We would like you to think in terms of providing useful material that educates potential patients and enhances the trust that potential patients will have in you and your practice. It is necessary to think of the pain points that patients are experiencing and how you can provide a solution to that problem. If you are a primary care physician whose focus is obesity, and you can help patients lose weight, and, more importantly, help them keep the weight off, then offer that information on a regular basis to potential patients. If you are an orthopedic surgeon specializing in sports medicine, provide information on injuries incurred by weekend warriors and focus on the prevention of soft tissue injuries. If you are a urologist and your area of interest and expertise is erectile dysfunction, speak to your patients about nonmedical, nonsurgical solutions to this common problem impacting millions of middle-aged men.

We believe the road to conversion is paved with expertise and education. You must see yourself as a virtuoso violin player playing on one of the world's finest violins. In this context, you are a creator of great value, a resource of good health that will positively change the lives of patients who become part of your practice.

Bottom Line: We hope that we have shown you that the one-page marketing plan is not a sprint but a marathon. Outcomes and gratification are deferred, but it all begins with a plan of action. In the next and final article of this series, we will discuss how to create a stellar experience for each patient who enters the practice so that patient leaves the practice as a raving fan. We will also discuss how to increase the lifetime value of patients who are generated by a successful one-page marketing plan.

REFERENCE

1. Dib A. *The 1-Page Marketing Plan*. Successwise. 2016:114.

HEALTHCARE CUSTOMER RELATIONSHIP MANAGEMENT PROGRAMS

The following programs offer customer relationship management capability:

- Zendesk (Zendesk.com)
- Salesforce (Salesforce.com)
- Monday.com (Monday.com)
- Scoro (Scoro.com)
- Hubspot (Hubspot.com)
- NetSuite (NetSuite.com)
- Nutshell (Nutshell.com)
- Quickbase (Quickbase.com)
- Freshworks (Freshworks.com)

Developing a One-Page Marketing Plan: Part III

In Parts I and II of this article we discussed two of the three phases of the one-page marketing plan. Phase 1 consists of finding your target market and crafting a message for potential patients. Phase 2 is converting the potential patient to a paying patient. This article will discuss Phase 3: creating raving fans who will promote your practice to others.

Tribe is defined as a group of people connected to one another by a leader who serves as the connector. Outstanding practices lead tribes of loyal fans, not just patients. If your practice has such fans, you have special patients who are promoters and cheerleaders for your practice. They will enhance your marketing message and escalate your reputation beyond what you might be able to do alone.

To create such an enthusiastic fan base, it is necessary to continually impress your patients about your stellar services. Practices with devoted fans make an effort to foster a lifetime relationship with their patients.

These practices make it very easy for their fans to interact with the doctors and the practice. These practices have a system in place that allows them to frequently and consistently create a stellar experience. It is necessary to have a strategy for building a following and make every effort to take very good care of those followers. You have to consider that each devoted fan leads to exponential results—each patient doesn't just add revenue on the first visit, but brings in repeated revenue, because he or she serves as a magnifier for creating new business for your practice.

DELIVERING A WORLD CLASS EXPERIENCE FOR THE PATIENT

There's an advantage to being small and flexible and having the ability to make decisions quickly. Large practices and large groups are stymied by their bloated bureaucracy, which has layers and a hierarchy of people that need to sign off on any decision that needs to be made. Smaller practices have the advantage of being agile and can respond to patients' needs and make decisions quickly and much faster than large organizations. More importantly, small practices can micromanage the doctor–patient relationship. As a result, the patient doesn't find him- or herself adrift in a sea of other patients, and the practice has an opportunity to offer a personal and customized interaction that is conducive to inspiring loyalty.

The first step in creating a fan of your practice is to find out what your patient wants. It is imperative to think about not only what the patient wants but also what the patient needs. For example, in an IVF practice, the woman wants to become pregnant and have a baby. Every woman who enters the practice wants that result. Now you hope can you give her what she wants but, if not, how can you give her what she needs? It is necessary to understand both needs and wants. They may overlap, but often they are completely separate. Our challenge is to motivate patients to do what they need to do to achieve the results they want and need. The take-home message is that we want our patients to achieve the results that both they and the doctors want. The benefit of reaching this goal is that patients who achieve their goals will recommend you enthusiastically to others, who are then likely to become patients in your practice. We've found the best way to encourage compliance is to divide the process into bite-sized morsels so that the whole endeavor doesn't seem so daunting.

In this age of technology, you have an opportunity to make healthcare frictionless. For example, make it easy for patients to make an online appointment. This is particularly important and attractive to millennials. Another friction point is for making payments to the practice. When this can be made easy and quick, your practice will be attractive to patients. Another method of reducing friction regarding payment is to provide prices of your services. There should be no secret about the cost of visits and procedures that you offer, and that information should be readily available to patients. Receptionists should be able to quickly quote the cost of each service the patient is likely to encounter. These prices should also be posted on the website. The take-home message is that the purpose of any new technology that is implemented into your practice is to eliminate friction.

INCREASING PATIENT LIFETIME VALUE

It is important to understand the lifetime value of a patient to your practice. The calculation for lifetime value is the average value of an appointment multiplied by the average appointments per year multiplied by the average number of years a patient is likely to remain in your practice.

The calculation of lifetime value = $V \times N \times Y$, where V = average dollar value of appointment, N = average number of appointments each year, and Y = average number of years the patient visits your practice.

For example, if you are a middle-aged otolaryngologist and your average patient is seen three times a year and each visit is worth approximately $150, and that patient stays within your practice for six years, then the average lifetime value of that patient would be $3 \times \$150 \times 6$, or $2700.

Conwell's classic story *Acres of Diamonds*[1] is about a farmer living between the Tigris and Euphrates rivers who wanted to find diamonds so badly that he sold his farm, left his family, and went off on a search that took him all over the world. His search was futile and ultimately led to extreme poverty, as well as the loss of his family. The new owner of his farm discovered a mother lode of diamonds on the farm that he had purchased from the original owner. The moral of this story is to dig first on your own property when seeking a treasure or, more succinctly, look first at what you already have. If you apply that maxim to your marketing efforts—look at your existing patients and make sure that they have a stellar experience before reaching out for new patients. Numerous studies have shown that it is far easier to satisfy an existing patient than to recoup the time, money, and energy required to attract new ones. Those studies indicate that a person is 21 times more likely to buy from a business or practice they've already used than from one they have never visited.[2] In other words, there can be plenty of productivity from your existing or past patients.

Nearly every practice has dozens—perhaps even hundreds—of patients who have fallen through the cracks and have missed appointments for follow-up examinations. In this pandemic era, large numbers of patients have been fearful of coming to the doctor and have skipped follow-up appointments.

More than one-third of adults report they've delayed or forgone healthcare either due to fear of COVID-19 infection or their physician offering limited services during the pandemic.[3]

An even larger portion (40.7%) of respondents with one or more chronic conditions reported they've delayed or forgone care, while 56.3% of respondents with both a physical and a mental health condition have failed to follow up with their doctor.[4]

Black adults were more likely (39.7%) to report forgoing or delaying care than Hispanic (35.5%) or White (34.3%) adults and more likely to report forgoing or delaying multiple types of care: 28.5% compared with 22.3% and 21.1%, respectively.[4]

The most common type of medical care delayed or forgone was visiting their primary care physician or specialist (20.6%) and receiving preventive health screenings or medical tests (15.5%).[5]

Respondents with one or more chronic health conditions, such as hypertension, diabetes, respiratory illness, heart disease, cancer, kidney disease, and mental health disorders, make up the vast majority (76%) of those who have delayed or forgone healthcare.[5]

Delaying and forgoing care isn't without its dangers: 32.6% of respondents say that doing so has worsened one or more of their health conditions or limited their ability to work or do other daily activities, according to the report.[5]

This would be a perfect time to institute telemedicine for those patients who have missed appointments. A primary care doctor probably has numerous patients who need follow up cholesterol testing and blood pressure monitoring. A urologist certainly has patients with low-grade bladder cancer who need follow-up office cystoscopies. Men who are using testosterone for hypoandrogenism require monitoring of the hemoglobin/hematocrit and PSA levels.

How should the practice keep these existing patients in the loop or within the practice? We suggest sending patients reminders by email, text messaging, or even snail mail. Modern technology makes it possible to send reminders automatically to patients who are likely to need follow-up appointments.

You can make your practice user-friendly by making your practice accessible. Tell existing patients that they can have same-day or next-day appointments. Another convenience is to offer early morning, late afternoon, evening, or weekend appointments. If you are delivering extra value that your competitors do not provide, your existing patients will remain loyal members of your practice.

We suggest developing a reactivation campaign. This consists of going through your patient database and identifying patients who need to return to the practice. You need to give them a strong reason to return to the practice. An example would be type 2 diabetic patients who are using finger sticks multiple times a day and you can offer them one of the small wearable devices that transmits glucose readings to their mobile phones.

When the electronic contact method fails, consider calling the patients and ask them why they haven't returned. Let the patient know you care about them and their health. Tell them you want them to return to the practice, and make it convenient for them to reenter the practice. Ideally a reactivation should not be necessary. But there are going to be situations such as the pandemic, hurricanes, floods, and other natural disasters that do make it difficult for patients to return to the practice. However, a reactivation campaign can be your "acres of diamonds" and significantly increase the lifetime value from your existing patients.

Conducting a reactivation campaign begins with looking at your patient database and retrieving names of patients who haven't returned for follow-up. Next create a strong offer to entice them to come back. In most healthcare practices, returning is beneficial to their health, and failure to come back may cause deterioration in their health and well-being. Finally, if they do call for a follow-up appointment, send them a thank you note indicating that you are looking forward to seeing them.

Take-home message: Stay connected with your patients who haven't followed up. Let them know that you are concerned about them, that you're available, and you will find that they will handsomely reward you by reactivation into the practice. On the other hand, if you don't reach out to them, then they will forget you and their health may deteriorate.

Repetition will lead to repeat visits and loyalty from patients. One contact is not likely to keep your name and the name of your practice for recall when patients may need your services. By sending patients regular reminders, newsletters, and emails, you become a familiar name, and it is more likely they will be calling for an appointment when they need your services. Reaching out to patients in your database can be easily automated with current technology to do the heavy lifting. This technology allows you to easily keep in touch and continue to develop and maintain a relationship through your customer relationship management system. Maintaining that connection can be as simple as a monthly postcard or text message.

ORCHESTRATING AND STIMULATING REFERRALS

Several decades ago, the concept of marketing and spreading the word about your practice was limited to "word of mouth" or what we call "hopeium," in which the doctor and the practices "hope" that patients who have had a favorable experience will walk out of the practice and tell others about that positive experience. That's a "sit and wait' approach to building and maintaining a practice. That approach may have worked a few decades ago, but it's a passive approach and you may wait a very long time for it to work while others are taking a more active approach and creating vocal fans who do the marketing and practice promotion on your behalf.

It was my own (NB) experience and my discussions with colleagues that asking for referrals is beneath us and akin to begging for business. It is possible to initiate the process by simply asking patients for whom you have delivered outstanding care and who have had a favorable result to share that experience with others. However, you need to give them the ammunition necessary to be your publicist.

Here is an example from one of the authors (NB). A patient returns for a follow-up semen analysis after a vasectomy, and he is found to be sterile—the outcome he and his partner desired. I follow up with a letter mentioning that I would appreciate if they would share their experience with other men who are in need of the procedure. I include several packets that provide education on vasectomy, and that I would give any of their friends a free consultation if they were considering having the male sterilization procedure. I am certain that these satisfied patients will know others in a similar situation and in need of family planning and will very likely share their experience with my office. I have been amazed how many satisfied patients will distribute the packets and how many men will even ask for more packets!

Remember, it is human nature to be attracted to people with the same likes, interests, and situations as oneself. Also, no man is looking to have a vasectomy. However, he is looking for a solution for a specific problem, i.e., no more children. My approach is to identify the problem and offer a solution that will solve that problem.

This process acknowledges them and appeals to their ego, because nearly everyone likes being acknowledged. Rather than appear to be asking for a favor, I am offering something of value that they can share with their family and friends. Trust me, this process is far more effective taking an extra dose of hopeium!

Bottom Line: We know we have covered a lot of ideas in our journey to create a one-page marketing plan. This is an effective approach to medical marketing that is well within the reach of every medical practice regardless of size, location, and current level of marketing and practice promotion.

There's a popular Chinese proverb that says: "The best time to plant a tree was 20 years ago. The second-best time is now." Basically, this means that if you want success and growth tomorrow, the best time to act is now. So, our final advice is start planting your One-Page Marketing Plan today!

You can get a free download of the 1-Page Marketing Plan at 1pmp.com.

REFERENCES

1. Conwell RH, Shackleton R. *Acres of Diamonds*. Harper and Brothers; 1915. Available at www. google.com/books/edition/Acres_of_Diamonds/O44DAAAAYAAJ

2. Gallo A. The value of keeping the right customers. *Harvard Business Review*. October 29, 2014.

3. Czeisler MÉ, Marynak K, Clarke KEN, et al. Delay or avoidance of medical care because of COVID-19-related concerns – United States, June 2020. *MMWR*. 2020;69:1250-1257. https://doi.org/10.15585/mmwr.mm6936a4

4. Claxton G, Damico A, Rae M, Young G, McDermott D, Whitmore H. health benefits in 2020: premiums in employer-sponsored plans grow 4 percent; employers consider responses to pandemic: the annual Kaiser Family Foundation Employer Health Benefits Survey of the cost and coverage of US employer-sponsored health benefits. *Health Affairs*. 2020;39:2018-2028.

5. Gonzalez D, Zuckerman S, Kenney GM, Karpman M. Almost Half of Adults in Families Losing Work during the Pandemic Avoided Health Care Because of Costs or COVID-19 Concerns. Washington, DC: Urban Institute; July 10, 2020. www.urban.org/research/publication/almost-half-adults-families-losing-work-during-pandemic-avoided-health-care-because-costs-or-covid-19-concerns.

CHAPTER 32

The Role of Technology in the Small Medical Office

SAKINA BAJOWALA, MD, AND NEIL BAUM, MD

The medical profession has embraced technology in the diagnosis and treatment of patients. We have become dependent on technology for imagining lesions as small as 1 mm inside the body. Our patients have benefited from bioengineered medications that are disease- and even patient-specific that have allowed us to create precision medicine and treat patients as individuals rather than as diseases or conditions. However, doctors have not made use of the technology that is available to improve the efficiency, productivity, and even the quality of care that they provide. With improved availability, affordability, and mobility of medical technology, small practices now have access to technologies once previously available only to larger organizations with big budgets and full IT departments. This article discusses the technologies that are available to small practices that result in significant improvement in the care that we offer our patients.

ELECTRONIC MEDICAL RECORDS

Electronic medical record (EMR) systems are now de rigueur in a modern medical practice, whether it be large or small. A comprehensive EMR saves on chart storage space, reduces paper consumption, and allows for remote accessibility while on the go. With the advent of "software as a service" (SAAS) EMR systems, small practices without large budgets can have access to an EMR on a subscription basis without needing to make costly upfront investments in the acquisition and maintenance of on-site servers. Remote data backup to the cloud is automatic, protecting patient data from the hazards of failed equipment.

For a small medical practice without extensive cross coverage, remote access to the EMR (via Web or remote desktop connection) allows the physician to stay caught up with lab results, phone calls, and charting while on the go. The SAAS model has dramatically improved the affordability of EMR systems, and some highly rated EMR products are free to the practice. However, affordability must be balanced with usability. Your EMR system can have a major impact on work flow and efficiency. Therefore, it is essential to select a system that is customizable to your practice and documentation style. Never commit to a system without first giving it a trial run.

PATIENT PORTALS

The most robust EMR systems are equipped with patient portals, which give patients secure 24-hour access to their health information from anywhere with an Internet connection. A full-featured patient portal will reduce physician documentation time, as patients can complete history forms on their own devices before they even set foot in the office. The front desk can import this information into the patient's chart, allowing physician review before the initial evaluation. Patient portals also facilitate collections with electronic statements and online bill-pay features. When the interactive features of patient portals are optimized, it is no longer necessary to use valuable time on the phone for nonurgent issues such as appointment requests and confirmations, medication refills, normal laboratory results, routine questions, or clinical updates. Having an interactive patient portal is now a Meaningful Use requirement for CMS, and can help your practice qualify for financial incentives and avoid penalties.

VIRTUAL VISITS

A variety of telehealth applications now enable HIPAA-compliant video conferencing and virtual patient visits. Although virtual visits are not a covered benefit under all commercial health insurance plans, many patients value the convenience and accessibility of such a service so much that they will happily agree to a reasonable out-of-pocket fee for virtual encounters. Virtual visits are no substitute for a comprehensive physical evaluation, but they are ideal for counseling sessions in which a physical exam is not necessary. These include pre-procedure counseling, the review of abnormal laboratory results, and nutritional/dietary education, among others. Virtual visits can be automatically recorded as mp4 files and then imported into the EMR. Using virtual visits effectively can improve patient satisfaction, reduce no-shows, and positively affect the bottom line.

INTERNET TELEPHONY

Voice over Internet protocol (VOIP) phone systems offer the features of pricey telephony set-ups at a bargain cost. HIPAA-compliant options are now readily available for voice, fax, text, and video conferencing. Using VOIP reduces expenses by leveraging existing equipment, and features regular software updates, keeping your phone system from quickly becoming obsolete. A well-configured VOIP system is highly flexible and customizable, allowing the administrator to easily change settings from a mobile phone or desktop application. Auto-attendant features help to direct phone traffic without requiring costly manpower. The ability to configure the system to simultaneously or sequentially ring on the office phone, mobile, and home phone increases portability and the patient's perception of your office's accessibility.

SOCIAL MEDIA

No discussion of medical technology is complete without addressing the enormous impact of social media on how patients access health information. In the United States, close to 75% of people look to the Internet for healthcare information, and social media networks can be important hubs for the dissemination of health education. With a modicum of effort, a small practice can have a professional and robust social media footprint, which can save thousands of dollars in marketing expenses while simultaneously being a source where patients can obtain high-quality health information.

Creating a Facebook page for the practice allows the office to share practice news and pertinent media reports, and also to engage with potential and current patients. Twitter, the microblogging service, is an excellent method for sharing links to journal articles, medical news stories, and succinct "pearls" of medical wisdom. Patients who "follow" the practice's Twitter account will instantly be alerted on their mobile devices when you post, enabling rapid communication of weather-related practice closures or last-minute appointment availability, for example. On YouTube, Google's video sharing service, practices can create their own "channels" to share original videos with the public. Topics can include provider interviews, anatomic explanations, demonstrations of medical device usage, and reviews of the risks and benefits of medical procedures. Having a library of videos will improve practice visibility, establish a personal connection with patients before they walk in the door, and reduce time spent on repetitive counseling (for example, as adjunct to written informed consent). One of the major benefits of having an effective social media strategy is that high-quality content will often be shared by patients from one social media platform to another, extending your practice's reach at a minimal cost.

INTEGRATED SENSORS

Sensors are an exciting development in medical technology. Medical monitoring devices have rapidly become more portable and affordable over the past few years, with many now integrating with and drawing their power from mobile phones. Electronic peak flow meters, glucometers, and blood pressure monitors can all input data directly into mobile applications, with data then shared to your office with the click of a button. Reviewing these data with the patient regularly can help your practice proactively monitor chronic health conditions, and qualify for certain insurance reimbursements.

SMARTPHONE APPLICATIONS

Let's not forget the piece of medical technology that we all already have in our pockets! With the right suite of mobile applications, your smartphone can be a portable and inexpensive pharmacopoeia, medical calculator, encyclopedia of clinical guidelines, medical journal, billing/coding reference, and voice recorder. With advances in voice recognition technology, mobile phones can also replace a transcription service for quick dictations.

ADDING TECHNOLOGY TO YOUR OFFICE

It can be overwhelming to a small practice owner to consider the various technologies available for implementation. A structured plan for the introduction of technology to the office can help to control costs, reduce frustration, and maintain workflow efficiency. First, it is essential to create a list of needs versus wants. A comprehensive phone system and EMR may be on your immediate "must-have" list, while a patient portal and virtual visit capability can wait. Allocate the majority of your technology budget to essential items, with the remainder reserved for wish-list items down the road. Gaining competency in one system at a time will keep your office humming with a minimum amount of workflow interruption, and will keep your staff from experiencing tech "burn-out."

Naturally, certain costs and downsides come with the implementation of technology in a small medical practice. The most obvious of these is the financial outlay required. Small practices operate on unforgiving margins, and typically do not have large reserves of cash available. Several studies estimate that the cost per provider for implementation of an EMR system can range from $15,000 to $75,000. A detailed discussion costs is available online at HealthIT.gov (www.healthit.gov/providers-professionals/faqs/how-much-going-cost-me). Converting practice operations to Internet-based technologies creates a dependency on reliable connectivity. Practices that "got by" with entry-level Internet speeds while operating analog systems will almost certainly need to invest in reliable high-speed connectivity packages and computers that can handle the increased workload of operating multiple technologies simultaneously. Failing to do so can open your practice to the risk of an office shut-down if your Internet connection goes down. The individual costs of telehealth applications, VOIP telephony systems, sensors, and mobile applications pale in comparison. However, even these small costs can add up and be a drain on the budget if they are not being utilized effectively. Therefore, it is essential to implement only those technologies that you anticipate will fill gaps in your practice and be used frequently enough to justify the expense.

Privacy concerns must also be considered. Select only HIPAA-compliant vendors, and obtain the appropriate business associate agreements to protect your practice from potentially costly privacy violations. As all systems have a learning curve, one must anticipate the need for training time and temporary hits to efficiency as new technologies are introduced to the office. Patients and staff may be resistant at first, but this can be overcome by designating a technology "champion" charged with communicating the benefits and addressing any roadblocks to successful implementation. Finally, we should keep in mind that even the most advanced technology will not compensate for lackluster clinical or customer service skills. Technology is a tool to help a patient-centered practice operate efficiently, and should enhance, rather than detract from, or replace, provider–patient interactions.

CONCLUSION

In the future, physicians will be required to embrace technology in the care they provide their patients. In the past, the cost of adding technology in small medical practices was prohibitive. However, today it is possible for small practices, including solo practices, to afford implementing technology that makes the practice more efficient, more productive, and can even provide patients with stellar experiences that will motivate patients to tell others about their outstanding experiences with you and your practice.

CHAPTER 33

Utilizing Web 2.0 to Bridge Healthcare Communication Gaps

Neil Baum, MD, and Brittney Bauer, PhD

Communication is critical to delivering accurate medical advice. In the overall healthcare process, timely, informed, and bidirectional communication is important not only between doctors and patients, but also between doctors and other doctors. In fact, 65% of medical schools now teach communication skills as a part of their common curriculum.[1] Not surprisingly, upon completion of medical training and entering into a medical practice, more time often is committed to the science of patient care and less consideration is devoted to facilitating this communication process. Resulting issues in intraorganizational healthcare communication are linked to a rise in medical errors. As Pirnejad et al.[2] point out, "Communication failures, particularly those due to an inadequate exchange of information between healthcare providers, remain among the most common factors that contribute to the occurrence of adverse drug events . . . [and] communication errors were found to be the leading cause [of in-hospital deaths], and were twice as frequent as errors due to inadequate clinical skills." Furthermore, patient–provider communication is vital to improving adherence to medical instructions, establishing good clinical relationships, and fostering patient satisfaction.[3] Prior research demonstrates that there is a positive correlation between effective patient–provider communication and improved patient health outcomes, and that effective communication can help improve a patient's health as much as the actual medication.[1] Given the central role of the communication process in healthcare delivery, this article seeks to utilize the capabilities of Web 2.0 to help bridge harmful communication gaps.

WHAT IS WEB 1.0?

The advent of commercial Internet usage enabled organizations to offer connected digital content and deliver this information to consumers with more timeliness, convenience, and detail than ever before. In the era known as "Web 1.0," online content consisted of static websites, resulting in a one-way flow of information from the practice to the viewer. In the late 1990s and early 2000s, websites were easily created by electronically moving the material from the practice's trifold, tricolor brochure to a widely accessible online platform. These ostensibly professional websites often were created by untried, self-taught Web designers who had little or no experience in building platforms specifically for healthcare purposes. These sites were inexpensive and even free to create, but they were not very effective in improving communication between the doctor and the patient.

Web 1.0 was focused on searches (i.e., the higher the site appeared on the search engine, the more visitors the site generated), which were assumed to translate into more patients calling to make an appointment. Importantly, Web 1.0 differentiated between organic versus nonorganic search results. Organic search results, positioned as content on the left-hand side of the search page, are those that appear because of their relevance to the search engine query. Nonorganic search results, also called pay-per-click, are actually paid advertisements that appear along the righthand side or top of the displayed organic search results (Figure 1). To reduce consumer deception, it is an accepted practice to identify content that is nonorganic by labeling the post an "ad" or indicating that it is "sponsored" by an organization.[4]

In an effort to more specifically target potential patients who may be interested in the practice, search engine optimization has the goal of placing the website on the first page of results for Google or any of the other search engines (e.g., Yelp, Bing, Yahoo). Search engine optimization is the process of improving the volume of traffic that is driven to your site through unpaid (i.e., organic) results, as opposed to paid (i.e., nonorganic) inclusions. This can be accomplished by making sure that content can be "crawled" by programs or automated script that visits websites and scans pages in order to create databases or entries for a search engine index by strategically crafting webpage copy that is autonomously searchable, and including terms that are likely to be of interest to potential patients.

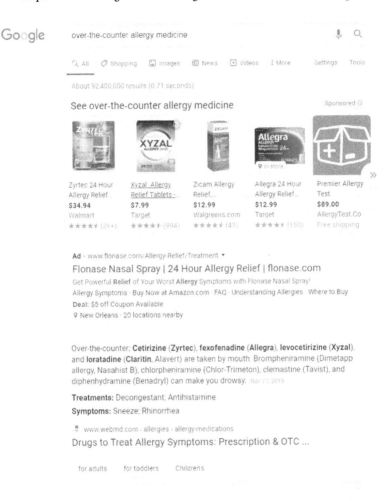

FIGURE 1. Organic versus nonorganic search results.

THE NEW ERA OF WEB 2.0

The term "Web 2.0" was introduced in the first decade of this century, and has been defined as "a collection of open-source, interactive and user-controlled online applications expanding the experiences, knowledge and market power of the users as participants in business and social processes."[5] When applied to healthcare, Web 2.0 uses modern cloud-based and mobile technologies to enhance communication via social media interactions and user-generated content contributed by doctors or the practice. In the early 2000s, following the widespread adoption of both the Internet and easy-to-use tools for communication, social networking, and self-publishing, media attention focused on increasing interest from patients, clinicians, medical researchers, and medical librarians in using these tools for healthcare and medical purposes.[6] These technologies have the potential to empower patients to have greater control over their own healthcare and decrease medical paternalism. However, the nature of Web 2.0 allows for the possibility of changing—perhaps even to the point of disrupting—the current model of healthcare delivery.

In particular, social media and blogs have caused a revolution concerning every aspect of social life and the medical aspects of patient care. Social media can be used to facilitate communication between communities of physicians and patients, or even to study the dynamics of blogs and their influence on patients' knowledge and information-seeking tendencies. Social media are radically changing the way we communicate and the information spreading into contemporary society. The term *social media* is defined as websites and Internet tools that allow for users' interaction through sharing information and ideas. These applications help facilitate communication among users by creating an accessible platform that is open to all. Social media also creates societies and networks based on socialization and participation. Hundreds of millions of users from different socioeconomic, political, and national backgrounds worldwide communicate using Web applications and technology. Blogs are personal websites consisting of thoughts, information, photographs, and personal ideas that are arranged in chronological order based on the most recent post. Most blogs allow visitors to add comments and ask questions about the content. Posting messages and commenting on blog entries form a direct line of communication between the blogger and the visitors. Blogs serve as a unique, self-publishing tool in consumers' hands, and offer a creative public space for conversations concerning health and healthcare.

When considered in the context of healthcare, Web 2.0 is often given the specific nomenclature "Health 2.0." The prominence of Web 2.0 in healthcare can be attributed to the availability and proliferation of applications across healthcare in general, and the potential for improving public health in particular.[7] Early examples included doctors, patients, and scientists utilizing a specific set of Web-based tools (e.g., blogs, e-mail listservs, online communities, podcasts, social media posts, videos, wikis) to provide accessible information to consumers. Using the principles of open source and user-generated content, the power of social networks was harnessed in order to personalize healthcare, collaborate, and promote health education.[8] Web 2.0 can incorporate multiple technologies specific to the healthcare industry, such as connected health, the EMR, mHealth, telemedicine, and the use of the Internet by patients themselves, such as through blogs, Internet forums, online communities, patient–physician communication systems, and other more advanced systems.[9] Thus, Web 2.0 is not only about healthcare providers having an increased ability to generate and disseminate information; it is also about patients being cocreators in this process.

DO PATIENTS BENEFIT FROM MEDICAL GATEKEEPING?

One might question whether or not patients being active participants in the healthcare process is a benefit for society. A key concept of Web 2.0 is that patients themselves should have greater insight into and control of information generated about them. One advantage is that it empowers patients to have greater control over their own healthcare and diminishes the age-old paradigm of "the doctors know best." Critics of these technologies have expressed concerns about possible misinformation and violations of patient privacy; however, as more patients become comfortable with the secure sharing of their health information, the concept of Web 2.0 is gaining more acceptance. Much of the potential for change that comes from Web 2.0 is facilitated by combining technology-driven trends such as the patient's medical records, which "may lead to a powerful new generation of medical applications, where patients share parts of their electronic health records with other patients with similar medical conditions and 'crowdsource' the collective wisdom of other patients and professionals.[10] Thus, Web 2.0 has the potential to promote collaboration between patients, their caregivers, medical professionals, and other stakeholders in health.[11]

In the not too distant past, patient records were recorded on paper or on an EMR that could be accessed only by a physician or other medical professionals. Physicians acted as gatekeepers to this information, telling patients test results when and if they deemed it necessary. Such a model operates relatively well in situations such as acute care, where information about specific blood results would be of little use to a nonmedical person, or in a general practice where results were generally benign. However, in the case of complex chronic diseases, including psychiatric conditions or diseases of unknown etiology, patients were at risk of being without well-coordinated care because data about them was stored in a variety of disconnected places and, in some cases, might contain the opinions of physicians who did not share their thoughts and opinions with the patient. Increasingly, medical ethics deems such actions to be medical paternalism, and these actions are discouraged in modern medicine.[12]

Consider a hypothetical example that demonstrates the increased engagement of a patient operating in a Health 2.0 setting. Let's imagine that a patient goes to see their primary care physician with a presenting complaint, having first ensured their own medical record was up to date by checking it using the Internet. The treating physician might make a diagnosis or send for tests, the results of which could be transmitted directly to the patient's EMR. If a second appointment is needed, the patient will have had time to research what the results might mean for them, what diagnoses may be likely, and may have communicated with other patients who have had a similar set of results in the past. On a second visit, a referral might be made to a specialist. The patient might already have had the opportunity to search for the opinions or recommendations of other patients regarding the best specialist to go to, and in combination with their primary care physician decide whom to see. The specialist gives a diagnosis along with a prognosis and potential options for treatment. The patient has the opportunity to research these treatment options and take a more proactive role in coming to a decision that takes into consideration the opinion of their healthcare provider. They can also choose to submit more data about themselves, such as through a personalized genomics service, to identify any risk factors that might improve or worsen their prognosis. As treatment commences, the patient can track their health outcomes through a data-sharing patient community to determine whether the treatment is having a beneficial effect for them, and they can learn about research opportunities and clinical trials for their condition. They also have the social support of communicating with other patients throughout the world who have been diagnosed with the same condition. Thus, Health 2.0 has the ability to put the patient in the center of the process of their own healthcare and works in conjunction with the other caregivers so that everyone is essentially on the same page.

WHAT WILL WEB 2.0 DO FOR YOUR PRACTICE?

To start, Web 2.0 ensures that you stay informed of the latest developments in your particular field of medical expertise or interest. These communication technologies enable medical education through podcasts and other forums to allow physicians to enhance their learning at any time that is convenient for them. In the Web 2.0 era, the Internet allows collaboration and helps patients receive the information they need to actively contribute to the conversation when consulting with their physician. Web 2.0 enables patients who use search tools to find out information about a particular condition, be it a common one or an esoteric diagnosis that the primary physician potentially has not seen. Notably, even at the earliest stages of Web 2.0's development, Google search engine results revealed the correct diagnosis in 15 out of 26 cases (58%, 95% confidence interval 38% to 77%).[13] Additionally, physicians can gain more detailed patient histories by having access to real-time patient-reported outcomes and continuously aggregating both patient and physician data for personal and scientific research. Data also can be aggregated for disease-specific communities and patients with rare conditions, with accurate information provided on treatments, symptoms, and outcomes, which may improve their decision-making ability or the likely success of carrying out scientific research such as observational trials.[14]

Of course, negative consequences from the use of Web 2.0 are possible. These might include issues around the loss of control perceived by doctors over patient information and safety, the dangers of patients acquiring or spreading inaccurate information, and concerns over medical ownership and privacy. Also, Google has limitations as a diagnostic tool for medical doctors, as it may be effective only for conditions with unique symptoms and signs that can easily be used as a search term. Studies of its accuracy have returned varying results, and it remains in dispute.[15] Finally, concerns exist about the quality of user-generated content leading to misinformation, such as perpetuating the discredited claim that the MMR vaccine may cause autism.[16] In contrast, a 2004 study of a British epilepsy online support group suggested that only 6% of information was factually wrong.[17] In a 2007 Pew Research Center survey of Americans, only 3% reported that online advice had caused them serious harm, while nearly one-third reported that they or their acquaintances had been helped by online health advice.[18]

Bottom Line: Web 2.0 creates two-way communication between patients and doctors or the practice. The concept allows feedback between both parties. As a result, patients are more involved and better able to participate in their healthcare decisions. This situation is better for patients and better for the doctor, who is now in the adjunct role, instead of the paternal role of "the doctor knows best."

REFERENCES

1. Thakkar S. Bridging the communication gaps between patients and providers. Veta Health. February 23, 2018. https://myvetahealth.com/bridging-communication-gaps-patients-providers/

2. Pirnejad H, Niazkhani Z, Berg M, Ba R. Intra-organizational communication in healthcare. *Methods of Information in Medicine*. 2008;47:336-345.

3. Olson DP, Windish DM. Communication discrepancies between physicians and hospitalized patients. *Arch Intern Med*. 2010;170:1302-1307.

4. Heilpern W. How 'deceptive' sponsored news articles could be tricking readers—even with a disclosure message. Business Insider. March 17, 2016. www.businessinsider.com/how-deceptive-sponsored-news-articles-could-be-undermining-trusted-news-brands-even-with-a-disclosure-message-2016-3

5. Constantinides E, Fountain SJ. Web 2.0: conceptual foundations and marketing issues. *Journal of Direct, Data and Digital Marketing Practice*. 2008;9:231-244.

6. Giustini D. How Web 2.0 is changing medicine. *BMJ*. 2006;333:1283-1284.

7. Crespo R. Virtual community health promotion. *Preventing Chronic Disease*. 2007;4(3):75.

8. Hughes B, Joshi I, Wareham J. Health 2.0 and Medicine 2.0: tensions and controversies in the field. *J Med Internet Res*. 2008;10(3), e23.

9. Caldwell A, Young A, Gomez-Marquez J, Olson KR. Global health technology 2.0. *IEEE Pulse*. 2011;2(4):63-67.

10. Eysenbach G. Medicine 2.0: social networking, collaboration, participation, apomediation, and openness. *J Med Internet Res*. 2008;10(3):e22.

11. Sarasohn-Kahn J. The wisdom of patients: health care meets online social media. California HealthCareFoundation. 2008. www.chcf.org/wp-content/uploads/2017/12/PDF-HealthCareSocialMedia.pdf

12. Bassford HA. The justification of medical paternalism. *Social Science & Medicine*. 1982; 16:731-739.

13. Tang H, Ng JHK. Googling for a diagnosis—use of Google as a diagnostic aid: internet based study. *BMJ*. 2006;333:1143-1145.

14. Frost JH, Massagli MP, Wicks P, Heywood J. How the Social Web supports patient experimentation with a new therapy: the demand for patient-controlled and patient-centered informatics. *AMIA Annual Symposium Proceedings*. 2008:217.

15. Amri M, Feroz K. Google searches help with diagnosis in dermatology. *Inform Prim Care*. 2014;21(2):70-72.

16. Venkatraman A. Garg N, Kumar N. Greater freedom of speech on Web 2.0 correlates with dominance of views linking vaccines to autism. *Vaccine*. 2015;33:1422-1425.

17. Health 2.0 : Technology and society: Is the outbreak of cancer videos, bulimia blogs and other forms of "user generated" medical information a healthy trend? *The Economist.* 2007;September 6:73-74. www.economist.com/technology-quarterly/2007/09/08/health-20

18. Metzger MJ. Making sense of credibility on the Web: models for evaluating online information and recommendations for future research. *Journal of the American Society for Information Science and Technology.* 2007;58:2078-2091.

CHAPTER 34

The Care and Feeding of Your High-Profile Patients

Neil Baum, MD

WHO ARE HIGH-PROFILE PATIENTS?

High-profile patients are more than the professional athlete or the high-ranking politician entering your practice. High-profile patients include movie stars, celebrities, entertainers, musicians, members of academia, Nobel Prize winners, royalty, heads of state, military leaders, very wealthy patients, heads of industry, best-selling authors, and also the family members and even the extended social network of these individuals. A high-profile patient may also be a luminary physician in your community, region, or the nation who has selected you to take care of his or her medical or surgical problems.

In essence, there is no single entity such as fortune or fame that engenders an individual as a high-profile patient, but rather the individuals' perception of themselves and of those around them that based upon their expertise, accomplishments, and contributions, they are considered to be part of a unique segment of society. There is no value judgment awarded for or against these individuals based upon these factors, and the "status" is not synonymous with preferential access or quality of care that is provided to the high-profile patient relative to any other patient seeking medical care.

ADVANTAGES OF PROVIDING CARE FOR HIGH-PROFILE PATIENTS

When your practice treats individuals who are highly visible and who share that they received care in your practice, you create an aura of a special practice. When a plastic surgeon performs a successful facelift or rhinoplasty on a Hollywood movie star, there's an abundance of positive word-of-mouth marketing. The same holds true when an orthopedic surgeon successfully operates on the knee of a famous athlete.

Even though doctors should know better, it is difficult to resist the allure of a high-profile patient. Doctors feel flattered to be chosen by high-profile patients, and they enjoy the prestige. Above all, however, patient confidentiality should always prevail; and as patients, their particular problems should never be used to directly benefit the treating physician or the practice unless approved by the patients.

Another advantage of caring for high-profile patients is that grateful patients may have financial resources with philanthropic potential and an inclination to create endowed chairs, fund research, and contribute to capital campaigns that can benefit other patients in your care.

Providing medical care to high-profile patients creates positive word-of-mouth marketing, which by association promotes your practice. Having high-profile patients is inherently ego-gratifying not only for the doctor and the facility where the care is given but also for the staff.

Some physicians who care for a high-profile patient have their photograph taken with the patient and place it on the wall of the office. Remember, it is mandatory to obtain permission from the patient to place the photo on your "wall of fame." We have seen offices that have sports memorabilia from a team throughout the office, which creates the image, fact or fiction, that these famous players come to the practice for their medical care. We have seen OB/GYN practices that provide obstetric care to the wives of famous athletes promote this image of themselves. Ethical marketing should always prevail with strong consideration for patient privacy.

WHAT ARE THE DISADVANTAGES?

The care of high-profile patients usually takes more time and energy than for other patients. The high-profile patient can be very demanding and request immediate access to the practice. These tendencies can have a negative impact on productivity and practice efficiency, and compromise the most common element of a physician's practice, which is delivery of healthcare to the general public.

Caring for the high-profile patient means being willing and able to provide care out of the traditional medical setting. You may have to go to the locker room, use a facility that is not one that you regularly use, make house calls, or go to the patient's hotel.

Some patients can be are very demanding, insisting that appointments be set at very specific times that are not typical work hours or expecting extraordinary attention. You and your staff may be tempted to acquiesce to these demands, whether they involve something as simple as a specific type of bottled water or something more important such as a particular medical procedure or prescription. An example is Michael Jackson requesting propofol, an anesthetic used in the hospital, from his doctor to help him get to sleep at home, leading to a medical disaster from improper medical judgment. Possibly the most important message is to deliver care that is evidence-based and in the best interest of the patient, yet remains sensitive to the particular system that the patient is embedded within.

Some practices see these patients at a time when there are no other patients present. This will ensure their privacy and create fewer problems, including leaks to the media.

Also, if you provide care for a high-profile patient, and the patient doesn't get the optimum result, the outcomes can become public. Negative news travels fast, and your reputation may be negatively impacted if the high-profile patient has a complication or a less than desirable outcome.

GETTING STARTED: KEEP COOL AND KEEP QUIET

When a high-profile patient has an appointment, you must maintain a professional atmosphere and not be star struck about his or her appearance in your office. However, you must always be a healthcare provider first and a fan second. Provide them with easy access to the practice through a separate entrance, and immediately place them in an exam room or the consultation office.

It is necessary to provide all patients with the same privacy considerations regardless of who they are. Remember, the high-profile patient has the same fears and concerns as your other patients.

The doctor is never the spokesperson for the high-profile patient; the patient will have a PR person and publicist that do that. If a patient wants it to be known that he or she is being treated for a medical condition, the patient will let the media know.

Also, it's important to educate and train your staff on how to handle celebrity patients. Remind your staff members of the importance of maintaining the professional barrier and not sharing any patient's medical information with friends and family.

It is important to never cross the line and make your role as a fan bigger than your role as a medical professional. The most important thing is not to fall into the trap of making medical decisions or performing a procedure that you are not categorically convinced meets the basic criteria of being evidence- or experience-based.

Typically, celebrities have assistants or managers who contact the practice to arrange an appointment. If a celebrity is in your town shooting a movie or a visiting sports team is playing in your city and the need arises for your practice's services, chances are the manager will be contacting your practice. Even this initial call demands privacy. We suggest that the file does not have the celebrity name, but rather the name of the caller.

You might take the extra measure of keeping the files in the doctor's office, which has both medical and financial reports. If word does leak out that your practice is treating a high-profile patient, the best way to deal with the media and even the general public is to simply deny it. Remember you must be an advocate for the patient even if that means not telling the truth to the media.

POINTERS FOR DEALING WITH HIGH-PROFILE PATIENTS

Following are some specific tips for dealing with high-profile patients based on a recent article in the *Cleveland Clinic Journal of Medicine*.[1]

Your entire staff needs to know about the high-profile patient who will be coming to the practice. Although you may know a famous athlete, a well-known politician, or movie actor, not everyone on the staff will be familiar with the individual and may not recognize the name or the person when he or she arrives in the office. If everyone knows that a VIP is coming, then everyone can be prepared.

There may be a tendency to apply shortcuts when caring for a high-profile patient. This is to be avoided at all costs. High-profile patients deserve the same approach as any other patient, and it is imperative that everything that would be done for any other patient is done for the high-profile patient. Any deviation from usual and customary procedures increases the possibility that care may be compromised. In other words, suspending usual practice when caring for a high-profile patient can imperil the patient.[2] Usually, the high-profile patient is relieved if the physician states explicitly, "I am going to treat you as I would any other patient in my practice."

Teamwork is essential for good clinical outcomes especially when the clinical problem is complex. I recommend appointing a "captain" who will be in charge of the team and who will serve as a spokesperson if there is to be communication with the media. Of course, any media discussion would require the patient's permission.

Think of a call from the high-profile patient or his or her agent as a call from the operating room, the ICU, or a referring physician. You will need to respond to these phone calls quickly if you want maintain the high-profile patient in the practice.

Managing the media is probably the most difficult aspect of dealing with high-profile patients, as the media will want medical information. A physician must always protect the confidentiality of the physician-patient relationship. Never forget that the release of health information is at the sole discretion of the patient or his or her designated surrogate. A successful communication strategy balances the public's demand for information with the need to protect the patient's confidentiality; however, patient confidentiality trumps the public's thirst for medical information on your VIP.

A high-profile patient may have his or her own physicians, trainers, and consultants from a sports team or other institutions. Most often, when an outside consultant confirms the current medical care, this can have the beneficial effect of increasing confidence and facilitating management. When a VIP patient involves his or her own physician, whose judgment and care the patient trusts, this represents an opportunity to engage the physician-advisor in clinical decision-making and thus optimize communication with the patient. Collegial interactions with these physician-colleagues can facilitate communication and decision-making for the patient.

Bottom Line: Caring for the high-profile patient can be a challenge and a detractor from your regular medical practice. However, it is the opportunity to enhance and grow your practice. Take the time and energy to feed and care for your high-profile patients: it's a great way to grow your practice, and you just may get a front-row seat at the Oscar's!

REFERENCES

1. Guzman JA, Sasidhar M, Stoller JK. Caring for VIPs: nine principles. *Cleveland Clinic Journal of Medicine.* 2011;78(2):90-94.

2. Adshead G. Healing ourselves: ethical issues in the care of sick doctors. *Adv Psychiatr Treat.* 2005;11:330-337.

CHAPTER 35

Project Management for Healthcare Practices: Costs and Timing

Neil Baum, MD, and Benjamin Swig, MPH, MBA

Creating a timeline and a budget is an important step in implementing changes in the practice. Estimating the cost and time required from initiation to completion is a daunting challenge for any medical practice or hospital. Implementing a new project requires leaving the comfort zone of the routine in order to produce a unique product, service, or result. A project is temporary: it has a defined time to begin and end, and a projected cost. Both of these issues—time and costs—have to be estimated with a degree of accuracy in order to accomplish a singular goal.

When projects are delayed or over budget, the problems often are a result of faulty estimates for the work involved and the related costs at the beginning of the effort.[1] Therefore, it is vital to gather accurate information from the outset and prepare estimates that will make the project successful, arriving at the destination on time and within the estimated budget.

Beginners to the concept of project management often are inaccurate. The time needed for completion often is underestimated because none of the contingencies that can delay the project are taken into account, and the cost of the project often is underestimated, resulting in cost creep or going over the budget.

Time delays and cost overruns also affect the morale of the team and result in finger-pointing and playing the blame game, as no one is taking ownership or responsibility for the delays or added expenses.

ORGANIZING A TEAM RESPONSIBLE FOR THE PROJECT

A successful project such as developing a brand for the practice requires a leader who can coordinate those assigned to various tasks to see that the project is completed in a timely fashion and within the allotted budget.

One of the ways of getting everyone on the same page is to develop a project proposal and then tweak or refine it over time. The proposal should address the following elements[1]:

- Goal or purpose of the project;
- Why the project is being implemented; and
- The objectives of the project.

At this early stage, the idea for a project will be carefully examined by the team leader to determine whether or not it benefits the practice or the hospital. During this early phase, a decision-making team, usually consisting of the office manager, the doctors, and someone from marketing, will determine whether the project can realistically be completed. Ideally, the goal should be synthesized into a single sentence. We believe that if you can't put your goal on the back of an envelope, you shouldn't initiate the project.

STARTING WITH A LIST OF TASKS

Initially, the team should meet and list all of the tasks that will be needed to make the project happen. We suggest that this meeting take place away from the practice or the hospital, to avoid distractions. Of course, all cell phones must be silenced during this meeting. The leader should ask everyone for tasks that they deem necessary for the successful completion of the project. Ideas should not be judged at this time; rather, free-flowing dialog should take place, with every idea written on a white board or a flip chart. One team member should be assigned to take notes and to prepare a summary or spreadsheet of the tasks. You want to try to identify all of the activities, tasks, and duties that the project will require in as much detail as possible. Figure 1 shows tasks necessary to create a brand for a urology practice.

CREATING A WORK BREAKDOWN STRUCTURE

A work breakdown structure (WBS) is a spreadsheet of all the work necessary to complete a project. A WBS is arranged in a hierarchy and

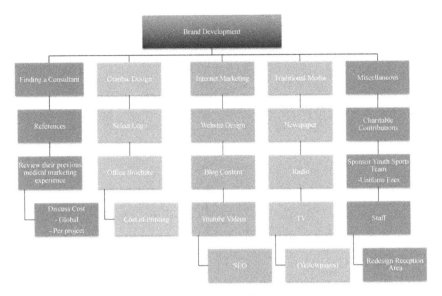

FIGURE 1. Brand development for a urology practice.
SEO, search engine optimization.

constructed to allow for clear and logical groupings, by either activities or results. The WBS serves as an early foundation for creating an effective schedule and for cost estimating. A project manager or leader will develop a WBS as a precursor to a detailed project schedule.

An example of a WBS for creating a shared medical appointment (SMA) program for the practice is shown in Figure 2. Most WBSs start with a description of the project, followed by a list of categories for accomplishing the project. These usually are the tasks that were identified at the initiation of the project. Under each category is the list of steps that must be taken to accomplish each of the categories.

DEVELOPING AN ESTIMATED PROJECT COST

For each activity in the WBS you need to calculate a cost. For example, creating a logo for the brand may be a one-time cost, and you should have a range provided to you by the logo designer. However, updating and maintaining the website and other social media for the brand will be an ongoing cost that will continue after the project has been launched and also after the completion of the initial project.

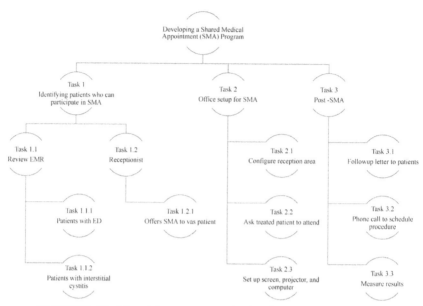

FIGURE 2. Work breakdown structure for developing a shared medical appointment (SMA) program. ED, erectile dysfunction; EMR, electronic medical record; vas, vasectomy.

Another method of assigning costs is to use historical data. If your practice or hospital has completed a similar project, such as an ad campaign to promote a service offered by the practice, the cost of the previous project may be available and may be at least partially applicable to the new project. Finally, the project manager can estimate overhead by applying a percentage based on how much overhead costs such projects typically generate.

A common technique for cost estimating is to list the resources you need for the project and then total their costs. If you have created a comprehensive WBS that includes all of the activities necessary for the project to be accomplished, then assigning personnel and costs to each activity becomes easier and provides the practice and the bean counters with a very close estimate of the costs involve. Typical resources include equipment, material, services, and labor. You can get costs for equipment, material, and services by consulting price lists or by requesting bids for the larger-cost items. Labor costs usually are computed at an hourly rate, and you can base the total costs on estimates from similar projects or ask for bids if you decide to outsource the work.

After preparing the WBS, you will need to assemble your team and ask them for their estimates of how much time will be required to complete their part of the project. We suggest that you ask them for a range, in hours or weeks or months, of the time they will need to create their component of the project. Using estimated hours is usually the best approach for smaller projects.

Your WBS will be essential in estimating the cost of the project. You will assign a dollar value to each of the action steps and for each category. You then add all of the costs for each category to arrive at an estimate of the total cost of the project. Table 1 shows an example of a cost estimate for finding a place to practice.

Table 1. Sample Cost Estimate

#	Activity	Duration (hr)	Cost
	**FINDING A PLACE TO PRACTICE**		
	Time and cost estimate		
1	Site selection and realtor	10	Paid by leasor
2	Redesign space with architect ($150/hr)	30	$4,500
3	Work with interior decorator ($100/hr)	30	$3,000
4	Select contractor	10	N/A
5	Review lease with lawyer ($200/hr)	10	$2,000
6	Grand opening ($100/hr)	5	$500
7	Signage ($100/hr)	2	$200
8	Obtain loan from bank	3	N/A
9	Insurance (Renters and Business Disruption)	5	N/A
10	Announcements ($50/hr)	5	$250
	Total:	**110**	**$10,450**

Think of your WBS as a farmer's fence (i.e., always under construction). It is never a document set in stone. It will need to be tweaked and altered as the project evolves.

CREATING A TIME LINE OR SCHEDULE FOR THE PROJECT

Two key features of a successful project are bringing the project to completion: (1) on time; and (2) within the allotted budget. Delay in time or budget overruns can wreak havoc with a project and result in even the

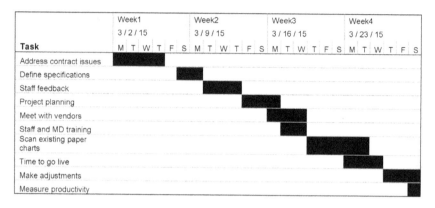

FIGURE 3. Sample Gantt chart for electronic medical record implementation. Black squares indicate when task is completed.

best-intentioned project becoming derailed or even aborted. The project manager can only fulfill the desired objectives if the estimates leading to the project schedule and budget are accurate. Methods for estimating project times and costs focus on simplifying the process and breaking it down into little steps. Such methods allow project managers to estimate the cost and duration of small tasks more reliably.

Each project should have a formal schedule that will serve as a guideline for completion of various aspects of the project. This might include time to assemble the team, time to create a budget, time to develop a website, and time to generate publicity for the project. Establishing a project management schedule involves listing milestones, activities, and deliverables with intended start and completion dates.

Numerous software programs are available that easily create a project schedule. One of the more popular scheduling programs for project management is the Gantt chart, a type of bar chart that illustrates a project schedule. Gantt charts illustrate the start and finish dates of the project. A sample Gantt chart for implementing an electronic medical record system is shown in Figure 3. The bars to the right of the activity indicate when the activity will take place, and the rightmost bar in the Gantt chart indicates when the project will be completed.

It is necessary to obtain buy-in from the team responsible for the project. Once the project is finalized and the WBS is created with a budget and a time line, the team must be apprised of the expectations and their commitment to seeing that the project reaches completion must be obtained. Frequent progress reports are essential to the success of the project. You will want to ask what was accomplished in the past week and what are the plans and expectations for the next week. It is a good idea to ask if there are obstacles standing in the way of completion of the project and what can be done to remove these roadblocks. Upfront commitment and frequent communication, both written and verbal, are necessary for a successful project completion.

SUMMARY

Doctors and practices are getting more sophisticated in their allocation of time and money for new projects. Over the lifetime of most physicians, there will be projects that will require careful planning and budgeting in order to determine the time to bring a project from idea to actual implementation. Also, it is important to have an estimate on the expenses for each project. By following the process of project management, these new ventures can be brought online in a timely fashion and within the allotted budget.

REFERENCE

1. Anderson MA, Anderson E, Parker G. *Operations Management for Dummies*. Hoboken, NJ: John Wiley and Sons; 2013.

CHAPTER 36

Viral Marketing in Healthcare: The Kind of Virus You Actually Want to Catch

BRITTNEY C. BAUER, PHD, AND NEIL BAUM, MD

With the recent COVID-19 pandemic, the world was forcefully reminded of the unmitigated power and persistence of a novel virus. Perhaps an effective way to fight such an outbreak is with a different kind of novel virus, one that instead of spreading infection propagates awareness and support. The "good kind of virus" we are referring to is spread through viral marketing tactics. Viral marketing is a strategy that uses network-supported word-of-mouth in digital marketing promotions.[1] In the healthcare sector, it lives up to its name by rapidly spreading information about a cause, practice, service, or medical professional with consumers through their social networks.

In the history of marketing strategy, viral marketing can be considered one of the new kids on the block. Traditional marketing media such as print, television, and radio have become common and effective tools in promoting healthcare services. However, modern technology now allows for digital marketing as an additional medium, and viral marketing is one such untapped marketing vehicle that is extremely popular in mass markets, highly efficient by nature, and places minimal demands on the organization's budget. It is viral marketing that allows medical practices to reach out to potential patients who may not otherwise be aware of the practice or its message. Viral marketing allows practices to access additional customers and enter new markets, thereby increasing the total number of potential patients who can avail themselves of the practice's services. Before discussing how to put viral marketing to work for the practice, it is necessary to clarify what viral marketing is and how it works.

WHAT IS VIRAL MARKETING?

The term *viral marketing* was coined by two venture capitalists to describe the rapid growth of an organization as a result of consumers spreading a message through their own word-of-mouth networks.[2] Their main observation was that viral messages spread organically, with spatial and network locality, very much like biological viruses.[3] The metaphor depicting viral marketing as a biological virus is largely due to the ideas that: (1) marketers should encourage consumers to disseminate content so as to create the potential for exponential growth;[4] and (2) the viral content's spread and effect on consumers is an inherently uncontrollable risk.

In a review of the viral marketing literature, Reichstein and Brusch[1] combined several existing conceptualizations of the phenomenon in order to provide a more comprehensive definition:

> Viral marketing is defined as marketing strategies that permit exponential distribution of content in network-based channels in the shortest time with comparatively little effort and additionally generate measurable added value through the content, which leads to a high cost-benefit effect.

The benefits of viral marketing are of enormous importance today because of the pervasiveness of virtual social networks through which viral content can be spread. An astonishing 2.94 billion people are estimated to actively use social networks, which represents more than one in three individuals worldwide.[5] Hence, organizations are advised to consistently attempt to create viral content on social networks in order to improve the perceptions of both current and potential new customers.[6]

DISCUSSION

How Does Viral Marketing Spread?

The traditional method of marketing a healthcare center by describing what the practice does and how it's different from other service providers in the community pales in comparison with the results of viral marketing. Conventional healthcare marketing often is predictable and uninspired—even when it uses modern technology to engage in digital and social media marketing. Just because the content is available online does not mean that it will go viral. The message and its delivery must be highly creative, while still conveying key information about the practice, in order to stand out and entice consumers to share the content with others in their social networks.

The advantage of inspiring viral marketing is that the creative content organically attracts people to the marketing message by using existing and potential patients to keep the message alive, without additional effort or expense by the organization. In a healthcare context, an effective viral marketing program can generate positive reactions or experiences for potential patients, and motivate them to share the experience with others in their social networks. The real value of virality is that the marketing message will perpetuate itself because others will be attracted to the creative content and want to engage in the experience.

Patients ultimately are consumers who are exposed to hundreds of marketing messages every day. Because it is not possible for humans to consciously attend to all of our sensory inputs at the same time,[7] most potential patients inevitably ignore most messages. With viral marketing, a message is able to break through the clutter of information overload that is common in traditional marketing communications. This gives the practice an opportunity to make a real impact on potential patients, which allows the marketing message to be much more effective. So, how do you create a viral marketing epidemic? According to Kaplan and Haenlein, [8] to make viral marketing work, "the right people need to get the right message under the right circumstances." The following section spotlights several viral cases that got these timing elements right.

Viral Marketing Cases

Perhaps the greatest viral marketing example of all time is the Ice Bucket Challenge for amyotrophic lateral sclerosis (ALS). The Ice Bucket Challenge, which began in 2014, was used to raise awareness and funding for ALS by having participants challenge friends to dump a bucket of ice water on their heads. The program was extraordinarily successful, enticing over 28 million people to join the virtual conversation by posting, commenting, or liking a challenge, and inspiring 2.4 million Ice Bucket Challenge–related videos to be shared on social networks.[9] As a result, $115 million was donated to fight ALS in just an eight-week period, an amount that funded over 200 research projects and global research collaborations; led to the discovery of five new genes, which spurred innovative therapies and drug trials; and helped 15,000 patients per year receive the treatments and care that they needed.[10]

The Ice Bucket Challenge gave everyone a fun way to get involved and give to a worthy cause. The challenge demonstrated the power of social media and how it could be effectively harnessed, directed, and managed to rapidly spread a message to the mass public. Most importantly, the Ice Bucket Challenge was a simple call to action with a stipulated time limit for those invited to participate. Participants had to accept and complete the Ice Bucket Challenge within 24 hours.[11] We contend that the time limit that was placed on the challenge created a sense of urgency and was one of the main reasons why the campaign spread so quickly.

Because the Ice Bucket Challenge was so successful, other organizations could play off the same idea in an attempt to create their own viral marketing campaigns. For example, ROI Online did this with their Nice Bucket Challenge. They built on the success and good intentions of the Ice Bucket Challenge, but added a unique twist of their own by filling the buckets with cold water bottles, food, socks, and toiletries to give to those in need.[12] Their campaign did not make as big a splash as the Ice Bucket Challenge, but it was another example of using a viral marketing strategy to communicate a message about improving health and well-being, and it generated some positive publicity for the organization.

Viral content should be timely not only in that it motivates consumer to act immediately, but also in its relevance and importance to society. We can see current examples of relevant viral content related to the COVID-19 pandemic. For example, there have been many stories during the last year about healthcare workers who risked their lives on a daily basis to care for COVID-19 patients. This presents an opportunity for the healthcare industry to use storytelling to highlight and bring awareness to the outstanding care that the practice or hospital provides. Healthcare, in particular, is a perfect candidate for telling the uplifting success stories of patients who were saved by the care of a medical center.

New York-Presbyterian Hospital is one of the best examples of a healthcare organization that shares these viral-worthy and heart-tugging stories. They frequently post *My COVID-19 Story* excerpts from their healthcare workers, as well as special messages to *Healthcare Heroes* (e.g., delivered by Bette Midler, Robert De Niro, Jennifer Lopez, New York Fire Department).[13]

Another example that recently went viral comes from Daniel Akinyemi, an ICU nurse in Montclair, New Jersey. Mr. Akinyemi had a COVID-19 patient on a ventilator whose husband mentioned that her favorite song was *Blue Bayou* and her favorite reading from the Bible was Psalm 23, so he sang the song and recited the biblical passage to her, and in an amazing recovery the very next day she was able to be weaned off the ventilator.[14] These types of messages have the power to capture widespread attention and bring positive awareness to the medical practice.

GETTING STARTED

As previously demonstrated, viral marketing strategies are extremely applicable for the healthcare industry because they have time-sensitive missions in both urgency and relevance to patients. For instance, the practice could offer a discount for a short period (e.g., new patient discounts) or come out with limited-time service offers (e.g., drive-through flu shots), which would create a need for immediate response from those interested in the practice's services. Furthermore, the practice could create innovative content that is related to pressing social or societal issues that are significantly aligned with the work of their organization (e.g., immigrant health and wellness). The ultimate purpose of using viral marketing in healthcare is to inspire patients to share the practice's content with others in their social networks so as to exponentially grow the pool of patients that can be assisted by or attracted to the practice. If viral marketing works, it creates a veritable buzz about the practice and its service offerings. Moreover, even if the content does not go viral, it is still reinforcing the practice's marketing mix and digital presence, which ultimately will build brand equity and benefit the organization in the long-run.

MEASURING RESULTS

The main goal of viral marketing is to attain exponential growth that results in high proliferation rates. This means that consumers must view the message, respond to the call for action, and share the content with others in their social networks. Therefore, as in epidemics and pandemics, the distribution rate of the viral content must be greater than one in order to achieve exponential growth. Kaplan and Haenlein[8] note that the exchange of electronic word-of-mouth—which is the driving force behind the distribution of viral marketing—is substantially easier to monitor than traditional word-of-mouth behavior, and allows for a more accurate analysis of its impact on tangible business outcomes such as new customer acquisition and profitability. The effectiveness of viral marketing efforts can be measured by comparing the number of online responses (e.g., likes, shares, comments, new posts) to changes in firm performance pre- and post-exposure to the marketing content. Thus, practices are better able to calculate return on marketing in a digital environment when employing these viral marketing tactics.

Viral marketing allows practices to break through the information clutter that bombards the public on a daily basis in order to have a real impact on potential new patients. Even if a viral marketing effort does not result in a new patient calling for an appointment, there is a good chance that it will help the practice gain exposure and build an enhanced contact list. For example, more people may sign up for the practice's newsletters and e-mails if they become interested in the online content. This enhanced e-mail list can generate future marketing opportunities for the organization.

Marketing, whether conventional or viral, often requires several contacts between the practice and new patients. It is not uncommon for a first message to capture the attention of potential new patients, yet not be strong enough to prompt them to immediate action. It is typically necessary to follow up with additional marketing efforts in order to influence behavior. After several contacts, it is more likely that the new patient will not only recognize the name of the doctor, practice, or hospital, but also have a more developed attitude towards that healthcare provider, which finally motivates them to become a patient.

Bottom Line: When it is done right, viral marketing can generate visibility and enhance the reputation of the practice, highlighting unique aspects that make the practice and its services attractive to the patient. Because viral marketing commonly relies on the concept of a word-of-mouth endorsement, the practice gains credibility with prospective patients in a very short period of time due to positive recommendations by those in their social networks. This enhanced credibility creates better opportunities to convert potential patients into actual patients. Thus, if exposure and rapid growth are the goals, then viral marketing in healthcare represents the kind of virus that you want to catch.

REFERENCES

1. Reichstein T, Brusch I. The decision_making process in viral marketing—a review and suggestions for further research. *Psychology & Marketing.* 2019;36:1062-1081.

2. Eckler P, Rodgers S. Viral marketing on the Internet. *Wiley International Encyclopedia of Marketing;* 2010.

3. Gupta A, Tyagi M, Sharma D. Use of social media marketing in healthcare. *Journal of Health Management.* 2013;15:293-302.

4. Wilson RF. The six simple principles of viral marketing. *Web Marketing Today.* 2000;70(1):232.

5. eMarketer. Q2 2019 Social trends. eMarketer. July 23, 2019. www.emarketer.com/content/q2-2019-social-trends.

6. Akpinar E, Berger J. Valuable virality. *Journal of Marketing Research.* 2017;54:318-330.

7. Musen G, Treisman A. Implicit and explicit memory for visual patterns. *J Exp Psychol Learn Mem Cogn.* 1990;16:127-137.

8. Kaplan AM, Haenlein M. Two hearts in three-quarter time: how to waltz the social media/viral marketing dance. *Business Horizons.* 2011;54:253-263.

9. Olenski S. 7 marketing lessons from the ALS Ice Bucket Challenge. Forbes.com. August 22, 2014. www.forbes.com/sites/steveolenski/2014/08/22/7-marketing-lessons-from-the-als-ice-bucket-challenge/#7b80e0347586.

10. Every drop adds up. The ALS Association. 2020. www.alsa.org/fight-als/ice-bucket-challenge.html

11. Trejos A. Ice Bucket Challenge: 5 things you should know. *USA Today.* July 3, 2017. www.usatoday.com/story/news/2017/07/03/ice-bucket-challenge-5-things-you-should-know/448006001/.

12. Brown S. Why has the ALS Ice Bucket Challenge been such a huge success? ROI Online. May 2, 2019. www.roionline.com/blog/blog/why-has-the-als-ice-bucket-challenge-been-such-a-huge-su.

13. A New Patient Experience: Inside the New York-Presbyterian David H. Koch Center. Health Matters. 2020. https://healthmatters.nyp.org/a-new-patient-experience/.

14. In harm's way. *The New York Times.* Updated August 1, 2020. www.nytimes.com/interactive/2020/world/coronavirus-health-care-workers.html.

CHAPTER 37

Patient Profiling Using Psychographics: Demographics vs. Psychographics and Why Culture Matters Most

Neil Baum, MD

PSYCHOGRAPHICS VERSUS DEMOGRAPHICS

Demographic information includes the basics: age, gender, race, address, insurance information, phone number, e-mail address, and occupation. Although demographics are still valuable and can be used as a starting point, they don't shed light on the attitudes and the mindset of your ideal patients. The demographics are merely the dry facts.

Practices are used to thinking only in terms of demographics, because dividing a market up by age, gender, ethnicity, and other broad variables can help to understand the differences and commonalities among patients. The thinking was "our target audience is 45- to 65-year-old women" or "we are launching a marketing campaign aimed at urban Latinos." Today, that thinking can be limiting your marketing efforts. Demographics only segments the patients that you are interested in attracting, but it isn't specific enough to be maximally effective.

Psychographics, on the other hand, focuses on the interests, attitudes, and emotions of a segment of potential patients—exactly the things practices need to understand to best promote their services to a particular segment of the population that the practice wishes to attract. To reach these ideal patients, you must know what or who they value most, where they get their medical education and medical information, and what content appeals to them.

Psychographics are like demographics on steroids. Psychographic information might include your patients' habits, hobbies, health-related experiences, and values. Demographics explain "who" your patient is; psychographics explain "why" they become part of your practice.

Psychographic segmentation divides the market into groups based on social class, lifestyle, and personality characteristics. It is based on the assumption that the types of products and brands and individual purchases will reflect that person's characteristics and patterns of living.

You can only reach your target audience effectively when you understand both their demographics and their psychographics. The combination of both sets of data starts to form your patient persona—a detailed picture of the patients you would like to care for in the future.

EXAMPLE OF PSYCHOGRAPHICS AND DEMOGRAPHICS IN A PRIMARY CARE SETTING

Let's look at a 45-year-old woman with multiple medical conditions. Her demographic information might include the following:

- Female;
- Aged 45;
- Address, telephone number, e-mail address, and insurance information;
- Married, with children;
- Dealing with issues of weight gain, diabetes, lack of energy or hormonal imbalance; and
- Household income $100K+.

Her psychographic information might include the following:

- Concerned with health and appearance;
- Wants a healthy lifestyle, but doesn't have much time;
- Enjoys going online in the evenings, big fan of Pinterest;
- Tends to favor quality over economy;
- Finds fulfillment in her career and family; and
- Values time with a small group of friends.

Looking at the two data sets, it's easy to see why you need both psychographic and demographic information. By using demographics alone, you have only a vague picture of your patient—you understand her challenges, but not where to find her and what really moves her to action. Psychographics gives you so much more understanding of the patient!

If you collect demographic information alone, you will have only a very hazy picture of this patient. Demographics provide you with information on how to find her and whether she has insurance to cover her healthcare costs. However, it is through psychographic information that you understand her challenges, and what really moves her to action. It is the combination of psychographics and demographics that gives you much more insight into your patients.

OBTAINING PSYCHOGRAPHIC INFORMATION

There are two effective methods for obtaining psychographic data: (1) interviewing your current patients; and (2) investigating your website traffic or analytics.

Interviewing Existing Patients

Start by thinking of your best patients. Next time you talk, ask them for a few more details about themselves. You can ask what they did over the weekend, if they have seen any good movies lately, found any great holiday deals, made any New Year's resolutions, and so on. Because we are physicians, we have the luxury of probing a patient's clinical, social, occupational, recreational, and emotional history.

Depending on your relationship with the patients, you can tell them exactly why you're asking and be more direct. In more than 40 years of practice, I've never had a patient fail to answer these questions or be upset about being asked for more information than their clinical history.

Want a larger sampling? Send out a patient survey and be honest—tell them you want to better understand what they care about. Most people are more than happy to share. This survey can easily be created on surveymonkey. com. The website is free, and it is easy to create a useful psychographic survey. You probably have collected e-mail addresses as part of your demographic queries, and you can easily send out your survey to your existing patients.

Psychographic segmentation starts with development of a questionnaire that uses attitudinal, values- and belief-based statements, to which patients react. Consider providing a range of responses—for example, from "Strongly Agree" to "Strongly Disagree." Once survey responses are gathered, a factor analysis using statistical clustering is used to identify response patterns that indicate natural clusters based on similar answers.

Once all survey data are analyzed, consistent groups—psychographic segments—are defined. Additional social media monitoring and analytics (discussed in the next section) can provide added insights based on trends in consumer interests and attitudes. Of course, the very nature of answering a survey requires respondents to consider their thoughts and choose an answer. When survey questions are focused on a specific topic, such as hours of operation or use of ancillary services, as with attitudinal segmentation, the results may be skewed because many respondents rationalize their answers based on societal norms or, in the case of healthcare, published facts.

Psychographic segmentation, on the other hand, may include completely unrelated and discontinuous questions about personal values or beliefs, so respondents are less likely to rationalize. However, the research team must make the effort to draw connections between psychographic insights and the topic of focus to make these insights actionable, which may require additional research.

After using quantitative marketing research to identify psychographic segments, conducting qualitative research (e.g., focus groups and one-on-one interviews) with members of each psychographic segment can help interpret the quantitative data from the perspective of each segment.

Investigating Website Analytics

If you prefer a more behind-the-scenes kind of investigation, there's no better way than using website analytics. The Internet has made capturing psychographic data much easier and relevant to both patients and practices alike. The Internet also makes it easier to find like-minded patients, even if they're from a different community or even a different country.

One of the best is Google Analytics, which also is free. Look at your existing website and see what the landing pages are where patients will start to look at your content. You can also see the bounce rate or how quickly the viewer left your site without looking at the content. Using analytics, you can determine what has moved patients to click, call, or schedule an appointment in the past.

USING PSYCHOGRAPHICS IN YOUR MARKETING

Getting the psychographic data is important, but really applying it to your practice is how you make it effective.

We've gathered some hypothetical data using the techniques outlined in the previous section, so now let's apply our data to our marketing strategy!

Once you understand what is important to the target patient, you'll know where to find her and how to motivate her. You'll know how to give her what she wants—that offering deep discounts isn't going to motivate her.

When developing and executing campaigns, content, messaging, and so on remember this: communication resonates with people that share the same psychographics (passion points, interests, and beliefs), not demographics. Getting the psychographic data is important, but how do you apply the data to your marketing and make it effective?

Let's continue with the example of the 45-year-old female with diabetes and obesity. Once you understand what is important to her, you'll know where to find her on the Internet and how to motivate her. You'll know how to give her what she wants—that offering free WiFi in the reception area isn't going to motivate her to be part of your practice. Instead, she wants to hear that your nutritional counseling service has worked for others in your practice with similar medical problems and how it will give her better health without a huge time commitment. So make sure you highlight customer comments to that effect.

When you know that she's spending her free time on Pinterest, you can stop spending money on Facebook or newspaper and magazine ads. Instead, use her love of Pinterest and share time-saving household and nutrition tips and give her ideas for fun things to do with family and friends.

Watch what gets repinned and analyze what that tells you about her. Did she love the one about the smiley-face veggie platters for an after-school snack? Give her more ways to help keep her kids eating well. If the "girl's night out" inspirational quote went over big, give her more ways to have fun with her friends.

When you know that career and family are important to her, you'll want to create content on your website or your blog that highlights the impact that good health has on job performance and also help with her self-esteem and confidence both at the job and when off the clock.

Knowing more about her hobbies and interests will help you when you need to choose a prize for your next contest, what to blog about, and what sorts of images to use in your next ad.

Using psychographics allows you to do smarter keyword targeting and move your website to the top of Google using search engine optimization. For example, targeting one message about your weight loss program for teenagers to parents who are searching for "childhood obesity" and another message to parents who are searching for "nutrition for teenagers" is likely to be one of the options that parents will discover if they are searching the Internet for solutions for their children's obesity. Once you know the key differences in what your patients care about, you can target Facebook ads to parents who've liked specific pages or identified particular interests; you can figure out the hashtags that different psychographic groups use on Twitter and target differently to those groups.

As with other forms of market segmentation, psychographic segmentation enables practices to identify patient groups based on shared characteristics. One key distinction is that psychographic segmentation focuses on what motivates individual patients—which can be more informative when developing marketing plans, wellness initiatives, or disease management programs.

When used in conjunction with demographic or socioeconomic data, psychographics enables practices to gain a clearer picture of both internal and external factors that influence patients' behaviors. These insights can also be helpful for hospitals and other healthcare organizations to understand patients' decision-making processes better and to improve the relevance of communication—whether designed to boost brand awareness and loyalty or increase patient engagement with the practice.

Bottom Line: It is critical for practices to invest in and understand the psychographics of a patient population rather than concentrating only on age, gender, location, and so on. The use of psychographics will help you develop not only the messages and marketing campaigns but also the services that your practice offers and that specific patients want and need.

CHAPTER 38

Learning from the Financial Industry: A Roadmap for Healthcare Practices

Neil Baum, MD

TURN SERVICES INTO PRODUCTS

The financial industry enables their clients to easily invest for their retirement and reach milestones with the client's financial goals and objectives at specific dates prior to retirement. Clients simply go to the firm's website and select the year they plan to retire, buy the recommended mutual fund, and enjoy the benefits of dynamic, lifetime asset allocation. In the past, before target date funds existed, people had to meet with their financial advisors to change the asset allocation in their financial portfolios as they aged toward retirement. The development of target date funds turned asset allocation from a service that typically required in-person annual discussions into a "set it and forget it" product that lowered costs and increased convenience.

In healthcare, Omada (www.omadahealth.com) similarly has turned services into a product. Omada packages complementary healthcare devices, services, and support into a turnkey offering that it sells to employers and health insurance plans to help people lose weight and reduce their risk of type 2 diabetes or heart disease. When people sign up for Omada's offering, they receive a wireless, digital bathroom scale, pedometer, resistance band, and tape measure. Customers also use a smartphone app to pair them with health coaches, who help guide them through health and wellness decisions throughout their day. By integrating devices and services with a well-designed digital platform and service experience, Omada has created an effective product that links participants' engagement to their clinical outcomes.

For example, Omada provides patients with highly trained coaches who are empowered with data to deliver guidance and healthcare advice from professional caregivers. Patients are given wireless scale to keep and offer smart device integration for seamless tracking. Those who decide to participate in the program are matched with a small group of peers for motivation, encouragement, and empathy. From meditation to medication, the program tailors the content to have an immediate and lasting impact. Omada empower participants to reach their unique goals through a customized to-do list. The result is that Omada has become the largest CDC-recognized digital diabetes prevention program and has inspired hundreds of thousands of participants to take their health into their own hands.

Another example is Pillpack (www.pillpack.com), a digital pharmacy "designed around your life," which turned the complex business of managing multiple prescriptions into an easy-to-use product. It sends subscribers customized packs of pills labeled with the date and time they're to be taken, and its mobile app pushes reminders and provides access to 24/7 customer service. Pillpack turned prescription management from a clunky, disconnected series of services into an elegant product that decreases trips to the pharmacy, eliminates sorting and counting medications, and reduces the chance of missed or incorrect doses.

INCREASE CONVENIENCE AND REDUCE COST

Historically, if you wanted to meet with a stockbroker or your insurance agent you had to make an appointment and get to the broker's office during his or her office hours. Today, of course, online brokers enable customers to manage their portfolio from home, at any time, on a 24/7 basis, at a fraction of the cost of a traditional broker, and with the added advantage of being much more convenient. However, you might have a problem trying to reach the online broker on the telephone!

Just as online brokerages pioneered virtual financial services, telehealth, which connects patients and clinicians by video and other digital technologies, enables patients to get a diagnosis, healthcare advice, and education, day or night, from the comfort of home.[1-3] More than 10 million consumers benefited from telehealth use in 2017, and insurance carriers are increasingly covering these visits, because they're both more convenient for their members and less expensive than office visits.[4]

Telehealth applies to patients with conditions requiring frequent follow-up visits and infrequent physical exams, and who have difficulty coming into the office. As with the financial industry, security is of paramount importance. Telehealth uses a secure video platform to connect with patients remotely, which is especially helpful if a patient is at a great distance from the hospital or the medical office. This technology is certainly applicable for patients who would not need to come into the office for in-person care and, therefore, avoids increasing overall utilization and reduces the cost of care. There is a movement for doctors to open up their schedules to see patients virtually, which makes the doctor more efficient and more productive.

Few recent trends in healthcare delivery have more power to improve population health, patient and provider experience, and hospital business models than virtual care. But for an industry reliant on, and in many ways limited by, brick-and-mortar facilities, this movement will mean significant disruption for providers. As more commercial and state payers offer telehealth coverage, and patients come to expect virtual care as standard practice, meeting the demand is quickly becoming clinically and financially imperative.

Like many hospitals, Brigham and Women's Hospital (BWH) in Boston is actively preparing for the era of virtual care in order to best meet patients' needs. The Director for Telehealth at BWH regularly hears about practices interested in offering virtual care services or receives patient inquiries about the telehealth programs. In spite of this growing buzz, however, virtual care at most practices and hospitals, including other academic medical centers, remains a future vision. For smaller or community-based providers, there is a greater need for virtual care but less interest in implementing the technology.

For virtual care to move from a pilot project to a standard service, the interested provider must answer five questions:

- Which clinical services should be offered virtually and why?
- Which technology tools will meet the demographic, clinical, and business needs for these services?
- Should telehealth programs be offered directly to patients or only offered through providers?
- How does virtual care create value for my practice or organization?

- How can this value be assessed from the patients' perspective as well as that of the organization?

Once these questions are answered, then the decision can be made to proceed with the implementation process.

Improving Access to Healthcare as Well as Improving Chronic Disease Management

The virtual care strategy can easily be started with video-based visits for outpatients with chronic diseases. Providers who see patients with conditions requiring frequent follow-up visits but infrequent physical exams, and who have difficulty coming into the office, are most likely to benefit. Patients who meet these criteria include patients with inflammatory bowel disease, diabetes, mood disorders, hypertension, ischemic heart disease, prostate disease, and airway disorders. The exam rooms and provider offices contain cameras that have a secure platform to remotely connect with patients. Providers must be willing to open up their schedules to see patients virtually, either during their clinical hours or during their nonclinical time.

The results of the pilot study at BWH consisted of approximately 600 visits that were conducted virtually, requiring about 200 additional hours for participating providers to see patients. Among patients surveyed after their initial encounter, 97% were satisfied with the experience and would recommend the program, and 74% felt that the interaction actually improved their relationship with their provider, allaying some of our concerns. The study found that 87% of patients said they would have had to physically come to the office to see a provider face-to-face if it weren't for their virtual visit.[4]

The program director believes that no-show rates will be decreased by offering virtual care, given the dramatic improvement in patient convenience. Increasing the time patients are able to spend at home or at work, instead of traveling to see providers, will be a major advantage for the patients. Moreover, reducing no-shows and increasing the number of patients who engage with their doctor will lead to improvement in quality and help reduce cost of care, such as hospital readmissions or visits to emergency departments. Finally, virtual care should result in a reduction of provider burnout, which currently affects nearly 50% of all physicians.[5]

E-Visits: Providing On-Demand, Virtual Urgent Care for Simple Symptoms

At the other end of the clinical complexity spectrum, a virtual care program is applicable for patients with common, acute symptoms requiring rapid triage and management who have trouble achieving access to their providers. For certain common and irritating symptoms, seeing one's provider in the office is often less important than obtaining quick access to care.

Broadening the Reach of Specialty Care

In addition to telehealth services offered directly to patients, virtual tools are available to improve care and communication among providers. Virtual visits solve daily problems in ambulatory care. For example, after reviewing the patient questionnaire and having a brief discussion with the patient, the physician makes the decision if a referral is necessary or if the patient should be advised to make an appointment to visit the brick-and-mortar facility. At BWH, virtual visits can be directed to a dedicated and responsive communication channel that can be ordered like any medication or test. Providers formulate a question and synthesize relevant information, and then route these requests to established specialists. The most common specialist teams were cardiology, endocrinology, gastroenterology, hematology, infectious disease, orthopedics, and urology.

The BWH virtual care program has two strategic aims, targeted at improving access and supporting primary care providers so that more primary care can be managed without actual face-to-face referrals, and to ensure that when referrals do take place, the specialty consultation is more effective and more timely for the patient. The results demonstrated that when a patient first virtually consulted with a specialist in that field, about 50% of the time, a face-to-face office visit was avoided. From a cost perspective, this means fewer unnecessary specialist visits, thus reducing healthcare costs.[4]

There will soon be a day when providers will be deciding not "whether" to offer telehealth, but "when" and "how much." Virtual care holds the promise of revolutionizing healthcare delivery, but it must be carefully guided through complex clinical, financial, and technologic decisions. The challenge has not been in finding opportunities for virtual care, but, rather, on focusing on those with the highest value and the greatest cost savings.

LEVERAGE BIG DATA

In the financial world, Mint (www.mint.com) aggregates financial information from disparate sources including banks, brokerages, and credit card companies to provide users with a comprehensive view of their finances. Based on these data, it provides targeted money management recommendations and advertisements for other financial products and services such as auto insurance, credit cards, and IRAs. By applying insights drawn from analysis of data from its 20 million users, Mint can recommend highly targeted financial products to individual customers that align with their financial goals and with their level of risk.

Similarly, Memorial Sloan Kettering Cancer Center partnered with IBM Watson and Quest Diagnostics to apply big-data analytics to cancer diagnosis and treatment.[5] After the genomic makeup of a patient's tumor is determined, Watson examines a vast and growing clinical trial and medical literature database and, applying rules created by leading oncologists, finds targeted treatment options for individual patients.

IBM Watson has harnessed artificial intelligence–based screening processes to automate data-driven clinical trial identification steps and increase the speed at which matches can be made between patient, tumor, diagnosis, and treatment. Using the analysis of unstructured and structured data to analyze both patient records and trial inclusion/exclusion criteria, Watson for Clinical Trial Matching enables oncologists to quickly review a list of potential trials for every patient, while supporting the clinical trial office in reaching enrollment numbers. Watson for Clinical Trial Matching enables clinicians to more easily and quickly find a list of clinical trials for an eligible patient. Similarly, it enhances the ability of clinical trial coordinators to find patients who are potentially eligible for any of the site's trials. The improvement in screening efficiency and more effective patient recruitment can help increase clinical trial enrollment targets and offer patients the option of a clinical trial for treatment. IBM Watson proactively identifies eligible trial participants to help maximize placement into suitable clinical trials, improve enrollment target success, and enhance treatments with relevant trial options.

PROCESS IMPROVEMENT

In aviation, in the 1970s pilots were the king of the cockpit. (They were like the surgeons of decades ago, who were like gods in their operating rooms.) These surgeons and those airline pilots did things the way they felt was best, which meant each did things in a different way. For plane crews, that variation resulted in unclear expectations and in accidents. The result of this behavior was a crash every five days, with over 2300 worldwide deaths in plane accidents in 1973. Standardizing work, clarifying roles, using checklists, and system design has dramatically improved safety and reliability. Major crashes are now rare.[6]

Atul Gawande made an eloquent argument to apply these principles to patient safety in *The Checklist Manifesto*.[7] Standardized processes (with allowances for patient-driven, individual variation where needed) have been regarded as anathema to medicine. Fortunately, this is changing. Today every surgery in the United States begins with the surgeon identifying the name of the patient, the name of the intended surgery, the side or organ that is going to be operated, the estimated time of the surgery, and the estimated blood loss. This has reduced wrong-side surgery from one in 115,000 operations (the average large hospital may be involved in one event every five to ten years) to a negligible level (CMS has not reimbursed hospitals for additional costs associated from wrong-side surgery since 2007). As a result, process improvement has become commonplace in most healthcare organizations.[8]

Bottom Line: Over the past 20 years, financial services have become much more consumer-oriented, and today healthcare is following suit by becoming patient-centric. But simply handing investors the yoke, alternatively known as a control wheel or joystick, and having them fly the plane solo wasn't the right idea. Having patients drive their own healthcare decisions without professional support isn't right either. As in financial services, effective consumerization in healthcare requires a collaborative partnership. The other take-home message is that the methods that we used in the past to provide care of patients will not be effective today. We don't use the same techniques for diagnosis and treatment of diseases and conditions that were effective 20 years ago because in many cases they are antiquated today. We have to make changes and put patients first and use the same technology that has improved the financial service industry to improve the care that we can provide our patients.

REFERENCES

1. How to Successfully Adopt Telemedicine into Your Practice. eVisit. http://pages.healthcareitnews.

com/rs/922-ZLW-292/images/How%20To%20Successfully%20Adopt%20Telemedicine%20 Into%20Your%20Practice_0.pdf?aliId=913083420.

2. Herendeen NE, Schaefer GB. Practical applications of telemedicine for pediatricians. *Pediatr Ann.* 2009;38:567-569.

3. Adamson SC, Bachman JW. Pilot study of providing online care in a primary care setting. *Mayo Clin Proc.* 2010;85:704-710.

4. Licurse A. One hospital's experience in virtual healthcare. *Harvard Business Review.* December 9, 2016.

5. Bresnick J. IBM Watson, Quest launch genomic cognitive computing partnership. Health IT Analytics. https://healthitanalytics.com/news/ibm-watson-quest-launch-genomic-cognitive -computing-partnership.

6. Mate K, Compton-Phillips A. The antidote to fragmented health care. *Harvard Business Review.* December 15, 2014.

7. Gawande A. *The Checklist Manifesto: How to Get Things Right.* New York: Henry Holt; 2011.

8. Kwaan MR, Studdert DM, Zinner MJ, Gawande AA. Incidence, patterns, and prevention of wrong-site surgery. *Arch Surg.* 2006;141:353-358.

CHAPTER 39

Lessons I Learned from a Bonsai Plant About Practice Management

Neil Baum, MD

I never thought a small-scale tree could teach me lessons about running a medical practice. I have always been fascinated with the beauty of bonsai plants, which are miniature full-grown trees, and my appreciation only increased when I tried to raise a bonsai cypress tree by carefully tending and pruning the plant only to have it suffer an early demise. I took good care of the plant, providing it with sunshine and shade as directed, carefully watering and misting it according to the instructions provided with the plant. Then, for some reason, its foliage started drying out and dropping—slowly at first, and then accelerating, until the plant was a goner. I was so disappointed when the leaves started drooping and then turned brown and finally dropped into the pot, thus highlighting my failure as a horticulturist. This article compares nurturing bonsai plants with the care and feeding of a medical practice.

ROUTINE TENDING AND CAREFUL OBSERVATION ARE ESSENTIAL

Bonsai plants often have problems that emerge when the routine is changed. Just like a dog doesn't like to go to the vet or even the "spa" when the master goes on vacation, bonsai plants don't take kindly to changes in their water or exposure to light routines. The same holds true in your practice. The practice doesn't run smoothly when you deviate from the routine or the schedule. If the doctors are to arrive at 8:45 and start seeing patients at 9:00, the staff is prepared, the patients are in the rooms, the phone is taken off of the answering service, and everyone seems to be on the same page. If the doctor decides to arrive at 9:30, check e-mails, return a few phone calls, and then begin to see patients at 9:45 or 10:00, there will be mayhem in the office. Patients become surly, the staff are agitated, and no amount of hurrying up can get the practice back on schedule.

The same applies to hospital operating rooms (ORs). If the OR expects the doctor at 7:30, and he or she shows up at 8:00, the entire OR schedule is now delayed, and other doctors, patients, and OR staff will be upset. This will have a trickle-down effect on everyone involved.

Let the bonsai plant provide you with a lesson on having a routine—rarely, if ever, should you deviate from the routine you and your staff have agreed upon.

PRUNING AND PRACTICE MANAGEMENT

Your bonsai is not a weed and will not grow and take care of itself without careful attention and even coddling, much like that which is required caring for a child. Pruning is the art of retarding the growth of the tree to keep its miniature status and size. To have a fuller, lower-growing plant, it is necessary to trim back the branches at certain defined angles.

How often do you review your balance sheet looking at your assets and liabilities? How often do you look at your EOBs or your denials of claims submitted to the insurance companies or to the CMS? A successful practice does not run on autopilot. It is imperative that you review the key performance indicators, the most important metrics that indicate the growth or the decline of your practice. When you identify problems, that is the time to consider pruning what isn't working, such as dropping low-paying payers and look to new sources of revenue, such as offering early morning hours, evening hours, same-day appointments, or Saturday morning appointments. Another example of pruning is to look at revenue cycle management,[1] and make sure that nothing is falling through the cracks. This process also ensures that you are going to be paid what you deserve. Pruning is a necessity for a healthy bonsai plant and a necessity for a healthy practice.

USING THE RIGHT TOOLS AT THE RIGHT TIME

The absolute essentials for caring for a bonsai plant are a mister, measuring cups, and small pruning shears. But if you really want to provide outstanding care of your bonsai plant, the experts recommend a soil moisture tester. You must have the right tools to provide optimum care for your plant.

You can enhance the efficiency and productivity of your practice if you make certain that the staff has the right tools, including the right technology. For example, is your website offering your patients the ability to make an appointment online? Does the website offer the demographic forms and the health questionnaire for patients to complete before they come to the office for their first appointment? This single feature can make the practice more efficient, and your patients will appreciate being seen on time instead of spending 20 to 30 minutes completing forms in the reception area prior to being seen by the staff and the doctor. You can also enhance the efficiency of your staff if the scheduler or receptionist can verify the patients' insurance online before their appointment.

As with bonsai plants, resources and tools can make all the difference in the world! Make every effort to provide your employees with the skills and technology to let them do great work and be their most productive.

THE RIGHT ENVIRONMENT HELPS

Attention to careful potting of the plant to ensure that the soil drains quickly and keeping a moisture tray underneath it will allow the plant to believe that it is growing in the exact same conditions as its natural habitat.

I have observed that happy doctors and happy office managers create a milieu that makes for a happy staff, who, in turn, give patients a positive experience. Sometimes, obtaining this atmosphere is as simple as changing the verbiage or language that is used. For example, if you call the area that patients enter when they open the door to the practice as the *waiting* room, you are almost creating a self-fulfilling prophecy that the patients will be waiting before they will be seen. However, if you change the term to *reception area,* you create the aura that is where patients are to be received and that they will be seen and processed very quickly. Changing this one term makes patients feel appreciated and that they are doing the doctor a favor by being part of the practice rather than the other way around—that is, that the patient is the one who is making the effort rather than that the doctor is doing the patient a favor by providing healthcare.

Another method of ensuring the right environment is to have regular staff meetings to identify problems and also use this time to compliment staff members for going the extra mile on behalf of patients. I refer to these as ABCD awards, or Above and Beyond the Call of Duty. It is the actions of staff that aren't necessarily in the employee manual that you want to reward, at least verbally, so that the behavior is repeated and that the staff know that their actions are recognized and appreciated.

GETTING ADVICE

Unless you are a bonsai authority you will need to periodically ask for advice on your beloved plant. You can't possibly know it all, and you will probably have to consult with a bonsai doctor when your plant exhibits signs of failing to thrive. Likewise, your practice will, on occasion, need to consult with an expert to solve employment problems, establishing a sexual harassment policy, or advice on taxes and investments. As with the bonsai plant, it's not a sin to ask for help. It just may save your bonsai and your practice.

BONSAI PLANTS ARE DELICATE

Too much or too little water will cause your plant to wither on the vine. The same applies to a doctor's reputation. Physicians spend their entire lives building and protecting their reputation. We know that the majority of our patients have a favorable impression of the doctor and the practice. An angry patient with a bad experience can wreak havoc on a medical practice. Today, a patient who posts negative comments about the doctor and the practice can have their invective seen by thousands of viewers with just a click of a mouse. Therefore, it is imperative that physicians take an active role in protecting their reputations. The best way to do this is to capture compliments from happy patients the moment they utter their accolades. This can be done with online surveys, or right after the patient's visit, before he or she even leaves the exam room. I use a kiosk from Context Media that allows me to create a patient satisfaction survey that the patient completes in the exam room. It takes the patient less than two minutes to complete the survey and adds to the glowing compliments about my practice that have afforded me 4.5 stars!

GIVING YOUR BONSAI A CHECKUP

The bonsai experts suggest that even if your plant is doing well, it might be a good idea to have another pair of eyes, fingers, and soil testers to look in on your plant periodically. The best bonsai authorities will make housecalls without being asked and give your plant a periodic checkup.

The most effective office managers and managing partners practice MBWA—management by walking around. They visit with the schedulers, receptionists, and scanners and see how they are doing. These leaders find out about their issues and concerns and serve as the eyes and ears of the practice.

You can't have an effective practice if you are moving from one crisis to the next and stamping out forest fires as they occur. You can be much more effective if you conduct regular staff meetings. The success of any medical practice begins and ends with the staff. A well-motivated, excited, and enthusiastic staff is the key to giving patients a positive experience every time they interact with the practice.

I suggest that you perform a regular performance review, perhaps every six months. I believe employees like to know where they stand and how they can improve performance on the job. Motivated staff members want feedback on their progress—even if there is a lack of progress. The best way to furnish this feedback is with periodic performance reviews.

Begin by asking employees what they like best about their work, what they like least, one or two areas that they would like to improve, and what you as office manager or physician can do to assist them in their professional growth and development. I suggest you provide the employee with a worksheet with these questions and request that they complete the worksheet before the performance review. I like to make sure that I end the performance review on a positive note. I tell the employees how valued they are and how much of an asset they are to the practice.

Bonsais and practices need fine tuning. Don't be complacent with your plant or your practice.

Bottom Line: Lessons for practice management are available not only in books and in MBA schools but also in the flora and fauna of our hobbies and desktops . . . if that's where you keep your treasured bonsai plant. My children are grown, and I am proud of their accomplishments. Now I'd like to try raising a bonsai plant . . . one more time!

REFERENCE

1. Dowling R, Baum M. The urology practice revenue cycle: how to track and manage it. *Urology Times;* October 30, 2011. http://urologytimes.modernmedicine.com/urology-times/news/ modernmedicine/modern-medicine-now/urology-practice-revenue-cycle-how-track-and-m.

CHAPTER 40

Hickory Dickory TikTok

SANJAY JUNEJA, MD, AND NEIL BAUM, MD

WHAT IS TIKTOK?

TikTok is a homemade application developed in China that uses interesting and unique special effects to create short-duration, attention-grabbing videos that have the potential to go viral. TikTok provides the potential to create 15 seconds of video that give users recognition and popularity. This free app provides opportunities to create creative, ultra-short videos for countless viewers throughout the world.

TikTok is the fast-growing social media platform ever created, with over a billion users. It is especially popular among users 16 to 29 years of age. As of April 2021, TikTok had reached over two billion downloads worldwide. Every month, more than 850 million unique users log in to the video platform. It currently has more than 30 million active users in the United States alone and was the most downloaded social media app in the first quarter of this year. All of this means it's something your practice should consider.

Here are some statistics worth knowing:

- TikTok is available in 75 languages worldwide. It is users' first choice to post and share 15-second videos.
- Out of more than 800 million active users worldwide, the United States accounts for 39.6 million, with India leading the TikTok pack at 119.3 million.
- The average time spent by users on the TikTok app is 52 minutes every day.
- TikTok users are between 16 and 24 years of age, with 50% of users younger than 34.
- The male-to-female ratio of TikTok users is 56% to 44%.
- The number of adults in the United States using TikTok increased 5.5 times from October 2017 to March 2019.[1]

BRIEF HISTORY OF TIKTOK

TikTok started as three different apps. The first was an app called Musical.ly, which launched in Shanghai in 2014. In 2016, Chinese tech giant, ByteDance, launched a similar service in China called Douyin, which attracted 100 million users in China and Thailand in just one year. ByteDance decided it was onto something and wanted to expand under a different brand—TikTok. So, in 2018 it bought Musical.ly and began TikTok's global expansion. There's little indication that TikTok is a flash in the pan.[2]

WHAT TIKTOK CAN DO FOR YOU AND YOUR PRACTICE

TikTok's major advantage is that it serves as a great opportunity to offer entertainment to your patients. Your only limit is your creativity. The program is safe and suitable for people aged 12 and older. TikTok provides the opportunity for any doctor to make interesting videos and gain instant publicity.

The app is free, and beginners don't require any specialized equipment to create videos. Everything can be accomplished with a mobile device that has video recorder capability. The TikTok app does everything for you, and the content you create has the potential to become almost instantly viral. The beauty of TikTok is its simplicity. You don't need specialized training in editing videos and adding background music while using this app. This video app offers you the simplest interface by featuring audio and video editing options for ease of use.

THE POTENTIAL FOR TIKTOK IN HEALTHCARE

Facebook and Twitter have held the attention of the public for more than a decade. The TikTok app provides another way to socialize with people online. Most users post their funny video edits with the intention of entertaining others. For the healthcare professional, however, TikTok could be used primarily for the purpose of patient and community education.

You can shoot a 15-second promo and upload it to attract potential patients. The main requirement to capture the attention of potential patients is to be relatable. This is your opportunity to present a new idea or concept that's succinct—less than 60 seconds—and is understandable to the average person.

Being able to share your content in your community is one of the greatest uses of the TikTok app. This app goes beyond merely texting and sharing content. You are able to post your videos instantly for anyone any time you wish.

TikTok does not require you to have any previous video experience or training. Do whatever you like and express yourself to your network of fans and let it reach the eyes and ears that appreciate your creativity and your message. Fame is just a few minutes away: the more viewers engage in your content, the more viral your posts become across the net. The best quality content deserves attention beyond boundaries, and attention is what everyone needs, after all.

TikTok has the potential to make learning about health fun. If a doctor comes up with a unique way of giving you a few facts about an illness in 60 seconds, it sticks.

THE DOWNSIDES OF TIKTOK

Some detractors will see this application as a waste of time and not an effective or meaningful marketing tool. Certainly, as with any new idea, especially in the realm of social media, there are disadvantages to using TikTok.

- Currently, TikTok is free to use. Because of that, it is loaded with ads that are annoying and sometimes lure users to pay. But—every app you download and install contains third-party ads and promotional content that have nothing to do with the application.
- The app has the potential to be hacked and used for nefarious purposes. For example, a Chinese email scam came to the attention of the U.S. Army, which instituted steps against the use of TikTok on government phones. This incident was triggered by a "me too" app called TikTok, which, when accessed, leaked some sensitive U.S. information. As a result, the Department of Defense had to take measures to avoid future risks.[3]
- Because this app tends to host more and more content, some children are demonstrating addiction and overuse of the app. Such addiction is resulting in distress among parents as well.
- Numerous users have displayed sensitive, distasteful, or violent content. In one case, a video displaying terror attacks against Israeli citizens went viral, but the video was quickly deleted by TikTok.[4] However, this example still causes concern among the rest of the world.

- *Wired* published a report of an incident in India where a man allegedly live-streamed his hate speech against a particular community (the Dalits) just a day before murdering a member of this underprivileged caste.[5]
- In the United Kingdom, United States, and India, TikTok also has grabbed attention for its rampant use as a tool for harassment. Trolls leverage this application to deliver distasteful, offensive, and often untrue remarks against people they disapprove of.

Social media apps have become a convenient tool for both expression of concerns and open mockery. Although everyone has the right to freedom of speech, you should be very conscious of the negative effects of defaming or disrespecting someone.

ONE DOCTOR'S EXPERIENCE

Author SJ is a hematologist/oncologist who uses TikTok as a source of education and entertainment with hundreds of thousands of viewers. He has been an active TikToker for over two years and posts a video every week.

Dr. Juneja realized that rather than using TikTok as a means for marketing, he could instead use the site to help disseminate credible information. He realized that TikTok could be a way to simplify and deliver what otherwise are fairly complicated topics. For example, he posted videos about cancer screening, the misconceptions regarding cancer treatment options, and common hematologic problems in young adults that could be missed by their primary providers. The number one factor that dictates whether something goes viral is how long the viewer stays engaged with the video before leaving the site. Holding your viewers' attention can be accomplished with a hook at the beginning—a statement you are trying to address, or a myth you are trying to debunk. One way to accomplish this is to use a trend or a sound bite that is being used by many others where the ending is known to take a turn or end with comedy.

Probably the most encouraging thing about social media has been the observation that millennials want to learn. They love to be knowledgeable. Explaining how to analyze a CBC and differential and the problems it could signify in terms of iron or vitamin B_{12} deficiency, restless leg syndrome, and fatigue and signs of chronic inflammation or sleep apnea resulted in comments from several viewers, months later, that an undiagnosed problem was discovered and treated after watching one of our (SJ) videos. It is not unusual for healthcare providers, from nurses to primary care doctors, to offer positive feedback and appreciation for being kept up to date on little idiosyncrasies or nuances that result in better care for their patients. Here is how powerful the exponential reach of this platform is: you may reach 20 patients that you see in your office, but a 60-second video can potentially reach millions of viewers. It is a way to extend and perpetuate our knowledge not just to families within a one-hour radius of our practice, but instead across the country and possibly worldwide. Dr. Juneja has found that TikTok provides benefits that extend far beyond the small circle of his local community.

Some of the reasons for delivering healthcare information through the medium of TikTok are the widespread deficits in healthcare literacy and the fact that large segments of our population don't have other access to credible information. Because of a serious deficit of healthcare providers, even in large metropolitan communities it may take two to six weeks before a newly diagnosed patient is able to obtain an appointment and receive answers or guidance from an oncologist. This leaves patients desperately searching for information online, with very little understanding of what does and does not apply to them. And despite the vast and comprehensive world that the Internet provides us, there is no regulation or system in place to discern fact from fiction. Anyone can post information on a domain they created and allege any degree of training and expertise.

Dr. Juneja first used TikTok as an educational opportunity and also included some levity and entertainment. Since then, Dr. Juneja has had thousands of messages from people on social media stating that the quality of their lives has improved because of a 30- to 60-second video that appeared on their homepage on TikTok. So many of our patients spend long days and long years with fatigue, depression, restless legs, and even neuropathy for reasons that are easy to reverse. For example, having an iron deficiency properly investigated can completely change a patient's life, leading that patient to emerge from a state of fatigue and inactivity and become energetic and engaged.

Bottom Line: At this time, few medical practices and physicians have embraced the use of TikTok as a way to communicate with existing and potential new patients. It can be mindless fun and a source of entertainment, but it also has great potential to educate a younger segment of the population.

REFERENCES

1. Mohsin M. 10 TikTok statistics that you need to know. Oberlo. February 2021. https://www.oberlo.com/blog/tiktok-statistics

2. Smith G. The history of TikTok: from Musical.ly to the number 1 app in the world. *Dexerto.* May 2021. www.dexerto.com/entertainment/the-history-of-tiktok-1569106/

3. Barrett B. Security news this week: the Army bans TikTok. Wired. January 4, 2020. www.wired.com/story/army-bans-tiktok-cloud-hopper-email-scam/

4. Animated video glorifying Palestinian terror attacks posted to TikTok. Jerusalem Post. February 6, 2020. www.timesofisrael.com/animated-video-glorifying-palestinian-terror-attacks-posted-to-tiktok/

5. Christopher N. TikTok is fuelling India's deadly hate speech epidemic. Wired. December 8, 2019. wired.co.uk/article/tiktok-india-hate-speech-caste

CHAPTER 41

Moving From Volume to Value: Part I

CHELSEA KATZ AND NEIL BAUM, MD

Every physician has experienced the many changes in the past two decades that have changed the way we treat patients. Most physicians would agree that healthcare is becoming overwhelmingly complex. Just a few years ago, a primary care physician practiced alone or in a small group, with a small staff of one or two employees for each doctor, read one or two journals a month, only occasionally requested consultation from a specialist, went to the hospital and made rounds on his or her patients early in the morning and also late in the afternoon, and could complete the paperwork in about one hour a week. These days of the solo practitioner or small group practices of primary care doctors are gone.

Today the healthcare environment is exceedingly complex and very difficult for nearly all physicians to navigate alone. For example, there are thousands of new drugs, treatments, and diagnostic tests, all of which require decision-making from the doctor, followed by achieving prior authorization approval from the payer before the patient can be prescribed a medication or have a test ordered. Each prior authorization can take 20 to 30 minutes to obtain. Computerization was supposed to make us more efficient but has resulted in the need to purchase expensive equipment, have IT support readily available, purchase expensive annual updates, and, in most cases, has led to a loss of productivity for physicians who have transitioned from paper charts to an electronic medical record. There is a steady erosion of reimbursements, rising overhead costs, and loss of income for most physicians. There are complex new regulations to follow, and acronyms are choking the desire and enthusiasm for many doctors to remain in healthcare. And, yes, there is always the fear of litigation and the expensive malpractice premiums that we must incur. Is it any wonder that physicians are experiencing burnout in increasing numbers? It is not difficult to understand that the medical community is unable to reach consensus on what to do with the current health insurance situation in the United States.

In the past, the physician received compensation based on the services he or she had provided to his or her patients, the traditional fee-for-service (FFS) method of reimbursement. For those physicians who have opted to be employed physicians, their compensation is often the relative value unit (RVU) metric, which has a specific value for each billing code.

The trend for the foreseeable future is to move from volume of care to *value* of care that we provide in outpatient treatment. This first installment of a three-part article discusses the current movement from volume to value. We first discuss the concept of value, and then in subsequent articles we will discuss the measurement of outcomes and determination of the cost of care for large populations of patients. In the second article, we will review emerging concepts and methods that will allow healthcare organizations to adapt to a rapidly changing future. In the third and final article, we will discuss the process of measuring the outcomes of care to complete the value calculation. We hope that these articles will give you tools that you need to help make the transition from volume of care to the value of care that you provide your patients.

WHAT IS THE CURRENT STATUS OF AMERICAN HEALTHCARE?

Almost 18% of the U.S. GDP is relegated to healthcare expenditures, which is unsustainable in the global market place. It is also of note that this very costly healthcare system does not come with a concomitant improvement in outcomes compared with Germany, England, Sweden, and Switzerland, which spend nearly 50% less than what Americans spend. Other Western countries also are struggling with healthcare costs. It is sophistry to believe that increased spending on healthcare will enhance or improve the outcomes.

Aside from the challenges faced by individual physicians, the overall state of healthcare in the United States necessitates changing perspectives on providing care. Currently, healthcare accounts for nearly 18% of the nation's GDP, which is considerably higher compared with all other economically developed nations, where healthcare accounts for an average of 9% of their

GDP.[1] We also spend about $9000 annually per capita. By comparison, countries such as Germany, France, and Canada average closer to $5000 per capita.[1] This high level of spending in the United States does not appear to significantly improve outcomes. In the United States, population health outcomes such as life expectancy and rates of chronic conditions are worse than in most other developed nations.[1] Whereas population health outcomes are only partially determined by healthcare, outcomes more closely related to care, such as rates of diabetes-related amputations, also are higher in the United States.[2] A study of our nation's healthcare system is a lesson in diminishing marginal returns—more spending has not equated to better health.

HOW DID WE GET HERE AND WHY CHANGE NOW?

What Are the Traditional Forces that Define and Shape the U.S. Healthcare System?

We have arrived at this point through a variety of forces that have traditionally shaped the healthcare system in this country. Healthcare in the United States is distinguished as a predominantly private, complex multipayer system that has focused on scientific and technologic advances. Insured patients do not bear the full cost of their medical care, due to coverage often paid by the employer, and so patients have no incentive to consume less in the way of services, nor are their providers given any incentive not to provide more medical services. In addition, competing special interests from physicians, hospitals, insurers, the pharmaceutical industry, and patient advocacy groups have all worked to strengthen their position in the policy landscape, sometimes to the detriment of high-value care. Each of these components contributes to the higher costs seen in this country, with little accountability regarding quality or outcomes measured or rewarded.

Although the rate of healthcare growth has slowed somewhat in recent years,[3-5] it does not appear to have reached a ceiling. As more of the economy's resources are devoted to healthcare, less is available for other goods and services. Although jobs within the healthcare sector generally are higher paying, if the overall growth of healthcare outpaces that of the rest of the economy, Americans will find themselves in the very near future less able to access and afford the care they need. American businesses also are faced with the burden of growing healthcare costs as they struggle to provide benefits to their employees and remain competitive internationally.[6] Not least pressing are concerns about the long-term solvency of public programs such as Medicare and Medicaid, because more expensive healthcare costs translate to higher taxes to cover these all-important programs.

Why Do We Need to Change?

Physicians may not consider all of these matters on a day-to-day basis, but they do affect their ability to provide healthcare and shape the care that is delivered. The FFS model often results in overutilization of low-value and unnecessary care.[7] FFS also can impede coordination of care for patients across the healthcare system.[8] This service model does not appear to be sustainable, especially as the number of elderly people[9] and those with chronic and complex health needs[10,11] increases in the population. As long as providers are rewarded for the volume of care delivered, as in FFS arrangements, instead of for the value provided, they are pressured to deliver more care, much of which may be unnecessary, and population healthcare costs will continue to rise without regard to improvement in patient outcomes. Both private and public payers of healthcare have recognized this and have begun to shift their payment models, which soon are going to be tied to outcomes.

Employers have recently started shifting costs to employees by requiring increased contributions to their premiums, higher deductibles, and the use of high-deductible health plans (HDHPs).[12] Enrollment in HDHPs currently consists of about to 29% of insured workers,[12] up from a mere 4% in 2006.[13] As more patients are enrolled in HDHPs and face the full cost for at least their initial care, these patients are more likely to demand transparency in costs, better results, and a clearer understanding of what they are getting for their increased payments.

Contingent upon changes with the current presidential administration, the Department of Health and Human Services is striving to have 90% of all Medicare FFS payments tied to quality or value by next year.[14] Medicare's new payment reform system, The Medicare Access and CHIP Reauthorization Act (MACRA), which goes into effect in 2018, will help the organization to reach that goal. MACRA consolidates previous quality reporting systems to streamline tracking and reporting, thus further encouraging value-based care over volume, or FFS. If previous policy changes are any indication, as Medicare goes, so too will private insurance, very quickly.

To this end, private insurers already have begun to experiment with alternatives to FFS reimbursement arrangements. The Affordable Care Act (ACA) further encouraged insurers to do so,[15] through initiatives such as the National Quality Strategy and the development of Accountable Care Organizations (ACOs). These organizations are increasing in number, and, regardless of the ACA's fate, private insurers will likely continue to pursue such alternatives, given the pressure they receive from employers and patients to rein in costs.

Indeed, whether physicians are ready for it or not, the time for change is here. Physicians who can demonstrate that they can adapt to new incentives by shaving costs while maintaining and improving their quality and their outcomes will be more competitive in the changing marketplace. The question then turns to how to measure success in the new environment of value-based care.

Why Is Quality Important, How Do We Define It, and What Should We Measure?

The importance of quality in healthcare may seem obvious. It is underscored by the Hippocratic Oath that physicians take to *non nocere* or "to do no harm." Poor quality of care can also mean higher costs—whether through providing unnecessary care that results in iatrogenic disease, or forgoing important preventive care that ultimately results in greater disease burden requiring more expensive medical care. Of course, quality matters to patients as well. Even though they may not always know how to assess quality, patients want to receive it. To this end, providers are likely to face competition based on the quality they provide. Who wants to go to a doctor with a one-star rating? But where would such a rating come from and what would it actually mean? As the forces at play continue to transition incentives from volume to value, quality of care also will increasingly be tied to provider payment, and properly measuring quality will be primary.

Defining quality in healthcare is not a simple task, in part because quality holds different meaning to different stakeholders[16] and is multidimensional in nature. However, the widely used Institute of Medicine (IOM) definition of quality encapsulates a broad understanding of quality as "the degree to which health services for individuals and populations increase the likelihood of desired health outcomes and are consistent with current professional knowledge."[17] This definition can easily apply to multiple perspectives, from providers to patients, to insurers to purchasers. The IOM further specifies that high-quality care should be safe, effective, patient-centered, timely, efficient, and equitable.[18]

However, as with anything of this magnitude, the devil in the details. The IOM definition can serve as a guiding force, but how it will actually be applied in practice is what matters to providers. The Donabedian model, which serves as the primary framework for most quality metrics, partitions quality of care into three measurable components: structure, process, and outcomes.[19] *Structural measures* refer to capabilities of an organization or provider, such as availability of electronic records. *Process measures* are activities carried out by providers, and often stem from clinical guidelines. The rate of providing retinal examinations for diabetes patients would be an example. *Outcomes measures* refer to the health state of patients as a result of their care and includes measures such as mortality rates, lab values, or patient functional status.

The three components are connected, as structure drives process, which in turn drives outcomes. Quality assessments largely rely on process measures because they are easiest to track and record. In fact, 182 of the 271 quality measures available to report through MACRA are process measures. Improving processes of care matters for improving overall quality, but the value of care is defined on the outcomes achieved.[20] The shift to value in healthcare will require utilizing outcome measures that stakeholders can agree upon for their ability to adequately capture the quality of care that matters to patients, physicians, and payers alike.

How Will We Improve Outcomes?

Proper measurement is the first step to improve outcomes. Tracking how patients fare can be achieved largely through electronic medical records. Before outcomes can be improved, providers first must know where they stand. Many physicians overestimate their performance on quality measures until they are provided with their performance data.[21] To this end, continuous feedback on improvement also must be available to providers. From this feedback, payers can reward providers not only for achieving specific quality standards, but also for incremental improvements. By providing ongoing feedback for progressively better results, instead of continuing to penalize for not meeting a benchmark, providers may be encouraged to find innovative ways to improve.

Because outcome measurements are the road map toward improving outcomes, they will continue to be relied upon as quality measures, but when they are tied to incentives, they have to be clearly shown to improve outcomes. Porter and others[22,23] are proponents of organizing care and assessing quality by condition, rather than by procedure, so that the complete spectrum of a patient's health needs is more fully considered by the providers who care for them. Bundled payments are another approach to reducing costs, as is incentivizing coordination of care across providers and specialties. Although bundled and capitated payments are not new to healthcare, new tactics, which will be discussed in the subsequent articles, can help avoid the pitfalls of previous attempts to curb costs.

Other approaches to improve quality include public reporting of outcomes, although research is mixed on the effectiveness of this method.[24,25] If patients can see how providers stand next to their peers, it may promote competition to improve quality. One of the problems with this method is that providers may find ways to game the measurement process. Also, even with clear definitions of measures, patients may still not know how to best prioritize them. Therefore, outcome measures that are important to patients will be an important consideration moving forward.

How Can We Continuously Improve?

Continuous improvement can be attained if we:

- Continuously assess and revise metrics to accurately reflect quality that matters to stakeholders;
- Assess whether process measures continue to reflect outcomes accurately;
- Revise standards and clinical practice guidelines concurrent with new evidence;
- Promote a learning atmosphere that is less punitive and more encouraging of success;
- Promote effective communication within and between organizations;
- Maintain and improve IT systems to accurately and efficiently capture care and outcomes; and

- Use outcomes that are easiest to track and difficult to manipulate.

Bottom Line: The healthcare profession is about to undergo radical changes. No longer will volume of patients seen or services provided be the metric for payment and reimbursement. Providers, payers, patients, and the government will have to make a big adjustment by moving from volume to value. In the second article of this three-part series we are going to discuss identifying the cost of providing care; the third part will address measuring outcomes. We believe that the success of a medical practice is going to depend on the speed at which the healthcare profession can make this transition.

REFERENCES

1. Organisation for Economic Cooperation and Development. (2016). OECD Stat (database). www.oecd-ilibrary.org/economics/data/oecd-stat_data-00285-en. doi: 10.1787/data-00285-en. Accessed April 24, 2017.

2. Organisation for Economic Cooperation and Development. *Health at a Glance 2013: OECD Indicators.* OECD Publishing; 2013. http://dx.doi.org/10.1787/health_glance-2013-en. Accessed April 24, 2017.

3. Hartman M, Martin AB, Lassman D, et al. National health spending in 2013: growth slows, remains in step with the overall economy. *Health Aff (Millwood).* 2015;34:150-160.

4. Martin AB, Hartman M, Whittle L, Catlin A. National Health Expenditures Accounts Team. National health spending in 2012: rate of health spending growth remained low for the fourth consecutive year. *Health Aff (Millwood).* 2014;33:67-77.

5. Cutler DM, Sahni NR. If slow rate of health care spending growth persists, projections may be off by $770 billion. *Health Aff (Millwood).* 2013;32:841-850.

6. Sood N, Ghosh A, Escarce JJ. Employer-sponsored insurance, health care cost growth, and the economic performance of U.S. industries. *Health Serv Res.* 2009;44:1449-1464.

7. Shen J, Andersen R, Brook R, Kominski G, Albert PS, Wenger N. The effects of payment method on clinical decision-making. *Med Care.* 2004;42:297-302.

8. Institute of Medicine. *Rewarding Provider Performance: Aligning Incentives in Medicare.* Washington, DC: National Academies Press; 2006.

9. Ortman JM, Velkoff VA, Hogan H. An aging nation: the older population in the United States. Washington, DC: US Census Bureau; 2014. www.census.gov/prod/2014pubs/p25-1140.pdf. Accessed April 24, 2017.

10. Wu S, Green A. *Projection of Chronic Illness Prevalence and Cost Inflation.* Washington, DC: RAND Health; 2000.

11. Centers for Disease Control and Prevention. Chronic Disease Overview. www.cdc.gov/nccdphp/overview.htm. Accessed April 24, 2017.

12. Claxton G, Rae M, Long M, Damico A, Whitmore H, Foster G. Health benefits in 2016: family premiums rose modestly, and offer rates remained stable. *Health Aff (Millwood).* 2016;35:1908-1917.

13. Dolan R. Health policy brief: high-deductible health plans. *Health Aff (Millwood).* 2016. www.healthaffairs.org/healthpolicybriefs/brief.php?brief_id=152. Accessed April 24, 2017.

14. Burwell SM. Setting value-based payment goals—HHS efforts to improve U.S. health care. *N Engl J Med.* 2015;372:897-899.

15. Patient Protection and Affordable Care Act. 42 USC §1395jjj (2010).

16. McGlynn EA. Six challenges in measuring the quality of health care. *Health Aff (Millwood).* 1997;16(3):7-21.

17. Institute of Medicine. *Medicare: A Strategy for Quality Assurance.* Washington, DC: National Academies Press; 1990.

18. Institute of Medicine. *Crossing the Quality Chasm: A New Health System for the 21st Century.* Washington, DC: National Academies Press; 2001.

19. Donabedian A. Evaluating the quality of medical care. *Milbank Mem Fund Q.* 1966;44(3) (suppl):166-206.

20. Porter ME. What is Value in Health Care? *N Engl J Med.* 2010;363:2477-2481.

21. Davis DA, Mazmanian PE, Fordis M, Van Harrison R, Thorpe KE, Perrier L. Accuracy of physician self-assessment compared with observed measures of competence a systematic review. *JAMA.* 2006;296:1094-1102.

22. Porter ME, Larsson S, Lee TH. Standardizing patient outcomes measurement. *N Engl J Med.* 2016;374:504-6.

23. Deerberg-Wittram J, Guth C, Porter ME. Value-based competition: the role of outcome measurement. *Public Health Forum* 2013;21(4):12.e1-12.e3.

24. Hibbard JH, Stockard J, Tusler M. Hospital performance reports: impact on quality, market share, and reputation. *Health Aff (Millwood).* 2005;24:1150-1160.

25. Fung CH, Lim YW, Mattke S, Damberg C, Shekelle PG. Systematic review: the evidence that publishing patient care performance data improves quality of care. *Ann Intern Med.* 2008;148:111-123.

Moving from Volume to Value: Part II

Every physician and hospital talks about the quality of the care that they provide to their patients. Most patients are satisfied with the care that they receive. Unfortunately, quality is rarely objectively measured. Also, medical professionals may claim to be "cost effective" when they have never determined the cost of providing care.

Achieving value for patients must become the priority for physicians and hospitals and everyone involved in patient care. In Part I of this article we defined value as health outcomes achieved per dollar spent. Value is what matters for patients and unites the interests of all involved in providing services for our patients. If value improves, patients, payers, providers, and suppliers can all benefit, while the economic sustainability of the health care system increases.

Value—neither an abstract ideal nor a code word for cost reduction—should define the framework for performance improvement in healthcare. Rigorous, disciplined measurement and improvement of value is the best way to drive system progress. Yet value in healthcare remains largely unmeasured and misunderstood.[1]

Futurists are forecasting a colossal shift in payments from volume to value. Most agree that the bloated U.S. healthcare system, which now is more than $3 trillion per year and accounts for 17% of the GDP, is unsustainable. Drug manufacturers are defending escalating drug costs on the basis of their value, defined as their efficacy and effectiveness in treating a condition. Insurers are pushing the shift of financial risk to providers to accelerate the volume-to-value transition, and Medicare is promoting value-based purchasing in its alternative payments program. The acronym MIPS, for Merit-based Incentive Payment System, has become part of the healthcare vocabulary; CMS clearly states that the "payment arrangement must provide for payment for covered professional services based on quality measures comparable to those in the quality performance category."[2]

CHARGES ARE NOT A SURROGATE FOR COSTS

Many physicians have structured their fees based on the way they are reimbursed. Unfortunately, that approach was doomed from the start, because it was based on the flawed assumption that every billable event in a department has the same profit margin.

Yes, doctors and hospitals can easily calculate direct costs, which include drugs, disposables, staffing, length of stay, readmission rates, and complications. It is ironic, then, that a standard definition of cost remains elusive when there is so much pressure from payers, the government, and now from patients with higher premiums and higher deductibles to rein in the cost of care.

Physicians currently are reimbursed on average estimates of relative demands (relative value units, or RVUs) on physician labor, practice expenses, and malpractice expenses in performing billable activities, which often are over-estimated regarding their complexity.

We need to abandon the idea that charges billed or reimbursements paid in any way reflect costs. In reality, the cost of using a resource—a physician, nurse, case manager, piece of equipment, or square meter of space—is the same whether the doctor is performing a poorly or a highly reimbursed service. Cost depends on how much of a resource's available capacity (time) is used in the care for a particular patient, not on the charge or reimbursement for the service, or whether it is reimbursed at all.

SEVEN STEPS FOR DETERMINING COST OF DELIVERING HEALTHCARE SERVICES

Time-driven activity-based costing (TDABC) is a way of determining the cost of caring for patients. The following sections describe the seven steps used in TDABC.

Step 1. Select the Medical Condition

Begin by specifying the medical condition (or patient population) that you are evaluating to determine the cost of caring for the patient. For each condition, it is necessary to define the beginning and end of the patient care cycle. For a condition that that has a short duration—for example, a patient having a vasectomy—you only to need to consider the initial evaluation, the procedure, and the follow-up visits to check the semen for absence of sperm. For chronic conditions such as diabetes, hypertension, or cancer, you might choose a care cycle for a period of time, such as a year.

Step 2. Define the Care Delivery Value Chain

Next, we specify the care delivery value chain (CDVC), which charts the principal activities or interactions of the patient with the all the members of the practice for a medical condition. The CDVC focuses providers on the full care cycle rather than on individual processes. This overall view of the patient care cycle helps to identify the interactions of the patient with the multiple caregivers providing care over the full cycle of care.

Step 3. Develop Process Maps of Each Activity in Patient Care Delivery

Next, prepare detailed process maps for each activity in the care delivery value chain. Process maps encompass the paths patients follow as they move through their care cycle. This includes all the personnel, facilities, and equipment involved at each step along the path. In addition to identifying the capacity-supplying resources used in each process, we identify the supplies, such as medications, syringes, catheters, and bandages, used directly in the process (Table 1).

Table 1. Cost of supplies need for insertion of testosterone pellets

0.3 x $45 Administrator = $13.50
0.4 x $30 Medical Assistant = $12.00
0.15 x $400 Dr. Baum = $60.00
Cost $50/pellet or $450.00/patient
Supplies = $35.00
Total Cost: $570.50

Step 4. Obtain Time Estimates for Each Process

Now estimate how much time each provider, nurse, receptionist, technician, or other resource spends with a patient at each step in the process. For short-duration, inexpensive processes that have little variation, consider using standard times for your calculations. Actual duration should be calculated for time-consuming, less predictable processes, especially those that involve multiple physicians and nurses performing complex care activities such as major surgery or examination of patients with complicated medical problems.

TDABC also is well suited to capture the effect of process variation on cost. For example, a patient who needs a laryngoscopy as part of her clinical visit requires an additional process step. The time estimate and associated incremental resources required can easily be added to the overall time equation for that patient.

Step 5. Estimate the Cost of Supplying Patient Care Resources

In this step, estimate the direct costs of each resource involved in caring for patients. The direct costs include compensation for employees, depreciation or leasing of equipment, supplies, and any other operating expenses. These data become the numerator for calculating each resource's capacity cost rate.

Next, we identify the support resources necessary to supply the primary resources providing patient care. These include supervising employees, space and furnishings (office and patient treatment areas), and corporate functions that support patient-facing employees. When calculating the cost of supplies, include the cost of the resources used to acquire them and make them available for patient use during the treatment process (for instance, purchasing, receiving, storage, sterilization, and delivery).

Finally, we need to allocate the costs of departments and activities that support the patient-facing work. We map those processes as we did in step 3 and then calculate and assign costs to patient-facing resources on the basis of their demands for the services of these departments, using the process that will be described in step 6.

This approach to allocating support costs represents a major shift from current practice. To illustrate, let's compare the allocation of the resources required in a centralized department to sterilize two kinds of surgical tool kits, those used for total knee replacement and those used for cardiac bypass. Existing cost systems tend to allocate higher sterilization costs to cardiac bypass cases than to knee replacement cases because the charges (or direct costs) are higher for a cardiac bypass than for a knee replacement. Under TDABC, however, we have learned that more time and expense are required to sterilize the typically more complex knee surgery tools, so relatively higher sterilization costs should be assigned to knee replacements.

When costing support departments, a good guideline is the "rule of 1." Support functions that have only one employee can be treated as a fixed cost; they can be either not allocated at all or allocated using a simplistic method, as is currently done. But departments that have more than one person or more than one unit of any resource represent variable costs. The workload of these departments has expanded because of increased demand for the services and outputs they provide. Their costs should and can be assigned on the basis of the patient processes that create demand for their services.

Project teams tasked with estimating the cost to supply resources—the numerator of the capacity cost rate—should have expertise in finance, human resources, and information systems. They can do this work in parallel with the process mapping and time estimation (steps 3 and 4) performed by clinicians and team members with expertise in quality management and process improvement.

Step 6. Estimate the Capacity of Each Resource, and Calculate the Capacity Cost Rate

Determining the practical capacity for employees—the denominator in the capacity cost rate equation—requires three time estimates, which are gathered from Human Resource records and other sources:

- The total number of days that each employee actually works each year;
- The total number of hours per day that the employee is available for work; and
- The average number of hours per workday used for non-patient-related work, such as breaks, training, education, and administrative meetings.

To calculate the resource capacity cost rate, we simply divide the resource's total cost (step 5) by its practical capacity (step 6) to obtain a rate, measured in dollars per unit of time, typically an hour or a minute:

$$\text{Monthly Practical Capacity of Resource} = \frac{a}{12} \times (b\text{-}c)$$

Step 7. Calculate the Total Cost of Patient Care

In the final step, the total cost of treating a patient is determined by simply multiplying the capacity cost rates (including associated support costs) for each resource used in each patient process by the amounts of time the patient spent with the resource (step 4). Sum up all the costs across all the processes used during the patient's complete cycle of care to produce the total cost of care for the patient.

We have provided two examples from Dr. Baum's practice. Table 2 presents the cost for an office visit for a new patient with urinary symptoms; Table 3 shows the cost of performing a vasectomy in the office setting.

Table 2. Cost incurred in seeing a new patient

0.3 x $45 Receptionist Allen = $13.50
0.4 x $65 Nurse White = $26.00
0.15 x $300 Dr. Baum = $45.00
Total cost of visit: $84.50
Reimbursement <$84.50 is going to be a loss; reimbursement >$84.50 will be a profit.

Table 3. Practice's cost of performing a vasectomy

0.3 x $35 Administrator = $10.50
Medical assistant to set up instruments = $12.00
0.5 x $300 Dr. Baum (includes semen analysis x 2) = $150.00
Supplies = $30.00
Clips
Suture (3-0 plain)
Ophthalmic cautery
Ice pack
Sterile gloves
Sterile drapes
"Brass bell" for patient to ring for his significant other!
Time-driven activity-based costing = $202.50

Other Uses of TDABC

TDABC predicts the volume and types of patients expected. If the practice participates in a capitated model, then it becomes imperative to know the costs of care and the various morbidity patterns of various population segments. This information may be difficult to obtain, but it begins with costing each aspect of care over an entire patient cycle. Now you can negotiate from a position of strength and better predict the profitability of participating in a capitated contract.

You can use TDABC to predict the quantity of resources required in hours to provide care for patients. This costing method also estimates the quantity of each resource needed to meet demand. The process can provide an estimate of monthly budgets simply by multiplying the quantity of each resource category required (e.g., nurses, medical assistants, physician assistants) by the monthly cost of each resource.

Bottom Line: TDABC provides one of the metrics that is necessary to determine value of healthcare. In the third and final segment of this article, we will discuss how to assess outcome data so that value can be calculated.

REFERENCES

1. Porter ME. What is value in health care? *N Engl J Med* 2010; 363:2477-2481.
2. Rutherford R. Thinking under Medicare's newest pay for performance program: making sense of the merit-based incentive payment system and the alternative payment models. *J Med Prac Mgmt*. 2017;32:320-323.

Moving from Volume to Value: Part III

WHY IS IT IMPORTANT TO MEASURE OUTCOMES?

Health outcomes are the results of care delivered. The goal of healthcare is to improve patients' health and their health-related quality of life. The goal of measuring health outcomes is to ascertain the best approximation of actual health and health-related quality of life that is affected by interaction with the healthcare delivery system. Without measurement and data collection, it is impossible to know whether the first goal—health—is being attained.

Getting a full picture of the quality of healthcare is important, but when it comes to assessing the value of care, outcomes are where the rubber hits the road. This is the measure by which we will be judged by our patients. Quality of healthcare is evaluated by three different types of measures: structure; process; and outcomes. Assessment of structure and process measures provides the understanding of what is happening during the course of care to affect outcomes or to peek under the hood and see the reality of the healthcare that we deliver to our patients. However, the end goal of assessing these three components is to improve health outcomes, and the reason why we even consider the other types of quality measures. Structure and process measures are a means to an end—better outcomes, which means better health for our patients.

Large-scale healthcare policy decisions are centered on achieving the Triple Aim in healthcare : (1) improving the patient experience; (2) improving the health of populations; and (3) reducing the per capita cost of healthcare.[1] Assessing and understanding health outcomes is integral to all three aims of improving healthcare .

Desirable outcomes are what patients care about and the ultimate goal of practicing medicine for physicians. Patients are less concerned about the process of *how* you practice medicine, and more concerned with how that practice affects them and their health. When choosing a hospital, a patient is less likely to care about the processes in place to prevent infection, and more about their own probability of acquiring an infection during their stay.

Outcome measurement is an essential part of the transition from volume- to value-based healthcare; without knowing the outcomes, we do not know what we get for the money that is spent on care. Insurers and employers are no longer blindly paying for all care delivered even though it appears on a fee schedule. Instead, they are relying increasingly on measuring outcomes in new payment models.[2] Pay-for-performance is one such model, but Accountable Care Organizations, shared savings plans, and bundled payments[3] also are examples of emerging models to assess and improve value—and all require measuring outcomes.

As health plans and federal payers (e.g., Medicare) are requiring data on process and outcomes, it feels daunting to record these details. It may feel as if there are endless hoops of paperwork and uncompensated time and energy, rather than a focus on patient care. However, it is important to see that recording outcomes is for the improvement of medicine and for individual physicians so that they can provide the best possible care. Medicine itself, while not perfect, is based on science and evidence, and assessing the practice of medicine should be no different. Decisions regarding what to do for patients and where to allocate resources, from single clinics to national policy, are guided by previous outcomes. These decisions must rely on solid verifiable evidence.

Physicians choose a course of care for their patients based on the probability that any of several different outcomes may occur. Without knowledge of where one is performing poorly or not as well as one should, how can one ever hope to change? The question then becomes what outcomes matter, and how should they be measured and reported?

WHAT OUTCOMES SHOULD BE MEASURED?

Currently, most of the quality metrics that are taken into account by policymakers, payers, and accreditors, such as The Joint Commission, are process measures. However, as the age of quality assessment evolves, outcome measures are taking a larger role in overall quality assessment.[4] As the evidence base in quality assessment grows, the process measures that remain in use will likely be those that are most clearly linked to actual outcomes.

Part of the pushback from physicians in measuring outcomes stems from the burdensome nature of the task. To ease the work, administrators and payers would do well to select from a larger body of goals and then prioritize a few actionable areas as early targets. This starts with a common understanding of what is meant by *outcomes*.

Defining health outcomes may seem intuitive—the effects of care on the health status of patients and populations[5]—but this can encompass a broad variety of measures. In the past, outcomes consisted of survival, length of stay, or readmission rates. Those metrics certainly are important, but now it will be necessary to go beyond those basic outcome measurements and start recording and documenting additional data that will clearly demonstrate superior and meaningful outcomes.

In considering which outcomes are meaningful, you need look no further than the patient sitting in front of you in the exam room. In the past, outcomes were measured from the provider perspective, and most healthcare organizations have been provider-centric rather than patient-centric. For example, doctors treating kidney stones might have been asked what percentage of patients were stone-free at 30, 90, and 180 days following a procedure to remove kidney or ureteral stones. However, the measurement of success arguably should include the patient's perspective of success, with questions like, "What percentage of patients are free of pain?" or "What percentage of the patients can return to gainful activity at 30 days?" and "What percentage are able to remain stone-free?".

Michael Porter[6] defines a three-tier hierarchy of outcomes that includes health status as the first tier, the process of recovery second, and the sustainability of health as the third. His examples include five-year survival among cancer patients (tier 1), time to return to work following hip replacement (tier 2), and incidence of second primary cancer (tier 3). Outcomes from one tier may influence those in other tiers. This can provide a useful framework for considering the broad range of outcomes and promotes consideration of the entire process of care delivery.

Value-based care will be the emphasis, and value depends on what matters to patients and how they perceive it. What matters to patients usually revolves around their quality of life, and may include things that physicians do not normally consider, such as, "How long did patients have to wait before being seen?" and "Did someone from the doctor's office follow up regarding the results of a blood test, x-ray, or other lab work?". Not only can these nonclinical metrics matter to patients, but they can influence health status outcomes. If a patient with a hernia has to wait three months for an appointment, the clinical outcomes may be negatively affected in addition to having a dissatisfied patient.[7]

Oftentimes, outcomes are organized around provider specialty. However, patients usually are more concerned about the full course of their care for a condition, rather than the isolated care received from a single provider. As Porter points out, in primary care settings, patient populations (e.g., people with diabetes, young women), rather than specific conditions, may be considered.[6] Assessing outcomes by condition, rather than just by medical specialty, can serve patients' goals, but payers also pay for the whole patient, and not a single provider.

As an example, patients with chronic hip or knee pain may need to see an orthopedic surgeon for consideration of a total joint replacement. But their care will involve multiple other providers, perhaps including a cardiologist, physical therapist, pain management specialist, as well as nursing staff. In order to measure the outcomes that matter to the patient, the full process of care should be considered, by condition, and care teams may help insure the best clinical practices and outcomes for the whole patient.

When teams are involved in patient care, it is not just the surgeon who is held accountable for the outcomes that are deemed important to the patient. Some providers may welcome this more encompassing view of outcomes, as one common complaint is that the results of care are dependent on far more than just what one provider can control. However, to ensure good outcomes, these different providers must work in a coordinated manner towards a common goal determined by the patient.

The International Consortium for Health Outcomes Measurement is developing standardized outcome measurement for disease categories, and has started with those that encapsulate the greatest disease burden. These sets are organized by disease category, rather than by provider specialty. Specific measures will continue to come from specialty practice guidelines, but these cannot be the only measures assessed.

In an era of information overload, it can be useful to start by focusing on outcomes for conditions of high disease prevalence and burden—cancer, diabetes, and heart disease. Another target for outcome measurement is those things that are the easiest to assess and measure correctly. To this end, if an outcome of interest is not readily available through the electronic medical record or other easily recorded place, then a proxy measure may be used until a better alternative is available.[8] For example, it might not be possible to assess prevalence of coronary artery disease, but preventive factors, such as cholesterol values, are accessible. Additionally, outcomes measures should be limited to things that can actually be affected by healthcare, and not those that depend on patient choice or factors completely out of the clinical realm of control.

HOW SHOULD OUTCOME MEASURES BE USED?

Outcome measures can be useful to both insurers and patients to help distinguish providers of high- versus low-value care. Payers can offer incentives to providers to improve outcomes by tying them to reimbursement schedules. Reported outcomes can be incorporated into public "report cards," or some other type of record, making the information available to patients and allowing them to make more informed choices about what provider they visit. In fact, the CMS is already using outcomes for both efforts, largely in hospital setting and for specific conditions.

Results on the use of payment incentives and public reporting in actually improving health outcomes are mixed.[9,10] Regardless, there is little indication that either is going away anytime soon. Additional work is ongoing to improve both efforts so that the actual goal of better outcomes can be achieved.

Although reimbursement changes and public reporting may seem frightening at first, the goal is to improve patient care and patient health. Providers can accept these assessments as a means to improve their own practices and to provide better care for their patients, rather than as a pejorative commentary on their work. To the extent that this can be achieved at the same or perhaps lower cost as the usual course of care, everyone wins.

GETTING STARTED IN MEASURING OUTCOMES

The first question on how to assess outcomes is: where does the information come from? Often data points already assessed for many patients can be applied, such as blood pressure for hypertensive patients, hemoglobin

A1C levels for those with diabetes, and cholesterol levels for patients at risk for heart disease. Claims submitted in billing and medical records contain large amounts of useful information. Measures related to patient satisfaction or timeliness of care would require additional efforts to assess, which may be administered or paid for by outside agents such as accreditors and insurers when they want to track that information.

A common worry is that patients with complicated medical conditions can make providers appear to be providing worse care than their peers with a different case mix. These patients should not be excluded from measurement, but appropriate risk-adjustment strategies can be employed to account for different health statuses. Another concern is that reporting may take time away from patient care. As standards change, it is important to make sure that efforts made to assess one type of outcome are not wasted in assessing the next one in the pipeline. In both cases, it may be helpful to keep the end goal of improved patient care and satisfaction in mind. Let's be honest, change does not often come without some growing pains, but the end result of improved outcomes should make the efforts worthwhile.

The benefits of outcome measurements are that they prevent overuse, underuse, and misuse of healthcare services, and also enhance patient safety. Outcome measurements also drive innovation and research and development, which enhances disease control and improvement in the patient's quality of life. By tracking outcomes, payers and providers are held accountable for providing high-quality care. When the outcomes are made available to the public or are transparent, patients can make informed choices regarding their care and can select providers who have stellar outcome data. Also, when outcomes are truly measured, there is competition among payers and providers, and with increased competition, prices are certainly going to decrease. Finally, patients with improved outcomes are more engaged in their care, more committed to treatment plans, and more receptive to medical advice.

Providers may feel resistant to measuring outcomes. It can be a chore to do so accurately, and at times difficult to see the benefits. The oath that each physician takes upon graduation is "Primum non nocere," or "First do no harm." Every physician we know believes that he or she does an outstanding job caring for patients. However, eschewing outcome measurement, on these and other grounds, is somewhat akin to 19th-century obstetricians taking offense at being asked to wash their hands to prevent infection in women after childbirth.[11] It is time for us to document this outstanding care, or its outcomes.

SUMMARY

The end results of outcome measurement identify patterns and trends and provide the healthcare profession with the effectiveness, or lack of effectiveness, of our medical interventions. By recording outcomes we can maximize favorable outcomes, and can minimize poor ones. Obtaining and recording outcomes enables us to demonstrate the quality of care and hopefully will lead to improved medical care.

Outcome measurement plays a pivotal role in medical decision-making for physicians, payers, and patients who are searching for high-quality medical care. It is outcome measurements that quantify components of quality such as clinical outcomes, patient satisfaction, and functional status of our patients.

REFERENCES

1. Berwick DM, Nolan TW, Whittington J. The Triple Aim: care, health, and cost. *Health Aff (Millwood)*. 2008;27:759-769. doi:10.1377/hlthaff.27.3.759.

2. Burwell SM. Setting value-based payment goals-HHS efforts to improve U.S. health care. *N Engl J Med*. 2015;372:897-899. doi:10.1056/NEJMp1500445.

3. Rosenthal MB. Beyond pay for performance—emerging models of provider-payment reform. *N Engl J Med*. 2008;359:1197-1200. doi:10.1056/NEJMp0804658.

4. Centers for Medicare and Medicaid Services. Hospital value-based purchasing. September 2015. www.cms.gov/Outreach-and-Education/Medicare-Learning-Network-MLN/MLNProducts/downloads/Hospital_VBPurchasing_Fact_Sheet_ICN907664.pdf. Accessed November 7, 2017.

5. Donabedian A. The quality of care. How can it be assessed? *JAMA*. 1988;260:1743-1748.

6. Porter ME. What is value in health care? *N Engl J Med*. 2010;363:2477-2481. doi:10.1056/NEJMp1011024.

7. Katz C, Baum N. Moving from volume to value: part I. *J Med Pract Manage*. 2018;33:271-275.

8. Proxy Measures. Duke Center for Instructional Technology. http://patientsafetyed.duhs.duke.edu/module_a/measurement/proxy_measures.html. Accessed November 7, 2017.

9. Jha AK, Joynt KE, Orav EJ, Epstein AM. The long-term effect of premier pay for performance on patient outcomes. *N Engl J Med*. 2012;366:1606-1615. doi:10.1056/NEJMsa1112351.

10. Van Herck P, De Smedt D, Annemans L, Remmen R, Rosenthal MB, Sermeus W. Systematic review: effects, design choices, and context of pay-for-performance in health care. *BMC Health Serv Res*. 2010;10:247. doi:10.1186/1472-6963-10-247.

11. Best M, Neuhauser D. Ignaz Semmelweis and the birth of infection control. *BMJ Quality & Safety*.2004;13:233-234. doi:10.1136/qhc.13.3.233.

CHAPTER 42

The Future of Medical Marketing

Neil Baum, MD

The marketing and promotion strategies of the past are not going to be adequate to promote practices in 2022 and beyond. The Internet is leveling the playing field of medical knowledge. Several decades ago, the doctor was the holder of all medical knowledge, and patients came to physicians for his/her advice and knowledge. Today, a motivated patient with a computer and Internet access can learn as much about the pathophysiology and treatment of heart disease or any other condition as a physician. Physicians, once viewed as the royal dispensers of specialized knowledge, now see patients who have researched their medical condition and arrive with a file full of studies and a course of action from credible websites.

Because it is possible that physicians no longer have more information than patients, it is our caring and compassion that will be important in helping patients follow our advice, be compliant in their follow-up, and improve their medical outcomes. Our new mantra should be "Computers (algorithms) will not replace us!"

Physicians may find the trends discussed in the following sections useful for marketing and promoting their medical practice, today and into the future.

TELEMEDICINE

Perhaps the biggest game-changer for medical practices since COVID-19 became part of the picture is telemedicine. The use of telemedicine has increased significantly since March 2020, when CMS waived requirements that limited telemedicine to distant site communication between patients and physicians and now includes all patients who have Medicare and Medicaid. Furthermore, CMS agreed to compensate physicians for virtual visits at the same rate as in-person visits.

Physicians now are able to provide safe and effective care without the necessity of examining the patient in person. For example, we estimate that nearly 60% of patients in primary care can be managed using telemedicine. Many patients, especially millennials, will be looking for healthcare providers who offer virtual visits using telemedicine. Practices that do not offer to communicate with patients by way of telemedicine probably will lose patients.

VIDEO MARKETING

Video marketing has been gaining a lot of attention on social media, especially in relation to healthcare practices. Video marketing is a healthcare marketing trend that is generating the highest level of engagement. Many prefer watching videos rather than reading about medical conditions. When done well, videos can help attract and hold the attention of viewers and improve your reach to attract new patients.

Short, content-rich videos of less than five minutes are the most effective. You can offer videos that focus on the topics that differentiate you and your practice from others in the area. Another effective type of video for healthcare marketing is testimonials from existing patients and from your staff, which helps build trust and credibility with current and potential patients.

If a picture is worth a thousand words, a video is probably worth more than 10,000.

Since the arrival of COVID-19, the medical marketing playing field has changed forever. We will no longer practice or care for patients as we have done in the past. Those doctors and practices that can accept change and can adjust will be the ones who will still have enjoyment, success, and balance in their work, all of which provide a defense against burnout.

PSYCHOGRAPHIC MARKETING

Demographic information, such as age, gender, race, address, and occupation, has been the requirement for becoming a patient in a medical practice and can be the starting point for targeting new patients, but it doesn't identify potential patients' attitudes and mindsets.

Demographics explain "who" your patient is; psychographics explain "why." Psychographic information includes your potential patients' habits, hobbies, health-related experiences, and values—information you need to promote your services to a particular segment of the population. To reach ideal patients you must know what and who they value most, where they look for their medical information, and what content appeals to them. With that information, you can create specific messages about your areas of interest or expertise and can make your practice attractive to new patients.

CYBERSECURITY

Cybersecurity is another consideration in the digital marketing of the healthcare practice. Healthcare faces greater cyber risks than other sectors because of inherent weaknesses in its security posture. Many providers think that they can defend themselves from cyberattacks, but that is folly.

The healthcare sector is an attractive target for cyberattacks for two simple reasons: it is a rich source of valuable data; and it is a soft target. Cybersecurity is not just about protecting data; it is fundamental to maintaining the safety, privacy, and trust of our patients. Effective cybersecurity must become an integral part of every medical practice.[1]

SHIFTING GEARS FROM ILLNESS TO WELLNESS

Nearly 18% of the U.S. gross domestic product is spent on healthcare—estimated at $3 trillion per year. Some suggest that one-third of that amount, or $1 trillion, is wasted with duplicated tests, services, and the cost of defensive medicine. Unfortunately, a huge gap exists between spending and outcomes. In fact, Americans lag near the bottom when it comes to health outcomes among wealthy countries.[2]

One problem is that today's healthcare system focuses almost exclusively on responding to symptoms and illnesses or after the patient becomes sick or injured. In the United States, we spend 97% of our healthcare resources on *disease* care.[3]

But another vision for health care is emerging—one that is focused on *wellness* rather than illness; that is proactive instead of reactive; and that focuses on population health rather than managing just a single patient with a single illness or constellation of illnesses.

Within the past decade, big data, analytics, and social networks, as well as advances in technologies such as wearable health-tracking devices, have given us the ability to learn more about wellness. That is the premise behind *scientific wellness,* which starts with a systems approach to analyzing highly specialized large datasets of individual human biomarkers such as genes, proteins, and microbiomes, and combines the results with personalized health coaching to influence the health of our population.

Just as the Hubble Telescope provided a new view into the universe, personal, dense, dynamic data sets will be transformational for providing new insights into both human biology and disease. This approach can help us better understand the genetic and environmental factors that determine our health status. Over time, this will enable us to identify the earliest transitions from wellness to disease, which is the key to both predictive and preventive care for individuals.

PRECISION MEDICINE AND PRECISION MARKETING

With an emphasis on personalized medicine, patients expect to be cared for to meet their individual needs. In addition to personalizing medicine, I suggest you consider personalizing marketing to ensure the right patients are receiving the right messages. I recommend that the same theory of precision medicine be applied to the practice's healthcare marketing efforts.

"Dr. Alexa" will see you now

Alexa, Amazon's virtual assistant, is primed to perform healthcare-related tasks. "She" can track blood glucose levels, describe symptoms, access postsurgical care instructions, monitor home prescription deliveries, and make same-day appointments at the nearest urgent care center. Alexa can look at a picture of a wound and give advice if additional care is needed.

Alexa also can assist with your insurance claims. Liberty Mutual Insurance launched the first- of-its-kind Alexa service that allows insurance buyers to navigate the policy purchase and management process purely by using their Amazon Echos.[4]

A new Alexa skill will help furnish patients with all the detailed information about the hospital they need before they leave from their home. This will enable users to gain access to real-time information about the hospital, including:

- Parking information;
- Visitor information;
- Important contact information;
- Bill payment information;
- Directions to the hospital and the closest urgent care facility;
- Info on how to view medical records; and
- Important things that you need to bring for your hospital stay.

Online Reputation Management

Physicians live and die by their reputations. We spend our entire medical careers polishing and protecting this status. The Internet has dramatically altered the way people gather information. It is sad but true that a single comment that takes only a few seconds for a patient to create and a single mouse-click to post on the Internet can be seen by thousands of visitors and ruin the reputation a physician has spent a lifetime building.

Never forget that your most precious asset is your reputation. Online physician reviews are positive 70% to 90% of the time.[5] However, physicians need to know the process of managing negative reviews. The best advice is to make sure you have many more positive reviews than negative reviews. That way an occasional negative review will not significantly detract from your online reputation.

Show Me the Money

A reasonable investment to make in marketing is 3% to 5% of the practice's gross revenues. However, marketers must be able to show that the money invested demonstrates a return on the practice's investment. It is reasonable to ask a marketing firm about the expected increment in new patients or how the marketing firm plans to position the practice on the first page of Google.

Bottom Line: If you plan to be in practice for the foreseeable future, you will need to embrace a few of these suggestions and implement them into your practice. Most of them are easily accomplished with minimal expense and have been tested in other practices and have been demonstrated to be effective. The toothpaste is out of the tube and can't be put back. That metaphor applies to medical marketing and practice promotion. It will not be enough to be a good diagnostician and provide excellent treatment for the medical conditions you treat. Patients are expecting a different level of care, and they expect the same convenience they receive from airlines, hotels, Amazon, the stockbroker, accountant, and the dentist. Doctors who embrace this change in the attitude of their post-pandemic patients are going to be the ones who succeed today and tomorrow.

REFERENCES

1. KPMG. Health care and cybersecurity: increasing threats require increased capabilities. KPMG.com. 2015. https://assets.kpmg/content/dam/kpmg/pdf/2015/09/cyber-health-care-survey-kpmg-2015.pdf.

2. Schroeder SA. We can do better—improving the health of the American people. *N Engl J Med.* 2007;357:1221-1228.

3. Hood L, Price N. Turn healthcare right-side up: focus on wellness not disease. *Psychology Today.* March 19, 2018. www.psychologytoday.com/us/blog/the-social-brain/201803/turn-healthcare-right-side-focus-wellness-not-disease.

4. Sakthive V, Kesaven MP, William JM, Kumar SM. Integrated platform and response system for healthcare using Alexa. *International Journal of Communication and Computer Technologies.* 2019;7(1):14-22.

5. Grabner-Kräuter S, Waiguny MK. Insights into the impact of online physician reviews on patients' decision-making: randomized experiment. *J Med Internet Research.* 2015;17(4), e93. DOI: 10.2196/jmir.3991